MAKE AMAZING

GAMES

Third Edition

MAKE AMAZING GAMES

USING FUSION 2.5

Third Edition

JASON DARBY

MERCURY LEARNING AND INFORMATION

Dulles, Virginia
Boston, Massachusetts
New Delhi

Publisher: David Pallai
MERCURY LEARNING AND INFORMATION
22841 Quicksilver Drive
Dulles, VA 20166
info@merclearning.com
www.merclearning.com
1-800-232-0223

J. Darby. *Make Amazing Games Using Fusion 2.5, 3/E.*
ISBN: 978-1-68392-700-6

The publisher recognizes and respects all marks used by companies, manufacturers, and developers as a means to distinguish their products. All brand names and product names mentioned in this book are trademarks or service marks of their respective companies. Any omission or misuse (of any kind) of service marks or trademarks, etc. is not an attempt to infringe on the property of others.

Library of Congress Control Number: 2021933057

212223321   Printed on acid-free paper in the United States of America.

Our titles are available for adoption, license, or bulk purchase by institutions, corporations, etc. For additional information, please contact the Customer Service Dept. at 800-232-0223(toll free).

All of our titles are available for sale in digital format at *academiccourseware.com* and other digital vendors. Companion files for this title can also be downloaded by writing to *info@merclearning.com*. The sole obligation of MERCURY LEARNING AND INFORMATION to the purchaser is to replace the book, based on defective materials or faulty workmanship, but not based on the operation or functionality of the product.

This book is dedicated to my wife Alicia and my children Jared, Kimberley, and Lucas, who are all awesome. Hello to my cats, crazy "Dexter," fur ball "Penny," and nose kissing "Sammy." Never a quiet moment to do work when they want feeding or fussing.

CONTENTS

PREFACE

Having always been fascinated by video games, I used to go to the local book shops as a teenager to buy gaming books. Though in many cases I didn't understand the complex coding syntax or the concepts they were talking about, I was just excited by the prospect of making my own games.

When I got the chance to write my very first book, the 1st Edition of *Make Amazing Games* way back in 2003 and 2004, I was writing it because of a love of video games that had been with me ever since I was a child, but also the immense satisfaction I had picking up a book that could contain the secrets to a hobby that I loved. Little did I know that after writing that first book I was going to go on a journey where I would end up writing books on different game genres and where I would work in the AAA games industry, working as a designer on multiple F1 games. Then, where I'd work on two flight simulator games and I would actually get to learn to fly a Cessna 152, taking off and landing (scary stuff let me tell you). Working on a Career mode for a Fishing game, learning all about trains for a Train Simulator, and finally working on a PS4 VR game for Sony (before it unfortunately got cancelled).

So even though the 3rd Edition comes from a place where I am now more experienced and knowledgeable about making games, the core of the book is still as relevant as it was when I wrote it back then.

"If you love video games how can you make your own?"

I hope this book can provide the same inspiration that video game books in the 1980s and 1990s gave me, and even if you don't release a game of your own to the public or work for a games company, you get to fulfill some part of the dream of making a video game.

Good luck!

Jason Darby
March 2021

ACKNOWLEDGMENTS

There are a number of people I would like to thank who have helped me write this book and have hopefully made it interesting for you, the reader. Firstly, my wife Alicia for being very understanding of all the time I have spent on my computer and gaming consoles over the years, as well as doing the editing of my text to make it as accurate as possible.

To Clickteam the creators of Fusion (as well as many other games making programs over the years) who have made such great products, that have allowed myself and thousands of like-minded others to really enjoy games creation.

Christian Burfelt, who created some of the original games that came with "Make Amazing Games," 1st Edition that we will be using as a base for the third edition. Thanks!

To Adam Lobacz who many years ago created the original graphics for Whack Em World Tour, which is the fourth game example in this book.

My son Lucas Darby, who started off using Clickteam Games Factory when he was 6 years old and can now program and create art. Lucas has redrawn all of the artwork for the example games so that they are relevant to today's higher resolution screens.

A lot of thanks must go to David Pallai, who was the president and founder of Charles River Media who gave me the chance to write the first edition of this book all those years ago (way back in 2003-2004). Without whom I would not have written so many books following that.

Finally, to my kids, Jared, Kimberley, and Lucas who have grown up a lot since the 1st edition and have been a constant source of nagging about finishing books and my indie games over the years… they have provided me with the inspiration I needed to get this new book written.

CHAPTER 1

VIDEO GAMES

In This Chapter

- Why Make Games?
- 2D or 3D Games
- Game Genres and Types
- Software Used in This Book
- About Clickteam

Games have been one of the most interesting aspects of computers since they began appearing in the home over forty years ago. Alongside spreadsheets and accounting programs (which were originally the core reasons for owning the PC), games began to quickly appear to take advantage of this new technology. Nothing is more satisfying than loading up your favorite game and, for example, being transported to a world that no longer exists, visiting a certain time in history and getting a sense of how people may have lived; flying an aircraft or driving a racing car; being a soldier fighting in a war; or even taking part in a sport you could never conceive of doing in real life.

Today's games bear no resemblance to the first simple games of the late 1970s and 1980s. They now have high-quality graphics and sound, complex stories and, in many cases, multi-million-dollar budgets, making the games industry more like the movie industry (and in fact the industry makes more than the movie and music industries combined). Games are big business, and one of the leading industries in which to find work.

Unfortunately, making games is still considered by many as a difficult thing to do, in which you have to spend years learning how to design and program in complex languages before you can even get a simple graphic moving across the screen! Even with today's advances in video game engines (which were extremely limited in both choice and ease of use way back in 2004 when the first edition of the book was released), it can still be overly complex. Doesn't sound like much fun if you're just starting out, does it? Most of us want some immediate response from the computer, not spending time to get "Hello World" written on the screen (the first thing most traditional programming books still try to teach, and not very exciting) or figuring out what a vector, material, or primitive shape is in a 3D game engine (if you don't know what that means, don't worry; we won't be talking about them in this book).

Many game programming books are aimed at the more professional user market—for example, games programming with C++, learning C# using games, and so forth. Typical game-loving people don't fit into the professional category or don't have the skills and, more importantly, the patience to learn traditional coding languages but would love to fulfill their dreams of making a game. In fact, many aspire to make games, but don't know if it's possible and don't know where to start.

This book shows you how it is much easier than you may have thought to make fun and exciting games. It also allows you to progress quickly and take an idea from concept into a fully playable game by the end of the book. In the later chapters, we look at adding more complexity to games with additional things like scoreboards, putting them on the Web, and building for different platforms. This book is squarely aimed at a beginner, a beginner at game creation or someone who has never used Clickteam Fusion 2.5 before. Game making can be a lot of fun, so you don't need to have aspirations to make a career of it or sell games that you've made (though many people do sell their games made in Fusion); you might just want to create a fun project for yourself or perhaps for your children. In fact, many game creators are actually just doing it for the excitement of other people playing the games they've created!

So, let us begin our journey in learning how to make and design games the easy way!

Why Make Games?

You may have many reasons why you want to make games, and using Fusion 2.5 is a great way to achieve many of them. Some reasons why you may want to make games include:

- You wish to make games as a hobby.

- You want to learn a new skill.

- You want to make games for your friends and family.

- You want a job in the games industry and want to create a portfolio of work to go with your CV.

- You wish to sell your own games.

- Perhaps you have an idea that you feel no one has done justice to yet, and you want to make that idea because it excites you.

- You are a teacher looking at getting students to learn useful skills such as storytelling, mathematics, art, and design while keeping them interested in the lesson.

As you can see, there are many reasons why you might want to make games (this list isn't definitive), but whatever your choice, it is important to ensure you enjoy the experience.

2D or 3D Games

Games can be classed as 2D, 2.5D, and 3D. The D stands for dimensions, and this relates to how graphics are drawn on-screen. So, a 2D game is usually where the game is presented on a flat surface (imagine looking down on a table from above and the table surface is your game area). This flat surface has two dimensions, an X and Y coordinate. You can see an example of a sprite within a 2D world/screen in Figure 1.1.

 A sprite is an image within your game that can also contain animations (moving parts).

To move objects around in this world, you have to use an X or Y coordinate. In Figure 1.1, you can see we have marked the direction of the coordinates, where X goes from left to right and Y goes top to bottom. So, if you want an object to be placed in the top left-hand corner of the screen, you would place it at 0,0. Depending on the screen resolution for your game (the size of the screen)—for example, a common screen resolution is 1920 x 1080—if you wish to place it on the top right, you would specify the X coordinate as 1920 and the Y coordinate as 0.

2.5D is a game that is in 2D (i.e., it only has X and Y coordinates) but the sprites are drawn in such a way to make you feel like it is a 3D game. Games using isometric graphics are considered 2.5D. You can see an example of this in Figure 1.2, whereby we have a cabin in the woods drawn at an angle; though it looks 3D the pieces are still only moving in a 2D plane (X and Y). Using such techniques can make your 2D game more interesting visually.

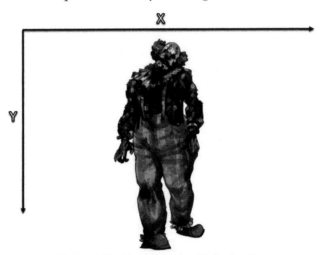

FIGURE 1.1 Zombie clown sprite – Trebuchet Games.

FIGURE 1.2 Cabin in the woods – Trebuchet Games.

3D is a game that has three dimensions. Most modern games that you'll play on a PC or console are most likely in 3D. That doesn't mean making 2D games is a waste of time, as they are still very popular for Websites and indie-style games, especially when using 2.5D. Certain genres can also be popular in 2D, such as platform or side-scrolling games (see Game Genres later in this chapter).

You can see an example of a 3D snow globe made using the Firefly plug-in for Fusion in Figure 1.3. You still have the X and Y coordinates, but now you also have the Z coordinate, which goes into the screen. You can move into and around the objects rather than have just a left to right view.

This book is all about making 2D (two-dimensional) games and does not touch on 3D game creation aspects. You can create 3D for Fusion 2.5 by using a specific paid-for plug-in (a separate piece of content) called Firefly 3D (go to *www.clickteam.com* for more details on the 3D Firefly object). The Firefly object isn't something recommended for beginners; get to know Fusion 2.5 before deciding to jump into 3D game creation.

FIGURE 1.3 Firefly 3D diorama – Clickteam.

3D is more complex in Fusion than 2D-based games, and as such is more complicated and time-consuming. For that reason, 3D games are outside the scope of this book. If you are interested in working in 3D in Fusion, you will need to learn the basics of how to create games before moving on to 3D.

Different game engines will use alternative dimension letters for the screen location within a game. They will all use X, Y, and Z but can change their position within the game world; for example, Y could move forward into the world while Z could be moving in a downward direction. For Fusion we are only concerned with X and Y, where X is left to right and Y is top to bottom of the screen.

Game Genres and Types

Before we look at how to develop and design our own games, we are going to take a quick look at different types of games that you could make. This list isn't definitive but includes most of the game types and genres that you might be considering for your next project; most can be made in Fusion in some way, and some are listed for completeness and to kick-start some ideas of what you might want to make (even if it's not possible to make a particular genre or type, you may be able to take some features and put them into your own game).

The games we have detailed are mostly ones that fit into 2D game creation. There are additional game genres and types that are listed that would be more suited to 3D game engines.

Some of the genres or types in this list could exist in multiple categories; for example, bat and ball could also be an arcade or retro game, but these are listed as separate entries.

Third Person/Third-Person Shooter

The types of games that you make might have various perspectives, for example, side-scrolling (from the side), top-down (from above looking directly below), or aerial (from the air). Third person is a term that refers to looking at the player-controlled character from a third person (i.e., not from the eyes of a character). This generally means looking at the player-controlled character from behind, sometimes directly behind or behind their shoulder. Many games use a third-person view, from racing games where you can see the driver's head to action games such as Uncharted or God of War.

A third-person shooter still uses the camera view from behind the player-controlled character but focuses on the shooting aspect of the gameplay.

Unless you are using the 3D add-on for Fusion, it's unlikely that you will be making a third-person game, and though in most cases this would be true if you were making a game involving a 3D world, you can definitely make a fake 3D third-person shooter using 2D elements.

Adventure Games

Adventure games have been around since the early home computers were available and are still extremely popular today. You'll find them on many different platforms, such as mobile devices, PCs, and consoles.

Early adventure games were called "text adventures," as they only displayed text on screen and the player had to use a bit of imagination to conjure up the image of the world they were in (an example of a text adventure can be seen in Figure 1.4).

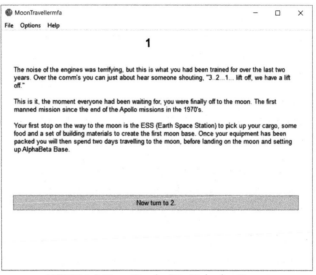

FIGURE 1.4 Moon Traveler 3D – Trebuchet Games.

It wasn't long after text adventures where they made the next logical step in gaming, and that was to include images to set the scene of the player's current position; these were called graphic adventures. From a design point of view they are the same as text adventures, but with graphical elements to help with directions and story. You can see an example of a graphic adventure in Figure 1.5.

From early graphic adventures the next step was a point-and-click interface where you could control a character and its interactions within the world using the mouse cursor. This would also include picking up objects and then using those objects within the world. You can see an example of a point-and-click adventure game made in Fusion in Figure 1.6.

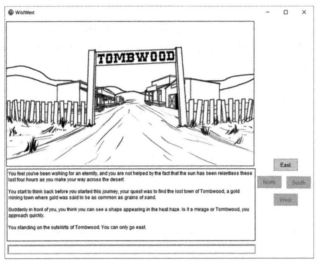

FIGURE 1.5 Wild West – Trebuchet Games.

FIGURE 1.6 Sherlock Bones – Trebuchet Games.

There have been other variants of adventure games over the years, as CD media became more popular; this allowed videos to be included within the games production. These adventure games were called full motion video (FMV) games. FMV adventure games use video to provide movement, animation, or actions within the game.

Arcade

Arcade games is a general term for games with a certain type of aesthetic and style that mainly originated from the late 1970s and 1980s, whereby you would put a few coins into a coin-operated machine (arcade machine) to play the latest games. The noise and sound of a room filled with arcade machines is something that cannot be easily explained, but it was an experience like no other. The games on these machines became very popular, and it was only a matter of time before they got recreated on home computers, and it was a massive part of the home computer revolution in the 1980s. Unfortunately, the arcade cabinet business is not what it used to be and, except for in places like Japan, it has mainly been taken over by gambling and slot machines.

Today when someone says a game is an arcade game, it has a certain type of retro/old-school gameplay; for example, the side-scrolling shoot-'em-up PS4 game Resogun felt very reminiscent of the game Space Invaders.

Arena

Usually called arena battle games, these are usually multiplayer based games within an enclosed environment where you battle with other players (PVP – player vs. player) or with bots (PVE – player vs. enemies).

Bat and Ball

A very popular type of game on the early 8-bit and 16-bit computers was the bat and ball style of games (an example is shown in Figure 1.7). You usually control a paddle and have to destroy blocks using a bouncing ball. There have been several variations of this type of game over the years in which several things have changed: the direction of the paddle/balls, various positive and negative effects when destroying certain blocks, and even 3D versions. As a game type there certainly are a lot of options for improving and adding new features, and you shouldn't have too many problems thinking up new ideas. As a starting point for making games, it's one of the easier game types to get to grips with and one of the first games we will explore in our game called "The Lab" (as shown in Figure 1.7).

FIGURE 1.7 The Lab – Trebuchet Games.

Board Games

Chess and checkers are just two examples of traditional board games that have been converted to the computer game format (a board game example can be seen in Figure 1.8). Though the classics are still extremely popular (they are also found on consoles such as the PS4), board games with more complicated story and depth have appeared over the last few years, and this is something that hasn't yet fully moved over to the gaming world.

Board games are more complicated than many genres because they require more complex coding for how the computer will respond to the players moves, so board games shouldn't be an early game type that you pick to make. It is recommended that you move onto board games once you have a better understanding of Fusion and have more experience of programming in the Event Editor.

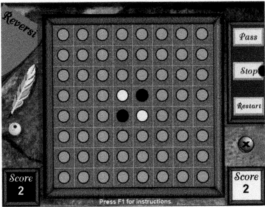

FIGURE 1.8 Reversi – Clickteam.

Card Games

There are two types of card games; first we have the traditional card games such as poker, blackjack, patience, cheat, rummy, and spider (an example of a card game is shown in Figure 1.9). These can be played solo with a computer-controlled AI or with another person. These types of games are also popular with online casinos.

The second type of card game is the "battle card" game. Over the last few years these have become extremely popular, and there are a number of high-profile games currently on different platforms and some with very high development budgets. This is where you collect cards and do battle with another player or computer-controlled AI. Your cards will determine the outcome of the battle. Cards will have different abilities, skills, or powers, some which will add certain advantages to you or give a disadvantage to the other player.

FIGURE 1.9 Card game – Trebuchet Games.

Battle card games do require a lot of design work to get right and can become complex, while in traditional card games the rules are already set out. So, if you are thinking about a card game, you might want to initially focus on the traditional card game, as it is easy to find the rules on the Internet. Once you have made a set of card pack graphics, you can also apply this to the many different card games that are available. So, one set of graphics can equal many different games.

Casual

Casual games are sometimes stated mistakenly as games that appeal only to non-gamers (the types of games your non-gaming parents or family members would play). The (incorrect) perception is that from a gameplay point of view, they are easy to play and don't contain any complex systems. That classification isn't really a fair argument, as they can be both complex and have a lot of depth. Casual games are usually about subject matters that are less serious and broader in appeal, and they could be said to primarily be on mobile platforms, but this isn't always the case. Puzzle games, card games, hidden object games, and endless runners can be classified as casual games.

City Builders

The clue to what a city builder is like is in the name. You are given a task to build a settlement, town, or city which may be in the past or in the future. These games involve strategy and moral-based systems (usually with regard to how the populace considers your city management skills). They usually contain research trees and collecting resources such as food, money, and mining. In Fusion, these games would be isometric or top-down.

Co-Op

In co-op games you play a game with another person for a common aim and work as a team. You can have more than a two-player co-op, and another term you'd see along with co-op is multiplayer (meaning multiple players playing the same game within the same server/world). The distinction between the two is that both are more than one person playing the same game within the same world, but co-op is working together as a group.

Driving

Elsewhere in this list is Racing, but driving games can also be noncompetitive games where the aim isn't to be first past the post to win a race. A popular type of driving game is more about the driving experience or completing a task. For example, Jalopy is a game where you take a drive across the former Soviet Union in a rusting old car; it's more about the journey and how you get there than driving fast from point to point. Other games which involve driving are Truck Simulator and Bus Simulator (you'll notice the word simulator mentioned later); driving and simulator are two game types that can be combined.

Endless Runners

Endless runners became popular on mobile and tablet devices. These are games that are exactly how they are named. You have a character who must traverse down a path, a path that never ends and will get more dangerous as you proceed. If you die you have to start again; the further you get, the more points you accrue. Either you score points by collecting items or it's based on time, though most games have multiple paths and something to collect (e.g., coins), as that is more interesting (as it provides a reward) than just a time-based scoring system that is just a number.

Fighting Games

There are two types of fighting games worth mentioning in this book; one type is side-scrolling beat-'em-ups. This is usually a left-to-right scrolling game, from point A to point B, with a story element attached to it. You fight multiple enemies at a time with different attack skills. These were extremely popular in arcades in the 1980s and could also contain platforms. In one particular game called Renegade, you could pick up weapons, do jump kicks, throw enemies off ledges, and kick enemies off their motorcycles, as well as face the boss (boss battles) at the end of a level.

The other types of fighting games are those that are currently popular on consoles. These allow the player to move to the left and right and are usually one on one or two on two. Though these fighting games give the appearance of 2D, there are normally 3D environments behind the players which can be interacted with. Still, it is possible to emulate much of a modern-day fighting game within Fusion.

First Person/First-Person Shooter

Earlier in this chapter we talked about third-person perspective, which was from behind the player-controlled character, so it makes sense that first person is from the perspective of the player character's eyes, looking out into the world. These types of games are not the standard types of games you would make in Fusion if you were thinking of a Call of Duty game, as Fusion is mostly a 2D engine, but there are games that create a fake 3D environment that presents the view as if it were from a person's perspective. A good example of this would be a game like Five Nights at Freddy's, whereby you play the job as a night security guard in a pizza parlor. You are viewing the world from a first-person point of view and can switch to viewing a security camera within the world. You aren't moving around the world in a traditional first-person game, but it's a great compromise and works really well.

A first-person shooter is a game such as the aforementioned Call of Duty, which involves the first-person perspective and gunplay. These are extremely popular and not really the type of game you should be attempting with an engine such as Fusion.

Flight/Flying

These games involve flying, either an aircraft or animal such as an eagle. In many cases these games could also be classed as simulators (mentioned later). There are a number of different types of flying games, such as side-scrolling and top-down (like the game we make in this book); these could be considered arcade or retro-styled games. In Fusion, you are looking pre-dominantly at 2D for flying games, but a very skilled Fusion user could in theory make an old-school 3D-based game.

God Games

These types of games were extremely popular in the late 1980s and 1990s. Many people attribute the creation of this genre to the company Bull-frog and in particular Peter Molyneux. The main aim of a god game is to take the role of a god or have the powers of a god, in particular be-ing able to hold sway over the populace and change the environment that these people live in. So in these types of games you can change the land-scape, make rivers, move trees, affect the weather, and cause lightning and fires. Two extremely well-known god games are Populous and Black & White.

Hidden Object

Hidden object games have been a very popular casual game in the last fifteen or twenty years. A scene is displayed with many different objects on-screen, perhaps a kitchen, for example. The player's role is to find the objects that are asked of them, so the word "Kettle," for example, might be highlighted, and the player needs to look over the scene to find the kettle; once they have clicked on it, the next object is then asked for. The whole task is usually timed, and if the player makes a mistake, they will lose some of their allotted time.

Initially, hidden object games were quite basic and were only about finding an object among a lot of other objects, but over time they have had stories added and more complex puzzle mechanics.

Horror/Psychological

Jump scares and scary bedtime stories are exciting and terrifying at the same time. Horror and psychological games are an interesting genre. Un-like some of the other types mentioned which might cover a particular type of gameplay experience, horror games can easily be a platform game, an adventure game, and so on. In some cases, it's more of a setting rather than a game type, but in the last few years there have been games that have created their own niche in the horror section.

A good example of this is a game called Five Nights at Freddy's, which was made in Fusion and became a massive hit. You star as a security guard who uses a security camera system and has to survive against animatronic characters.

Isometric

This is a graphical style that sits between 3D and 2D. It is generally a 2D game style but can also be done in a 3D game engine. It's putting the perspective of the player's view above an object and to the side so that you can see more than just a single flat plane; rather than just seeing the front of a building, you see the roof and two of its walls. It is a nice graphical style that lends itself to retro and indie game development very nicely.

JRPG

This is an RPG (role-playing game) in the Japanese style (see RPG for more information).

MMO

MMO stands for massively multiplayer online, which means many people playing online on the same world at the same time. Though many games are multiplayer, MMO is a big scale, whereby you can meet up with people from all around the world and take part in many quests and adventures. One of the biggest MMOs is World of Warcraft, where you can travel to different areas via boat, riding a creature, or by flying animal. The game has a massive amount of content that has been added to over the years with content expansions.

In Fusion, you will not be able to make a game like World of Warcraft because its scope, scale, and graphics are beyond what any small group can do, but it is possible to create a 2D MMO game, and this has been done by a few users over the years. It's not a simple or easy undertaking and not something you should attempt early on in your game creations.

Music Based

Music based games have been popular for a quite a few years now. We've had games where you can sing along to your favorite pop stars, play a plastic guitar or drum kit, do dance moves on dance mats, and even become a DJ. Though plastic instrument music-based games have come and gone, music themed games are still very popular; one such major success was the game Beat Saber.

Party Games

You might for a moment think party games are games with a group of friends, so isn't that just co-op or multiplayer? Party games is a term generally used to describe sitting around the sofa with a group of family or friends playing a game that contains many mini games to keep the party entertained, just like you would at a party.

Platform

Most gamers at some point have probably played a 2D-platform game (an example is shown in Figure 1.10). These are games that have the player navigating through an environment which contains ladders (to move up and down), platforms (to provide jumping between points), and traps. Using a combination of these can create an addictive and challenging gameplay experience.

Platform games have had a bit of a resurgence over the last few years in both 2D and 3D game worlds. It's nice to see some classic remasters such as Crash Bandicoot make an extremely successful return and a number of new games appearing on consoles that take a nod back to the classic games of the 1980s and 1990s.

Making platform games in Fusion isn't difficult from a code point of view, but to make a good platformer from a design point of view can be quite time-consuming, especially when taking into account difficulty levels within the game, as it can involve precision placement of objects such as traps and enemies to get the platform feeling right.

FIGURE 1.10 Robin Hood – Trebuchet Games.

We will be looking at how to make the platform game Robin Hood later on in the book (as shown in Figure 1.10.).

Puzzle Games

This is quite a broad subject and covers many different game types in both 2D and 3D. Puzzle games are games where you have to use logical thinking to figure out a particular solution. In terms of 2D games, you'll find many puzzle games on mobile devices and tablets. The most popular ones are games such as Threes, Candy Crush, and Candy Crush Saga.

Do not be deceived by puzzle games just because they might initially seem straightforward graphically. To make a successful puzzle game can take a lot of work. The game will need to be graphically enticing (rewarding to the viewer). They can contain many levels and you'll need to keep adding new features as the player progresses through the game; this can be additional graphical styles or story levels. There are many puzzle games on the market, so even if you are making a puzzle game for fun, you'll need to make it interesting to get people to play it.

 Some puzzle games can have thousands of levels.

Racing Car

One favorite type of game on old computers such as the Commodore Amiga and Spectrum was top-down view racing car games. Various tracks, bonuses, and great computer AI (Artificial Intelligence) would make for an exciting and increasingly difficult set of racing tracks. The great thing about racing car games is that you can add a lot of depth to the gameplay by adding items such as weapons to destroy other cars, weather conditions, car upgrades to make them faster, single races, or tournaments. So, you shouldn't get stuck thinking of things to add to make it more interesting.

 When considering what genre of game you are going to make, consider a type of game that ideas flow easily from. If you are struggling for ideas early on in your game creation, then it may be better to pick another game genre; you can always come back to your other ideas at a later stage if you have more ideas to add to them.

Real Time Strategy

Real time strategy games are games whereby you need to make tactical decisions within the game in real time. Initially these games were war games but soon moved onto games that involved 2D/3D units, such as Dune, Caesar, and Command and Conquer. These games mix real time decisions with unit creation and deployment.

Retro

The term retro changes with each decade, but it basically means games that are old and in an old style (and probably a style that is no longer being made). So, if you are forty years of age a retro game to you might be Space Invaders or Pong, while if you are a little younger you might consider games on the PlayStation 1 as being retro. Usually, games that are fifteen to twenty years old or more can be considered retro.

Roguelike/Roguelite

Roguelike games have become popular in the last few years, mainly due to their size and difficulty. In many cases they are dungeon-based games (dungeon crawler is another term you may hear), with levels of various difficulty. The dungeons are usually procedurally generated; this means that the levels are automatically created by the computer and will change on every playthrough. This means you get a fresh dungeon every time you play. Difficulty wise the games also have permadeath, so once you are dead then it's game over.

Roguelite is very similar to Roguelike and so may still have procedurally generated maps, but it may not be as harsh in terms of permadeath or have as complex strategy systems, meaning that it's a bit more casual and easier to play.

Role-Playing Games (RPG)

Role-playing games (RPG) originate from the time when people used to play traditional pen-and-paper role-playing games such as Dungeons and Dragons. You would have a DM/GM (dungeon master or game master) who would tell the story, and then the players would tell the dungeon master what they intended to do. The key aspect of role-playing games was the player characters were generally very detailed, with information on when they were born, where, what happened to them, and why they were like they were. This information provided players the background in how to play the character in certain situations, much like an actor taking a role of someone they've never met but knowing precisely what they would be like in a particular situation.

Two other key components to role-playing games are that the character's attributes were finely detailed, including how much health, luck, and dexterity they had as well as a set of abilities or skills. This is where player characters do a particular task well; in a Call of Cthulhu game, for example, that might be reading ancient text or pistol skill, while in a medieval style game it might be lock picking, the ability to read Latin, or skill at short swords. RPGs are considered stat heavy, which means lots of different bits of data can have an impact on the player's game and how they may go about doing a particular task, such as whether a character can wear heavy armor, carry lots of equipment, or use a particular weapon or spell.

You can make a side-scrolling, top-down, or isometric-styled RPG in Fusion, and keeping track of stats and skills can be done through a number of different methods such as arrays, INI data files, and variables, which will be discussed in Chapter 3.

Side-Scrolling Shoot-'Em-Ups

This was a favorite type of game in the 1980s, and it's still a popular format of game for indie game makers. In fact, a 3D scrolling shooter called Resogun was very popular at the launch of the PS4.

This type of shoot-'em-up game would normally have the gamer playing a space fighter pilot defending the earth against wave after wave of alien invaders (an example shown in Figure 1.11 is Fighter Pilot, which you'll be making later). The game could scroll from left to right or bottom to top and it also could include bonuses for destroying a wave of enemy fighters, including shield and weapons upgrades. Very predictable stuff but entertaining

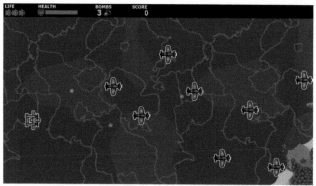

FIGURE 1.11 Fighter Pilot – Trebuchet Games.

all the same. These types of games are relatively easy to create; in fact, once you have done the scrolling, most of the hard work is done (except for having some original graphics, of course).

 You will see the word "indie" throughout this book, which relates to the term independent. In the games industry there are a number of meanings to this, such as ownership of a company. For the sake of this book, it means a game made by one or a small number of people who are not necessarily professional and not necessarily selling their game.

Sims

Don't confuse the term sim games with the game Sims from EA (though there is a connection) or modern simulation games. The word sim was used as shorthand for simulation on the early Amiga/PC computers, though in today's context it's not the same as a "simulation" game that you'll see in the marketplace. "Sim games" was a term coined in the 1990s, whereby a games core feature would be doing something that mimics real life, and can mostly be attributed to legendary game designer Will Wright. He made games such as SimCity, SimEarth, and SimAnt as well as the aforementioned The Sims. These games would contain calculations behind the scenes to work out how your choices would impact the world that you were playing in.

Simulation

Simulation games are about trying to depict a real-life scenario in a video game format. They may not 100% accurately represent real life but take parts of it, either because of complexity or because certain aspects are not interesting to play. You can play the more serious simulation games that, for example, accurately depict the inside of a boat and mimic the controls in real life or more mundane tasks such as working in an office or restaurant. The term "simulator" has changed over the years; originally it would be related to more serious activities, but recently it has seen a surge in more comedic settings. You can now play simulation games such as Job Simulator, Cleaning Simulator, Car Mechanic Simulator, and Goat Simulator to name a few.

Sports Games

This group is a catchall for single or team-based sports such as football, baseball, basketball, running, horse riding, and so on. You can also mix sports games with strategy games, but for this group it's more about performing the sport (e.g., physically kicking or hitting the ball with a character rather than telling the player what to do and managing the team).

 Though certain car racing events are considered a sport, we've kept that in its own dedicated group, as it's a common 2D game that can be made in Fusion.

Stealth

Many games contain elements of stealth, though very few are based solely on the concept. On the whole, making stealth games (or at least as part of a game) is an extremely complicated task, and many modern games don't seem to be able to strike the right balance. Games such as Assassin's Creed and Spiderman both have stealth sections, and many people agree that they are not the most enjoyable parts of the game. There have been a few games built entirely around stealth as the core mechanic, but these are few and far between.

Steampunk

Steampunk has been quite popular in the last few years. Taking artistic style from the late 1800s and early 1900s, it then mixes this up with futuristic weapons and devices. It's a weird combination that just seems to work. The Order 1886 is an example of this genre, whereby it took the grim environment of London in the 1800s and added in high-tech weapons and werewolf-type creatures mixed in with a narrative of the Knights of the Round Table. Though some would have preferred a realistic representation of London in the 1800s (including the life and times of such people), it was an interesting concept with great art style, which unfortunately just couldn't make it all gel together in a cohesive package.

Strategy

Strategy games involve thinking about a particular situation and working with and amending stats to get a positive outcome. Common strategy games can be war games where you move units on a map and engage the enemy (battles then take place based on unit strength and locations) or management games such as a football game where you try to put the best players into positions and watch the game unfold.

Survival

These games focus on harsh realities of the environment or world they put you in and how you might try to survive. Food and resources can be scarce, and there are elements of grinding the resources to make your situation better. Normally you can combine resources to make tools or equipment, such as a better shelter or the ability to make or mine other objects.

Turn Based

These are games that require you to take a turn and then wait for someone else to take their turn before you continue. Some games have elements of turn-based mechanics within them, while others may make this the core gameplay element. Board games are usually turn based; in terms of other types of video games, military or war games are usually highly turn based.

Visual Novels

Visual novels sit in two camps, one which has very little gameplay and just tells a story where the player may make decisions; it's mainly about the story. The other may include some elements of decision making and multiple endings. On the whole they are extremely text and graphic heavy, much like a graphical adventure game, but generally with less complicated game mechanics.

Walking Simulators

Walking simulators are games that strangely involve lots of walking. It's a term that has appeared over the last few years for games in which the player will inhabit a character and move around an environment solving puzzles. Examples of such games are What Remains of Edith Finch, The Stanley Parable, and Gone Home. In Gone Home, you arrive home to find that there is no one there. So, you move around the environment, reading messages, and so forth to figure out what has happened. These games are generally more about the narrative (story) than complex gameplay puzzles.

War Games

There are a couple of different types of war games that are available to play; one type is the strategy, map-based movement of units which can then turn into a battle within a 3D environment, such as the excellent Total War series. You then also have the old-school, hex-based war games, which are unfortunately not as popular these days, where you move your 2D units on a hex-based map grid and see the battle unfold in real time.

Software Used in This Book

The product that we will be using to create our games is Clickteam's Fusion 2.5 (an example game loaded into Fusion is shown in Figure 1.12).

There are other game creation tools that you could use to make games which will not be covered in this book (as otherwise this book would be many thousands of pages). We have selected Fusion as the software to use for a number of reasons:

- The product is relatively cheap to use (there is a free version which you can use to test out your game ideas).

- It is relatively easy to use (especially for the beginner game makers who are reading this book).

- You can create commercial software with it, which is a bonus if you do decide to continue with making games and decide you want to make a business out of it.

- Development time is a lot quicker than using scripting or traditional programming languages for the beginner.

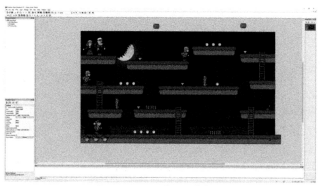

FIGURE 1.12 Fusion – Clickteam.

About Clickteam

What is Clickteam? Clickteam is the development group behind The Games Factory, Multimedia Fusion (now just called Fusion), and Install Creator (as well as many other programs). Having used Clickteam's games creation programs for many years, I wrote the first edition of this book way back in 2004. Creating a third edition made it an easy decision to write about the latest version, Fusion 2.5. Using its event-based programming language (which has been mimicked by many other game creation tools over the years), it's a quick and easy way to get your games up and running extremely quickly.

Clickteam provide a limited feature free version of their software so that you can make your own games and then build a HTML version that you can upload to your Website. So, you can get to learn the product before deciding if you want to purchase the full version.

You can find out more information about Clickteam and its products at the Website *www.clickteam.com*.

 The book covers the Windows Steam edition of the limited feature free software version. There are also separate download files for windows and Mac available in the companion files. Please note that the Mac edition works only on specific versions of the Mac OS. Visit https://www.clickteam.com/clickteam-fusion-2-5-free-edition for more information.

Summary

Now that we have touched upon game types and the tools that we are going to use to create our games, hopefully the creative juices are starting to flow and you have some idea of what you would like to make. Don't rush off just yet to begin making your game, as in the next chapter we will be looking at how to grow those simple ideas into full-blown games. Most people have more than one idea, so we will also be looking at getting you to make a decision on the type of game you want to make based on set criteria.

CHAPTER 2

BASIC GAME DESIGN CONCEPTS

In This Chapter

- Why Design?
- Product Design and Planning

I n this chapter, we look at why you might want to spend a little more time thinking about what type of game you want to make, and how you would go about considering how to choose what to create.

Why Design?

You're probably itching to make your first game and to just get on with it. That's not all bad, as it's good to be enthusiastic about a subject you are involved in. But before you get on with making your own game, let's ask a simple question—"How many people do you think start making a game and then give up?" Unfortunately, there are no stats for such a question, but we can guarantee that the world is filled with people who have had an idea for a game but never got it past the starting blocks of just an idea; there is also an ever-growing number of games that have stopped being worked on before they were completed. Making games is no different than any other creative medium; you could say the same for writing a book, writing a song or album, and so on. Many people have aspirations but ultimately fail to start or finish a project.

Not finishing a project is a problem that occurs quite often, and Fusion users have even given it its own name, the "Click Curse." Many games being made with these types of programs get dropped because:

- The idea was too complex for the skills of the developer at that time, and they got stuck and couldn't get past the current issues and so gave up.

- Badly written code, which means that the developer has probably taken the long route to making their game. They notice that it could have been easier to write a little way into development and decide to make the game easier by replacing their old code with the new, super-efficient program, but then realize it's too big a job.

- They find that the game doesn't work as well with the original story after they have begun making it and prefer another idea and decide to make a new game.

- Being too ambitious. Someone who has made no games before and hasn't done any design but tries to make an online role-playing game first is likely to run into problems.

- While working on their project they have a hardware failure and lose some of their work and give up because they then find it too much effort to recreate work they've already done.

Even though many people who have wanted to make a game have failed, there is also a large number of people who have succeeded; some of these people have been able to make their games easily, while it might have been a struggle for others, and they may have been close to giving up one or a number of times through the development of the game. Making games (depending on the size and complexity of the game) can be difficult. Gaming Websites have mentioned "crunch" and "burnout" among issues affecting people who work in the games industries AAA market, but these issues can also be seen by people who are trying to make a game in a small team or on their own.

Making a game (even for fun) can be:

> **Tiring:** If you are working full time and come back from work, you don't necessarily want to come back and work. You probably want to

spend time with family, watching TV or playing games. Time is precious and sometimes you just want to relax.

Lonely: If you are working on your game alone and are working on it full time, then it can become quite lonely doing everything yourself and not being able to talk to anyone about the technical details of what you are doing and how you should do it.

Distracting: You are working on your game and suddenly you realize that football is on or you want to check out the latest gaming news on your favorite gaming site. Suddenly you find that three or four hours have passed and all you've done is look at Websites rather than make progress.

Time-consuming: Sometimes even the simplest of games can take longer than expected. If you are new to making games, then you have to take into account learning the software that you intend to make games with, learning new skills, and so on.

Frustrating: Bugs and coding issues cause your game to take longer to make but also really push your brain cells and cause great frustration (especially when you find the problem that took two days to fix was really easy to fix and was fixed in five minutes).

So, what does this all mean? Well, making a game, be it for fun or for profit, is difficult and has pitfalls along the way, which means people give up. A bit of planning before you start can reduce some of these issues and hopefully prevent failing to finish a project, which if you ultimately want to release a game is what you should be aiming for.

In this book, you'll be creating four different games. This will give you a head start in learning how to make games using Fusion. You will not need to use this chapter for these four games, but understanding how it applies to making games will help you once you have finished this book and are ready to start making your own.

AAA is usually associated with expensive, large-teamed games and relates to the quality of the final product (production values). You can still be a small team and work on AAA games, but it's generally less likely to be the case.

This book is aimed at making games in Fusion and is not a design book, so we've kept this section light and easy to follow. There are many techniques and ways to go deeper into this; keep an eye out on www.jasondarbybooks.com for more information on these subjects in the future.

Keeping it Simple

If you are new to making games, then it would be recommended that the first few games you make after you have completed this book are simple and small. If you decide to make a complicated game while still learning the basics of the software, then you are most likely going to struggle. Imagine yourself as someone who is trying to become a runner. You cannot go from not running at all to running a half marathon. You can try and could probably achieve it by walking most of it, but you'll probably get injured or hurt yourself. This is the same as making a game; you might achieve it, but it'll take you a lot longer and you will have many struggles along the way. Keep it simple and make something that'll teach you a new skill. Just don't try to go from zero to hero in a short period of time, as it's the easiest way to fail.

Product Design and Planning

In the early days of the gaming industry, it was common to have game design documents that were over 100 pages long, but this started to become quite unwieldy, and as time went on the documents became smaller and were limited to shorter PowerPoint presentations with bullet points or using spreadsheets to contain most of the data. One of the reasons for this change was that as you make a game, the design, structure, and data can change a lot, and having to keep documentation up to date was extremely time-consuming for the designers. It would also lead to lots of confusion, as in trying to keep the overall document correct, bits of data spread throughout the 100 pages would easily get missed or not updated.

The second is the iterative approach, which many companies follow these days. This is where you have a basic concept, you create a prototype, and iterate (keep making changes to it) until you feel that it's something you'd want people to play. Both design methods have their issues, but for an indie developer or someone who is making smaller games, a mix of the two or following the iterative approach is the best option.

So, this section of the book is going to take a simple approach to picking a particular game idea and designing it. You'll be glad to know you won't be writing any 100-page design documents. No matter what type of game you are going to make, be it for friends and family, for profit, or for any other reason, you can pick and choose ideas in this chapter that you like the most to help you design your games. Use what you are comfortable with and which areas will help you make the game as easily as possible; there are no right and wrong answers to the best method of game development in tools like Fusion.

Figure 2.1 shows the order in which you could approach your game design.

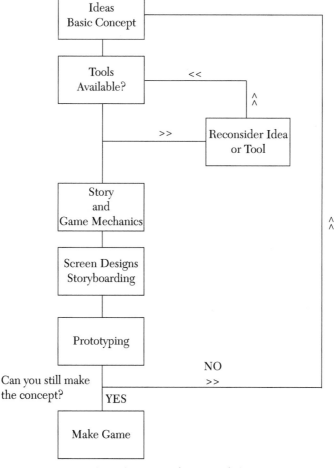

FIGURE 2.1 Approach to game design.

The Ideas

So, you have an idea; in fact, you are likely to have more than one. One of the major problems of wanting to make a game is having too many ideas. Therefore, which one should you choose and start to put a lot of time and effort into? Even a small project will require you to invest some time and effort in the game design, even the tiny games you might make for the Internet or free download.

You may have many good ideas, but you have to be a bit more objective and realize that you cannot implement them all at once.

The best way to do this is to complete a simple table of game ideas, as shown in Table 2.1.

TABLE 2.1 Organizing Your Game Ideas

Game Type	Idea	Technology Concept	Rating	Difficulty
Car Racing	You are a budding race-car driver wanting to become race champion. Before you can compete in the world championship, you need to win the regional heats.	Top-down scrolling	High	Medium
Sim	You are a WWI pilot who has just joined your squadron and must take to the skies as soon as you arrive.	Story-driven 3D flight sim	Medium	High/ Impossible
Scrolling	Aliens have invaded a small town in your local area. A band of citizens cannot simply stand by and watch the impending disaster. A small team armed with weapons goes in search of the alien menace.	Isometric scrolling	Low	Medium

Using Table 2.1, set out all your current game ideas; even if it's a silly or half-thought-out concept, write it down. Ideas shouldn't be judged at this point, so it's a good idea to keep notes of all game ideas in one place. The reason we make this table is to begin to reduce our ideas to a select few; that way, we can really make inroads into what we really want to make.

The table is then split it into five columns. Although the table is simplistic, we don't want to get into any minor detail at this stage. In fact, we want to keep it simple and not write too much; later, we will expand on the ideas of those games that deserve more time and effort.

The columns are separated as follows:

Game Genre: Categorize the game type into one of the standard gaming groups, for example, RPG, war game, flight simulation, isometric, first-person shooter (FPS), etc.

Idea: A brief overview of what the game is about; at this stage, we are keeping it simple. Just a quick overview of the story and the aim of the game.

Technology Concept: What game technology will the game use? This could be top-down scrolling, side scrolling, 3D FPS, etc. This is to give you an idea of what might be required from the tool you intend to use to make your game. It's not a good idea to make a 3D FPS if the product you're choosing can only make 2D games.

Rating: How high do you rate your idea? How excited are you at the prospect of making this game? If it's a low rating, it's not worth spending time and effort to make, as you will probably get bored and give up.

Difficulty: It's time to be honest about your skills in your chosen game-making product. Many people on the game-making forums have never used a game-making product and want to make an online role-playing game or something similar that is just too complex. If you really think the game idea is too difficult, put that aside, as you don't want to start a project and then struggle with the concepts. This is meant to make your life easier, not for you to deceive yourself into thinking you can make anything you want. There is no shame in admitting that an idea at this stage is too difficult, because later it might not be, and you'll have the idea on paper.

After you have reviewed the table and found the highest rating game that strikes you as the most interesting (there may be more than one), you are ready to continue. However, before you get all excited and start making the game, you need to make sure that the game-making tool is capable of carrying out your idea!

 Remember to use the "difficulty" column to decide between multiple high-rating game ideas.

Tool Choice

You have the game you want to make reduced to a few choice game ideas, or perhaps just one. Before you rush off and start it, take a few minutes to check that your ideas are compatible with the game-making tool you are using. In this book, we are going to be using Fusion 2.5, which is specifically for 2D games; therefore, if you selected a 3D FPS, this wouldn't be the right tool for the job. It is very important that you understand both your own capabilities and those of the tools you are going to use.

Investigate your product choice thoroughly before starting any project. This includes making sure what any compiled program created with it runs on, and any other specifications that might affect your decision, including whether your computer powerful enough to run on it, and any licensing rules regarding distribution.

The Story and Game Mechanics

Once you have a basic idea and the tool that you want to make it in, the next stage is to start breaking down the game story further so you have an idea of what might happen and the player's journey through the game. This will also allow you to start thinking about the game mechanics and features that you would include. Game mechanics can be thought of as the things the player will do and how they will do it. For example, in a game like Assassin's Creed, this could be the climbing mechanics, how the player will interact with other characters, or how combat will work. How these mechanics take form may be defined by the story, or in fact the story may change based on what you find works best for the player.

Your story doesn't have to be unique or new; as long as the idea is well presented, you should be fine. Spend a little time writing your story, as this is the key to what will be included in your game mechanically. At this point, you don't need to go into too much detail, as it's just a scoping exercise to make sure you have an idea you ultimately like. You might find that once you have done this, you no longer like the idea and don't want to make it.

If that's the case, you have succeeded, because no one should make games they don't want to make.

 When writing the basic story and game mechanics, be very careful, as this is where feature creep can appear. Feature creep means adding more features as you move through the process, which can turn a small game idea into a massive, complicated game and something that you'll never complete.

From the list of game ideas, let's pick "car racing" as an example. The story plan goes something like that shown in Table 2.2.

TABLE 2.2 Story Plan

Game Name	Car Racing
Story	After working seven years at the local carting center (where you practiced your driving skills during your lunch hour), you are now convinced you can compete in the world's deadliest and most dangerous racing event, "Death Racer." Unfortunately, entry to the event is very competitive, and people have to compete in the regional heats for a chance to be in the ultimate racing event and win the ultimate prize.
Initial Game Details	You will need to complete six regional heats (tracks) and be in the top ten drivers to be promoted to the Death Racer event. You will get points if you appear in the top three of each regional heat. Additionally, you will be awarded cash prizes, which you can then spend on car upgrades or a new vehicle. If you come last in any regional heat, the game will end. The Death Racer event is one track that contains some of the most dangerous obstacles you come across in the entire game. There are fifty drivers competing in the heats. The top ten drivers with the most points get promoted to the Death Race. There are computer-controlled heats in which you will not compete, but the computer generates the results.

So, even at this stage, you have an idea of what your game is all about and what is contained in it.

- Six regional heats in various locations
- One final track once you have progressed through the heats' car upgrades
- Track obstacles

- Prizes

- Car repairs

- Computer-controlled drivers

- It is a dangerous sport

Game Mechanics and Systems

Now that you have your initial story and basic game details, you'll need to break the game down further, so you know what types of game mechanics and systems you want to include. Using the list of items generated from your story plan, you need to get into some more detail by creating a list of features. This list will then be our starting point for creating our game; once you have created it, you will need to review it, and you may decide to remove or add extra items.

So, brainstorm. Write every little bit of game idea down, regardless of whether the idea is far from good or ideal. The list is very useful for confirming all the things you want in the game.

Let's take a look at your game list:

Dangerous Racing
     Weapons
          Forward Firing Missile
          Rear Firing Missile
          Laser
          Mine
     Obstacles
          Oil Slick
          Water
          Fall off Track
     Weather
          Snow
          Rain
          Sunny

Car Improvements
    Engine
        Speed (Turbo)
        Power
    Bodywork
        Durability
        Damage
        Other Cars Bounce off
    Tires
        Breaking
        Cornering
        Affected by Oil, Water, and Track Conditions

This is just a small example of a game features list, which could in theory run into a number of pages. "Why so many pages," you might ask? Especially if you are doing iterative design? Even in iterative development you still need to have a basic understanding of what you are making. Making your list as complete as possible could save you lots of time later. If some of the items are too difficult to code or perhaps just too much work, you can always mark them as version 2. You may be asking the question, "Why did you say there was no need to write a large game design document and here you talk about making a big list?" The basic features/systems list isn't the same as writing an extensive game design document (GDD). A GDD will contain lots of information and detail about the game; it might include things like art requirements, voice over (VO), and text that will be used, as well as the general game mechanics. This document will be very detailed, while the game mechanics list detailed here may take one to five pages and is just a bulleted list.

The whole point of this exercise is to structure what is going to be in the game and what is not going to be in it. You can certainly make changes to this list, but be aware of feature creep; it's more likely that you'll remove items from this list than add new ones to it.

 Changes to the way the game plays are considered acceptable if it makes the game more enjoyable once some initial user feedback has been received. However, it isn't a good idea to add new features when the game is close to being released, as this is a surefire way to delay it further.

So, let's look at a couple of examples of detailing the mechanics of the game.

Car Types

At various stages of the game, you will be able to purchase a new car or upgrade your current one.

Cars will have various starting stats, which can then be upgraded, but each car will have limits on how far it can be improved.

Table 2.3 is an example of the breakdown from the description.

TABLE 2.3 Car Levels

Car Type	Engine Start	Tires Start	Speed Start	Bodywork Start	Cost
X1	Lvl – 1	Lvl – 1	Lvl – 1	Lvl – 1	Default
Speeder	Lvl – 2	Lvl – 2	Lvl – 1	Lvl – 1	$150
Hoffe-E1	Lvl – 2	Lvl – 2	Lvl – 1	Lvl – 1	$200
Panther	Lvl – 1	Lvl – 2	Lvl – 2	Lvl – 2	$350
Turbo-x	Lvl – 2	Lvl – 2	Lvl – 3	Lvl – 2	$550
Win Fusion Etc.	Lvl – 2	Lvl – 3	Lvl – 3	Lvl – 2	$700

You can then break it down even further to detail each specific level of component so that is also easy to program when you get to that point.

An example of the further breakdown is shown in Table 2.4.

TABLE 2.4 Car Speeds

Speed Level	Top Speed
Lvl – 1	8 Mph
Lvl – 2	12 Mph
Lvl – 3	15 Mph
Lvl – 4	17 Mph
Lvl – 5	19 Mph
Lvl – 6	22 Mph
Lvl – 7	24 Mph
Lvl – 8	27 Mph
Lvl – 9	30 Mph
Lvl – 10	35 Mph

This probably seems like a lot of work, but for simple games, it might only take you twenty minutes. For a bigger game, it might take a few hours or even days to document the features of what's going to be in the game. Without detailed game mechanics and story information, you're going to spend much more time programming the game to try to get it to function correctly.

When doing this in an iterative approach, you would work hand in hand with the prototype to figure out the elements of the data needed and what those values are by constantly testing and playing the feature. There is nothing wrong with getting an initial starting list and breaking that down; just don't spend lots of time thinking about whether the data you have written is balanced, as you wouldn't know that until you've got it in game and are playing it.

 Once you have created your data, you'll need to balance your game as you continue to develop and test the game. This is quite normal, and you may find you'll need to add new mechanics or remove others.

Prototyping

Before we get into designing what our screens would look like, and so on, it is worth mentioning "prototyping." This is a very popular technique in game making where designers with the help of programmers will try out certain ideas and game mechanics to see if they'd work. You can come up with an idea, but you can find that once you have put it into the game it just doesn't work as expected, and if you've spent six months making it, that can really be disappointing to have to remove it and start redesigning again. There are various different types of prototyping, some which can be done separately to the game in their own levels, whereas some others might just be inserted quickly into the game code to try out.

For example, you might be making a game where you have combat. Perhaps you were making a World War II game and you have various weapons and enemy types. You may make a combat arena which just contains basic environmental elements but where you can pick up each weapon and try it. You might also be able to change the data for that weapon live, so you can try out different settings to see what feels right. A game which involves hand-to-hand fighting might have a basic arena where you can fight against various enemies. If your game contains lots of platforming, such as climbing or jumping over objects, you may have an area that tests out the various elements of navigation.

 When creating levels (i.e., the environment that your player would navigate around) a common term used in prototyping is white or gray boxing.

 Gray or white Boxing is a technique used in 3D games where you build a test area of the world using white or gray boxes to represent the 3D assets. So, if you want to test out movement and jumping over walls, you might have your character model fully rendered but the wall would just be a single-color box.

Screen Design

Now that you've completed the story and game mechanics, you need to understand how the game is going to look, which will give you an idea of how each screen (frame in Fusion) or level will appear. This allows you to cast a designer's eye over the recommended structure and ensures that everything works correctly from a usability and layout point of view. If someone else will be making your graphics (this isn't uncommon), the screen design is also for his benefit, so you should create the designs how you want them to look and then send them off to the graphic artist to generate.

Game Map

The game map is a simple yet effective way to break your game into sections, levels, or areas of the game. This will also include main menus, level menus, end-of-game screens, or high-score tables. Using a single letter-sized piece of paper (you may need to stick more together), map out the main parts of your game and where they link (see Figure 2.2). The example in Figure 2.2 is from the forthcoming game "Dead of Day" from Trebuchet Games, which contains simple single-use screens (i.e., a menu screen, options, credits) and a multi-use function screen so, for example, the game screen contains moving through the world as well as additional features such as inventory and map.

You can see from the diagram how each screen connects and how it relates to other screens around it. An example of the game flow as seen in Figure 2.2 starts with a main menu screen, and from that screen you'll have three options, Load Game/Continue, the Options screen, and the game's credits.

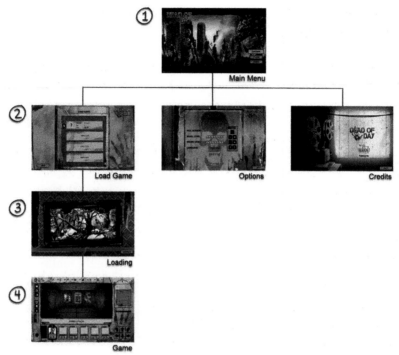

FIGURE 2.2 Game map showing connections between screens.

On each box within the game map we have signified the name of the screen, which should give you an idea of the aim of each screen; the "Loading" item (numbered row 3) loads in data for the game but displays a pretty picture to the player while the "Game" item (numbered 4) is where the core gameplay takes place.

 In Figure 2.2, an actual game is used with completed graphics for the game map to give you a better idea of how the screens connect together. In most cases you would just use words in each box (such as Loading Screen, Game, etc.) to signify the role of each screen.

Screen Map

The screen map takes the process to the next level, whereby you start to draw each screen. This is the detail part of the drawing/design process and could take a while for you to complete it. It is very important though, as this makes you think about what each screen will look like and what components of the game will appear and where (this can be seen in Figure 2.3).

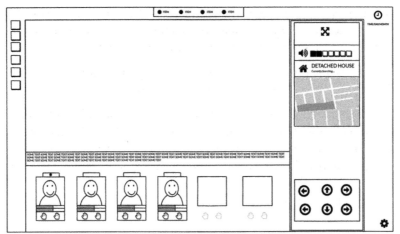

FIGURE 2.3 Screen map detailing everything on screen.

You may find that when you do this, you will suddenly realize that there isn't any room left to put other graphics or it just doesn't work on paper. This is another step that clarifies what you are trying to do before beginning to write the code.

Paper Testing

This might sound a little strange at first, and you might not want to do it. As with everything mentioned so far, it's a very useful process to follow and will help reduce errors later. Most people understand that testing is done at the stage at which the code has been written and the game is ready for its beta testers, so this may seem alien as a concept. Paper testing is very easy to do and not very time-consuming, but again it's something that could save you time and effort in the long run, so why not just try it? Taking what you drew in the screen map and game map sections mentioned previously, we now play the game on paper. Starting at the first box on the game map, imagine you are playing your game and follow the process through. You will need to do this a few times to take into account different routes that the user might take while running your game.

For example, you might want to look at:

- Is it easy to navigate to the start of the game?

- Is it easy to get to the options (keyboard redefine, sound options)? Are all of the options on a single screen or on multiple screens? If they are on more than one, do the screens connect well, and is it easy for the player to navigate back to the main options screen?

- What happens when the game is over, if the game player loses all his lives or decides to quit? Make sure your game allows the player to exit at any time. Does trying to exit go to another screen?

- Are there any other screens that are missing? Examples are tutorials, loading screens, and further gameplay elements.

Once you have done this, you may have to go back and amend your game and screen maps. If you do, make sure you go through the paper testing once more to ensure that the changes do not adversely affect the game. Paper testing is very effective for making sure you have the right screens at the right place and that you have designed your navigation between screens correctly. It will soon show up if you have made any major mistakes anywhere in the entire design process.

Graphics

Only a small percentage of people can make good-looking graphics and animation. If you are one of the few, that's great, and it will be very helpful when you design your game layout and graphics to be used in the game. If you are not, you will run into some issues, so here are some ideas of where you might be able to get some material for your programs.

You can choose from a number of options when looking for graphics:

Fusion 2.5: The full version of Fusion comes with a large collection of graphics that you can use within your games. They may not suit the final game that you are making, but if you are going to prototype or try to get a working version of your game ready before looking for an artist to help you, using the inbuilt graphics can be very helpful.

Graphics libraries: There are a few graphics libraries available on the Internet, some of which are free to use while others have options to purchase. Again, make sure you read the small print on the Websites, as some sites say that if you sell/distribute over 10,000 items of any one product, you will need a different license agreement. You may not want to worry about this right now, but you still should consider it, as you don't want to pull your product off the Internet because you cannot afford the licensing fees. Make sure you know what costs are involved before you start; that way, nothing will be a shock to you when and if you get past those levels.

Make your own: You may be a good enough artist and have the right tools for the job. If you decide to make your own graphics, consider the impact this might have on the time scales for making your game. This will definitely have a bearing on if you have the time, effort, and patience to complete the project, as making graphics can be very time-consuming. If you cannot draw, then still consider putting in placeholder markers using your own skills; waiting for an artist to make art before you code is not a sensible way to make a game, as once the art is done and you begin work you may find additional issues and have to change your game and go back to the artist to make revisions.

Get someone else to make them: One of the challenges of making a game is to get help from other people, especially people you have never met. If you can find a graphic artist to help, make sure you understand how he works, and come to an agreement on time scales. Most graphic artists won't accept work unless there is some form of demo or game in existence. Don't try to get help when you have only written the story, as many artists won't bother to reply to the requests for help at that point. They need to know that you are serious about the project before putting their own time and effort into the work. Even if you cannot draw you can still use "Designer Art," which is in the place of real art but still allows you to complete the coding of the game, so you can show people how it will work.

Sound and Music

Very much a secondary thought in game creation, but still an important aspect to consider, is the sound and music you are going to have in your games. Although not as important as the graphics or gameplay of your game, think about watching a movie without sound, and your overall opinion of the film would definitely go down. Sound and music give a game atmosphere and make it appear more professional, if done correctly. The problem with sound and music is that they have the same problems that come with graphic creation: most people can't make their own and need to find someone or something to supply them.

Fusion 2.5: In the full version of Fusion are many music tracks and sounds that you could use in your game. Music is more specialized, as you want to match a certain sound to a particular time in the game. Definitely take the time to browse the installation files to see if there is anything you could use, as this is definitely easier than some of the other options available to you.

Sound libraries: There are a number of excellent professional Websites that you can listen to for purchasing and downloading a range of sounds and songs. Although you are going to have to spend money, you will be able to pick the exact sounds you want in your game. Always read any licensing text off the Website concerning using sounds commercially; most are okay but read the small print to make sure, as many sites have different rules and pricing for different soundtracks.

Make your own: A few years ago, this would not have been practical unless you had some form of sound equipment (MIDI) and a talent in music creation. Today, however, a number of products are available that can help you make music and sounds relatively easily. With a good microphone and some household equipment you can make you own sound effects.

Get someone else to make them: The same issues exist as with outsourcing graphics; make sure you have a specific time scale for completing the work, and understand the scope of the work and what kind of budget you have.

Summary

As presented in this chapter, take some time when planning the design of your game, even for the smallest of projects. This ensures that you keep to a good development time and stay within budget (if any). If you are creating a small game, the process doesn't have to be as intense or in-depth as some of the suggestions written here. These are only recommendations, and you can amend them to suit your way of working. By doing so, you might not make millions or be an instant success, but it will certainly make your life easier and make sure you are focused on what you are trying to do.

Remember, we all have different success levels; for example, if your plan is to make your game fun and enjoyable for friends and family, that's your success criteria. These concepts will help you even if you are creating for a small audience, so don't think you need a big plan to put some structure into what you are making. You don't need to be making the next Red Dead Redemption or Call of Duty to use a common-sense approach to game design and game making.

CHAPTER 3

BASIC PROGRAMMING CONCEPTS

In This Chapter

- Traditional Programming Languages
- Traditional Programming versus Fusion
- Programming Terms and Concepts
- Pseudocode – Programming in English

You now know how to design the basics of your game, and soon you will be shown how to make your own games using Fusion 2.5. Before you begin, this chapter discusses some of the programming concepts used within Fusion. Although Fusion doesn't use traditional programming like C++ (or other languages), you are still going to be exposed to some concepts used in everyday programming languages. Finally, we discuss how to write your programs in pseudocode, so you can easily convert it to any other language you might learn in the future.

Traditional Programming Languages

Programming languages have been widely available to the general public since the beginning of the 1980s (before this, the hardware and software would have not been cost effective unless you were a medium-sized business). Today, there are many different programming languages you can choose from to make a program, game, database, or application. Not all programming languages can be used efficiently for game creation; for example, you might consider using C++ to make your game's engine, but you wouldn't use COBOL or Pascal (two really old database coding languages). Nearly all programming languages on the market require some form of text/code entry to make "your" program.

An example of the more traditional-based programming languages is shown in Figure 3.1; the code displays the text "Hello World" on the screen.

```
// Create a blank window
DefaultWin=New Window (1920,1080);

WriteLn ("Hello World");

While(TRUE)
{

}
```

FIGURE 3.1 Code example.

Once the code has been entered, the programmer would generate a file that would run on the operating system they are developing for (normally, this is an executable file, but other languages and programs do have other types). What you will notice from the basic "Hello World" code is that it seems straightforward to put text to screen. As programs get more complex and are expected to do more, coding becomes much more complicated.

Traditional Programming Versus Fusion

The major benefit of using Fusion over the traditional languages is that the actual programming is hidden behind a GUI (graphic user interface) front-end, which makes it easier to program and much easier to understand and manage your code (using code comments and groups).

Some of the benefits of using Fusion over traditional code include:

- Traditional code and concepts are hidden behind an easy-to-use GUI front-end. Results from creating programs are seen much quicker than when using traditional coding. Therefore, you will stay more focused and will be more excited, as you will have something on screen very quickly.

■ Creating games in Fusion means you are still being exposed to programming techniques and concepts. For example, you will still learn about sprites, loops, arrays, INIs, and more.

■ Although not as powerful as some traditional-based languages, Fusion is specifically designed for making games. Thus, you get the power of its drag-and-drop programming system, which will allow you to make games with animation, action points, destruction, and movement (also many more functions) without the need to write your own engine using another programming language. The major benefit of this is that the code has already been written for you, and all you need to do is write your game idea!

■ Fusion helps break the game into manageable chunks so you can concentrate on different aspects at different times.

Over the last few years, there have been many successful Fusion developers and programmers. Many users haven't realized what tool was used to make the games. Who cares what makes your game, as long as it does what you want it to do? Just because it only takes a few minutes to get a graphic onscreen and move it around, compared to perhaps many minutes or hours with traditional coding (obviously, this wouldn't be the case if you were an experienced C++ programmer), does it really matter? If you have a time restraint, and Fusion can do what you need to do, why make life more difficult for yourself?

Programming Terms and Concepts

Before we begin making our programs, it will be very beneficial for you to understand some of the terms and concepts we will be dealing with in this book and within Fusion, so you won't have to struggle with terms when moving "full steam" on your project.

Arrays

Arrays are a way of storing and retrieving large amounts of data in an organized format. They are very efficient for storing data for many different reasons but can only contain text or numbers in each array file (in Fusion's point of view; this may not be the case in other languages). There are typically three types of array dimensions: one-, two-, and three-dimensional.

Each piece of data is stored in a location within an array file and is called upon when needed. The array can also be written when the program is running, which means it can be used to save real-time data. You could think of an array as a less sophisticated database; in some respects it is similar to a spreadsheet that stores data.

The most basic type of array is a single (one-dimensional) array, which is just like having a row of boxes one on top of each other that contain data (which could be text or numbers). To access the relevant data, you would specify its location within the array, which in the case of Figure 3.2 would be [X2]. Why is it X2 and not just 2? Well, in each type of array we define a letter and a number in Fusion.

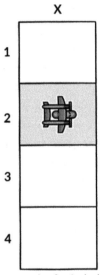

X

1

2

3

4

FIGURE 3.2 An example of a single dimension array.

The image of the plane is being used to signify data and would not contain a graphic, but it could contain a pointer to a graphic file (this would be the folder location and filename). Remember, the array can store either numbers or text, but not both (when using Fusion's default array options).

A 2D array is slightly more complex and allows you to have a typical grid-like data structure very much like a spreadsheet, and it is usually called the [X,Y] dimensions, as shown in Figure 3.3. X goes from left to right, and Y goes from top down.

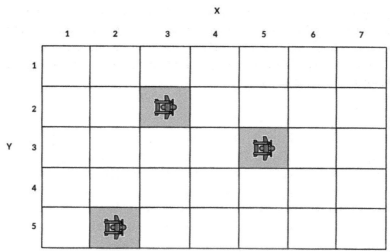

FIGURE 3.3 A 2D-array example structure.

As most people are familiar with programs similar to Microsoft Excel, a 2D array is not a difficult concept to understand; you are basically placing your data in a structure that has rows and columns (the X,Y axis). So, in Figure 3.3 we have data in (3,2), (2,5), and (5,3).

Finally, we have a 3D array, which is again a more complex type of array, and one you will find very useful for your game making. Think of a cube shape, and that will help you understand the basic structure (see Figure 3.4). With a 3D array, you need to specify three numbers, an [X,Y,Z] axis, to locate the data.

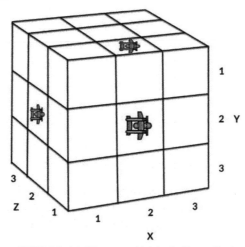

FIGURE 3.4 A 3D Array, which looks like a cube.

The main considerations between a 2D and a 3D array are that with 2D, you are dealing with a flat sheet of paper with rows and columns of data. A 3D array is shaped more like a cube (could be a long or tall cube), and each block (rather than cell or face) contains the data. In Figure 3.4, you have data in (2,2,1), (1,2,2), and (2,1,1). So, although, for example, in Figure 3.4 the plane icon is on the top, it really inhabits the whole of the cube; it is shown on the top to show how the data could go backward into the shape. Remember its X, Y, and then Z.

Although arrays are quite efficient and a basic 3D array doesn't use much hard disk space, it is a good idea to only pick the one you need and not move up to the next type unless necessary. Arrays can get quite complex, so keeping with a 2D array where possible will also help make your program understandable if you were to stop programming and come back to it after an extended period of time.

We need to discuss one more concept concerning arrays that you will come across, 1-based and 0-based indexing. As you know, each array item is numbered by its axis (e.g., x and y), but a 0-based or 1-based index would state whether the numbering begins with a 1 or a 0.

Figure 3.5 shows how the 1-based index works; in the first example, the first item in that array is [1] and then [2]. In the second illustration, you would be accessing [0] and [1] instead. It is very important to remember which index you have selected, because if you try to read and write to a 0-based index and have selected a 1-based index, it will not work (you will not get any error messages to suggest otherwise).

With Fusion, you have the benefit of putting multiple array files into your game, so you can break your game down into smaller and easier-to-manage files. This allows you to create a small array file and make sure it works and

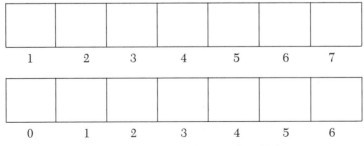

FIGURE 3.5 An example of a 1- or 0-based index.

that your game is reading/writing the data correctly—then, you can move on to the next section. If you create a single massive array file, you might find that it doesn't work, and the more data you are dealing with, the harder the testing becomes. When you start to break your program down, ensure that you make many comments in the program so you know what you did. This will help you when you go back to a project after a break.

INI Files and Data Files

INI files are basically text-formatted files that computer programs can read. These were used quite extensively in older versions of Windows to contain information about the operating system, but less so these days as they were replaced by the registry. Most traditional programming languages do not call them INI files anymore, but configuration or data files. It is very common to store information relating to configuration and program settings in an INI file (see Figure 3.6). An example of the INI file in use within a game is "Dead of Day"—we use the INI file to store the current sound and music levels, and if the game is in full screen or windowed mode. We also use the INI files to store the game's save information as well as current statistics used for achievements.

```
[HQ_Resources]
Food=0
Water=0
Fuel=0
Medicine=0
Wood=0
Electronics=0
Metal=0

[Mission_Resources]
Food=0
Water=0
Fuel=0
Medicine=0
Wood=0
Electronics=0
Metal=0

[HQ_Cabin_Starting_Values]
HQ_Defence=1
HQ_Storage=1
HQ_Food=2
HQ_Water=2
HQ_Health=0
HQ_People=1

[HQ_Cabin_Current_Values]
HQ_Defence=1
HQ_Storage=1
HQ_Food=2
HQ_Water=2
HQ_Health=0
HQ_People=1
```

FIGURE 3.6 An INI file in use showing stored game information.

The biggest issue with using INI files for storing the game's save data is that they are not encrypted. So, a player could access the file and change data to help them play the game quicker. For example, you may store the player's current gold; imagine for a moment if they were able to go in and increase that value, allowing them to buy all of the best equipment. This would potentially make your game unplayable. Using other objects, you can encrypt the INI file so that the player cannot read the data and so cannot make changes to it.

Flags

Flags signify on and off states. They are very useful for many simple situations and shouldn't be overlooked. For example, do you want to check if a door is open or a light switch is on? If so, a flag can show you the state of that item very simply and allow you to check its state. There is no restriction to the type of game a flag is used in, and they can be very useful in many different situations. For example, you might want some flags to signify when the adventurers have triggered a trap. Therefore, once it had been triggered, you could then specify that the trap was now off so it didn't happen again. In one of the games you will be making, a flag is used to see when a certain event has happened so it can initiate some alternative code.

Local and Global

In the programming world, local and global refer to variables and how they are defined within the program, whether available to the entire program or just a certain section of the code. Fusion is not much different in concept from using a traditional text entry-based coding language; in fact, the ideas are the same. Local means using an object or code for a single frame, and global means that the information is available to the entire program. Fusion has a number of global options, including global events and global values.

Loops

You will often need to instruct the program/game to do the same thing several times in a row. This is called a loop and is very useful when you want to draw some items on screen or do something repetitive. It is also much easier to write a loop to do this rather than write the lines of code separately without a loop. As an example, perhaps you are trying to make a crossword game and have to display a 17x17 grid of pictures on screen to represent the crossword puzzle boxes. There are two ways you could achieve this: you could write seventeen lines of code to represent each row of boxes, or you could use a loop, which would achieve the same result in two lines of code. Hopefully, from that example you will understand what the power of a loop can do for your programming; it will simplify your code, and you won't have to write as much to achieve the same result. You will also find that reducing your code makes your program more efficient, which means in the long run, it might actually take up less space and run faster. However, more importantly, the less code you have to write, the easier and quicker it is to debug (find issues with) your program.

Random

Randomizing numbers or lists is a common task in programming languages. A random number, for example, is a number chosen at random (you don't know up front what number will be chosen). Perhaps you are making a dice game and are thinking of using a six-sided dice. You use the random feature to simulate the player rolling the dice and getting a number between 1 and 6. Every time you roll the dice you want the number to be chosen at random (i.e., not the same number each time), and so this is where you use the Random feature. In Fusion if we wanted to simulate a die, we would use the following:

Random(6)+1

We put this text string within the Expression Evaluator (this will be discussed in Chapter 5); the word Random tells Fusion that it will be generating a random number, and the number in the brackets is the range that we want to pick from. Finally, the +1 will add a further 1 to the result. You may be wondering why we have a range of 6 and a +1 to add to the result. The reason is that the Random feature uses a 0-based index. All numbers chosen start from 0, so if you put the number 6 in brackets, it will pick from a range of 0 to 5 (6 numbers). If you were to put a (7) this would select from 0 to 6. So, in the case of a 6-sided dice where you need a number from 1 to 6, always adding +1 will give you a resulting range of 1 to 6.

Variables

A variable is a piece of data the computer will store that will change (or more specifically, can contain something different from when the program started). This could be either a string (text) or a numeric (number) variable. At the start of a program, you would normally set these to blank so you don't have to worry about incorrect data being passed to your program. This is normally called initialization and is a process in which you set all variables and other data to specific data.

What can a variable hold? Basically anything. If we had a program that asked a user two questions:

- What is your favorite number over 10?

- What is your favorite number under 10?

We would need two numeric variables to store the response from the user input. As a group of people queue up to enter the details, each user could enter a different number. The reason for a variable is that the number entered could be different each time. We could also store string variables (where it stores text in the variable rather than a number):

- What is your name?

- What is the name of your pet?

Some examples of variables that can change could be:

- Current Date and Time

- Player's Score

- Player's Health

- Resources collected

- Enemies destroyed

An example of a variable in use within Fusion is the counter object (we'll discuss objects in detail in Chapter 6) which is used when you want to put a changing number into a game. This could be used to count down the time or the number of lives the player still has left. Fusion has an object for this type of thing, and all you need to do it set the starting number and then keep amending it when you need to (e.g., when the player has lost a life).

Pseudocode – Programming in English

At many colleges and universities, taking a computer science course could mean learning a number of programming languages, including C++, C#, Pascal, Visual Basic, and COBOL. Some people find programming easy while others find it time-consuming and complicated. If you are one of the people who has never really got to grips with programming or are starting out, then pseudo programming might be of help, as it can really help you understand what you need to do within your program with regard to coding. If you have never programmed before or don't think you are good at it, this is a great way to become a better programmer. The main problem with programming is that it can be a bit daunting until you've had enough practice.

Now, of course, Fusion doesn't use text programming, and although pseudocode is most useful for those types of languages, we can still put it to good use to understand what we need to do in our program. Pseudocode is also very good for giving you an idea of how you should structure your program, and it will help you with what areas you will need to put into it to get it to work. Let's take a simple example of what you want a program to do and then rewrite it in pseudocode. First, we want to make a program that displays a message on screen, and when you press a key (any key), it will disappear. So, let's break it down into what needs to happen.

1. Start of the program

2. Text message appears on screen

3. Another message stating "click any key."

4. User presses any key

5. End of program

So, you have now written your first pseudocoded program, and it's practical in any language—Pascal, C#, or even Fusion. Each language has its own rules for what you would need to do in each section, but you can understand what you will need to look for within the product documentation or help file. We will now go through each of the options and see what it means to our program. The start and end of the program should always appear in your pseudocode, as these will always happen. The options in between are what you want to happen in your program, so in this example we are putting text to the screen, showing another message, and responding to a key press. Once the key press has been completed, the program ends.

This is pseudocode at its most basic; for it to be more useful, we need to be a little more descriptive in what we are trying to achieve and how we will do it within our programs.

1. Start of the Program

2. Setup Screen, initial objects, variables, and initialization

3. Text message appears on screen

   A. Specify location on the screen

   B. What text do we want

4. Place another message stating "click any key"

   A. Specify location on the screen

   B. Place text on screen

5. User presses any key

   A. Await User Input

6. End of program

7. Close and remove objects and close window/screen

The great thing about pseudocode is that it can make quite complex code much easier to write and create. You will notice that some pseudocode is indented; you can do this to separate groups of code that work together, making it easier to read. Once you have converted your program to pseudocode, you can then go to each line and transfer it into Fusion or another language.

Summary

Understanding the concepts in Fusion is very useful if you decide to learn another programming language. A number of Fusion users have gone on to become prolific C++ programmers, and the catalyst for that was these types of programs. My son started on Fusion when he was around six years old, and now at eighteen he knows various traditional programming languages and is already a better programmer than me. Sometimes it can just be a case of understanding a concept, so once you know what it is all about, you can then apply it in the real world. Do not underestimate the benefit of learning the basics, as it will definitely come in handy later if this is something that you wish to pursue.

CHAPTER 4

FUSION BASICS

In This Chapter

- Structure of a Game
- Game Creation Process in Fusion

I n this chapter, we discuss basic game creation concepts and what you are likely to see in any game you might download or play. We also cover some of the concepts and terminology you will be exposed to later in this book.

Structure of A Game

In game development, a number of settings are available to programmers to make their games look more professional and give the players more control over the way the game behaves in their PC/Mac and Web environments. An example of this could be games running in a window, full-screen games, menu bars, and minimize and maximize options. In this section of the book, we go through the options available in games today, so when you start to program them yourself, you will know if these options would be useful. These are issues you should consider before beginning development of your games, as you might have to rework your program at a later stage if you decide to do things differently.

Some of the areas that you will come across in your development time include:

Full screen: The majority of modern games use the full screen to display their game. With full screen enabled, you will not be able to see any part of the Windows/Mac operating system screen (e.g., the desktop or taskbar).

Application window: Certain types of games prefer to use an application window to display their game rather than the full screen. This allows game players to continue to use the desktop and any programs they might be running (e.g., email). Card games and board games (chess, solitaire) are common games that run in an application window (see Figure 4.1).

Headings: If you are running your game in an application window, you can include a heading bar where the name of the game (or application) is displayed (see Figure 4.2).

Menu bar: When running your game in an application window, you can include a menu bar. You might be familiar with this concept, as they are included in many applications within the Windows environment. A menu bar allows the player to click on different bits of text and select options from a menu system (see Figure 4.2).

Minimize button: In the top right corner of an application window is the minimize button, and clicking on it can reduce a game to a small bar on the taskbar. Clicking on the button (it will be an icon with the product's name on it) again will then restore the game to the desktop area (see in Figure 4.3).

Maximize button: In the top right corner of an application window is another button that allows you to maximize the game to the whole area of the desktop (this is not the same as full screen, as you can still access applications and the taskbar using this option). The maximize button can be seen in Figure 4.3.

Close button: Another option when using an application is the ability to close it. The close button is in the top right corner of the application window and appears as a cross icon with a red background (see Figure 4.3).

Thick frame: If an application window has a thick frame, it means that it can be made larger or smaller using the mouse.

FIGURE 4.1 A game running in an application window rather than full screen.

FIGURE 4.2 The heading bar is at the top, and the menu is directly below it.

FIGURE 4.3 The three buttons signify minimize, maximize, and close.

Figures 4.1, 4.2, and 4.3 are from a Windows operating system. These will look different on a Mac, but the concept is still the same. If you are using the free version of Fusion, you will not be able to generate a Windows or Mac executable and will not have these features available when creating a HTML5 version, as these are specific desktop application features. They are mentioned here for completeness so if you decide to purchase the full version of Fusion you will understand what they are.

Game Creation Process in Fusion

Creating games in Fusion follows a very simple process which can be described as follows:

Frames: These are the screens of your game.

Placing Objects: Objects contain special code that is specific to a particular task.

Creating Code: You create code in a graphical interface that resembles a spreadsheet in a screen called the Event Editor.

Testing: Running your game and seeing where issues exist, then fixing them.

Games created in Fusion are comprised of a series of frames. These frames can be defined as a particular aspect of the game you are creating, perhaps the main menu, the game itself, or a frame for the high scores. The frame system provides a simple and easy way to break your game into sections; for example, you could create a frame for every level in your game, so each could be different. Frames make it easier for you to get other people involved in the development of your game, as you can get them to create the different sections and you can then import them into your final game structure. If you are working on your own, the frames system allows you to pick any area of the game, program it, make sure it works, and then move on to another area. If a particular aspect (frame) is causing a problem, you can still continue to program and leave the difficult frame for another time. The frame system provides an easy way to visualize the structure of your creation much more than using traditional programming languages. When you first open Fusion, no frames are present, and when you create a new game, it creates a single frame for you to get started with. If you have already designed the structure of your game, you can add new frames immediately to the program and rename them appropriately (by default, they are "Frame 1," "Frame 2," etc.). Each of these newly created frames will be blank, as you will need to put graphics on them. To move between frames, double-click on the frame name in the workspace toolbar, or use the next frame option in the navigate menu toolbar (this will be covered shortly).

Each game created in this book contains three frames: one for the main menu, one of the actual game, and one for all the high scores.

 If you decide to use multiple frames for the levels within your game, remember this does add complexity to your coding as you'll need to take information from one frame to the next, such as lives, current score, bonus points, etc.

 When making your own frames you may decide to have multiple layered screen elements within the same frame. For example, you could have a separate frame for the game screen and an options screen. You could also put both elements on the same frame. There are benefits and disadvantages to both, for example memory requirements and handling many graphics on the Event Editor.

Graphics and Objects

Once you have created your frame structure, you can then move on to the next stage of game development with Fusion, which is placing your graphics and objects on the play area. The most common way of doing this is to draw your images externally and then import them into Fusion. It is also possible to create a library of graphics or use the inbuilt supplied graphics and drag and drop those onto the play area. A number of objects can be placed within Fusion that can display images (objects are discussed later in the book), two of which are the Active object and the Backdrop object. If you want to use graphics that will be moving on the screen (e.g., a spaceship or a bullet), you would use Active, and if you want to have an image that is not going to interact in the game (e.g., a background image), you would select Backdrop. After inserting a graphical object, you can double-click on it to open the Picture Editor, where you can then import any images you have created. As discussed in the next few chapters, a number of different objects can be added to a frame to add extra functionality. Each object has its advantages and uses within a game, and you will need to try them to see how you can use them (many of them are self-explanatory). There are some functions built into Fusion, and you don't have to insert an object onto the play area to use them; for example, input (keyboard and mouse), sound, and movement between frames are just some of the built-in functions you can access via the Event Editor using code.

 The play area is where the player will play the game; in Fusion you can have an on-screen and off-screen play area. This is presented in Fusion with two different colored backgrounds.

Event Editor

Once all of your graphics and game objects are in place, you need to do one more thing to get your game working: you need to tell Fusion what to do with these objects, and what happens when the player does something specific (clicks with the left mouse button, uses the arrow keys, etc.). This requires you to create a number of actions for each event that can happen from within the Event Editor using Fusion's point-and-click programming language. Coding in the Event Editor is straightforward and powerful. Each object has its own set of actions and conditions that can be accessed through the Event Editor, giving game developers a large number of possibilities in their creations.

Summary

In this chapter, you were given a brief summary of the three main areas of game creation within Fusion. First was the creation of frames, which are the building blocks of your screens or levels. Then we discussed objects, which are placed on each of the frames and provide functionality within your games using joysticks, graphic objects, video, and sounds. Finally, once you have placed your objects on your frames, you would then begin to code your games using the Event Editor.

CHAPTER 5

FINDING YOUR WAY AROUND

In This Chapter

- System Requirements
- Program Installation
- Starting Fusion for the First Time
- Menu Tour
- The Editors
- Making More Space

In this chapter, we will be installing the Fusion application and learning the interface. This is very important if you want to quickly start making games and understand where to click when making the example games included with the book. By the end of the chapter, you will understand how to access each of the screens and why you might want to use them.

System Requirements

You need to consider two areas of system requirements when using Fusion: the system requirements for installing the product on your machine, and the requirements for the machine on which your completed game is going to be installed.

Installation Requirements

Table 5.1 lists the general system requirements for installing Fusion. Although these are the minimum required to install and run the product, a faster and better machine will improve the overall performance and speed of the product.

TABLE 5.1 System Requirements for Installation

Minimum Requirements
Operating System – 8 and Windows 10 (older OS's may also be supported)
Dual Core Processor
1GB RAM
Must support minimum of Direct3D 9
650MB Free hard disk space
Broadband Internet Connection

 The minimum requirements should meet your installed Operating System minimum requirements. Where possible you should exceed the OS minimum requirements.

Runtime Requirements

Though you can only create a Web game with the free version of Fusion, if you upgrade to the paid version then you'll need to take into account giving the user a compiled Windows or Mac build of your game. Runtime requirements are much more complicated to work out compared to system requirements (requirements for running the Fusion tool on your machine) because they are based on the size and complexity of the game. For example, a simple game with a single graphic that moves across the screen would have different runtime requirements than a game with hundreds of graphics and sound. To know what specifications you should put on your product, you will need to test it on a variety of hardware platforms. Finally, whenever you are specifying runtime system requirements, make sure your minimum settings match at least the operating system minimum requirements.

Program Installation

We will be using the free version of Fusion, which is available on Steam and as a standalone installation file in the companion files. The book covers installation via Steam, if you already own the full version standalone or use the standalone version in the companion files, the installation process will be different. Please consult www.clickteam.com about how to install the product.

You can download the Free Edition of Fusion available on Steam.

- Type *https://store.steampowered.com* in a Web browser.

- Click on the green "Install Steam" icon in the top right-hand corner of the Steam Website. Then follow the instructions for installation.

- If you don't have a Steam account you will need to create one; if you have an account you will need to log into Steam.

- Once Steam has been installed and you have an account, there are two ways of accessing the Free Edition of Fusion; first you can go to a direct link:

  https://store.steampowered.com/app/478960/Clickteam_Fusion_25_ Free_Edition/

- Or you can click on the "Search the store" box and type in Fusion Free. This will list a number of products; select "Clickteam Fusion 2.5 Free Edition" to take you to the store page.

- Click on the green Free button to start the install process (you may need to scroll down to see this button).

- Information about the space that the install will take will appear as well as the default installation directory; click on the Next button and it will begin downloading the files and installing.

- Click on the Finish button when it appears to close the Steam dialog box.

- Go to the Library | Software drop-down menu to display all software that is currently installed or downloading. Click on the product name in the product list bar on the left-hand side of Steam. If the Free Edition does not have a % number next to it, this means it has finished downloading and the blue Launch button will be available on the product page.

With the free version you will be able to create and run your games locally so you can test them and see how they look, and you will be able to export to HTML5. HTML5 is a Web-based format, meaning you can put your game on a Website and allow other people to play it using a standard http Web address.

With the Free Edition version, you also get a Royalty Free commercial runtime, meaning you can make and distribute any games you've created free of charge.

 Only certain features of the HTML exporter are supported, and more in-depth features are reserved for Fusion 2.5 standard or Fusion 2.5 Developer.

 The books figures in this chapter are based on the Free version of Fusion 2.5. In Chapter 20, we will be detailing features available in Fusion 2.5+; if you are running the free version these items will not be available.

The free version has a number of restrictions compared to the full Fusion 2.5 release product, such as:

- Does not include certain editors, such as the Event List Editor or the Data Editor.

- You cannot create project files.

- You cannot use Alpha Channels.

- You cannot embed binary files into the project.

- You cannot buy exporters which allow you to export to other platforms; you'll need to purchase a copy of the software to allow you to extend your platforms further.

- You cannot use AVI or TGA file formats.

- Develop your own extensions in C++.

Even though the Free Edition has some limitations, it still has enough features for you to be able to put your game together and test it, which is extremely useful and can help you decide if you then want to purchase the full version.

Starting Fusion for the First Time

To start Fusion, double-click on the Fusion icon on the desktop. Fusion will now load and appear on-screen, as shown in Figure 5.1. The Fusion program can be broken into a number of separate sections (see Figure 5.2).

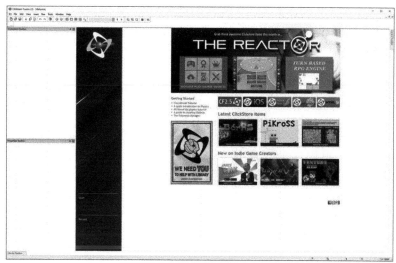

FIGURE 5.1 The Fusion main screen.

FIGURE 5.2 Breakdown of the main sections in Fusion.

1. **Menu Text toolbar:** Item one in Figure 5.2 is the menu bar, which is where you can access all of Fusion's creation, configuration, and display options. To reveal the options, click on the menu text and select a word from the drop-down menu. Some items will be grayed out, which means they are disabled, because you cannot set an option while in the current screen. Items will become enabled when you are in the correct screen.

2. **Menu Button toolbars:** Item two in Figure 5.2 is the Toolbar, which is a graphical icon used to move to another screen, to another editor, or to change an option. There are a number of toolbars that will appear or disappear depending on the screen you are currently in.

3. **Workspace toolbar:** Item three in Figure 5.2 is the Workspace toolbar, which contains the building blocks for each level.

4. **Properties toolbar:** Many items within Fusion have property settings, allowing you to configure the look and the way they interact within your game. Every time you click on anything that has configurable properties, it will appear in item four in Figure 5.2.

5. **Editor area:** You will use a number of editors within Fusion; for example, the Storyboard, Frame, and Event Editors all appear in item 5 in Figure 5.2. When you first start Fusion and there is no file loaded, it will display some help and news information; it will also provide you with a way to create a new application or option a previously generated one.

6. **Library toolbar:** The Library toolbar contains images and objects that you can use within your game. By simply using drag and drop, you can move an item from the library into your game. The Library toolbar is shown in item 6 in Figure 5.2. When first starting Fusion the library toolbar will be collapsed; if you move your mouse over it, it will expand, and by clicking on the pin icon you can stop it from collapsing.

7. **Layers toolbar:** The Layers toolbar will show you all of the different layers you have in your game for that particular frame. This is very useful when you want to put different graphical images and objects at different levels (on top of each other). Consider this like using layers within a graphics program; having objects and graphics on a higher layer will put them above other objects within the frame. The Layers toolbar is shown as item 7 in Figure 5.2; as with the Library toolbar, it is initially set to collapsed when starting with a blank application.

Fusion Tour

In the following pages, we will take a quick tour around the different areas of Fusion in more detail.

Menu Text Bar

The menu bar is at the top of Fusion's application window and looks like a row of text. Clicking on any of these words will reveal a pop-up menu, an example of which is shown in Figure 5.3. The menu bar contains a number of configuration and display settings for you to choose. Some of the items have an underlined first letter (e.g., the "F" in File), which means that you can access the menu option using a shortcut key. The shortcut key can be enabled by holding down the ALT key and then selecting the underlined letter you want to access. For example, if you wanted to access the File menu, you could use the shortcut ALT and then "F" to make the pop-up menu appear.

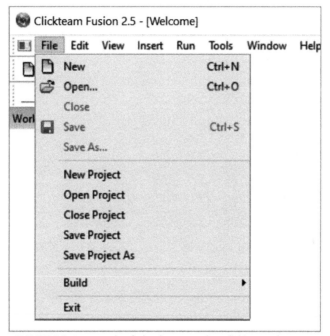

FIGURE 5.3 An example of what happens when clicking on the menu.

Consult Fusion's help documentation on any specific option within the Menu bar for more information.

Menu Button Toolbars

The menu button toolbars provide you with a number of graphical icons to quickly access common features within Fusion. This can be file maintenance such as loading and saving, UI convenience such as zooming into various screen items, runtime settings such as running and debugging your level and, finally, quick access to the various editors.

The toolbars available in Fusion include:

- Standard
- Workspace
- Properties
- Navigate
- Run
- Editor
- Layers
- Library

The Standard Toolbar

The Standard toolbar exists on all screens that you will navigate to within Fusion (see Figure 5.4).

FIGURE 5.4 The Standard toolbar.

There are nine icons in total which are (from left to right):

New: Creates a new game.

Open: Opens a previously saved game or example. A dialog box will appear, and you will need to browse to where the programs are located. Fusion can open a range of file types, including previous versions and library files created with Clickteam's older software.

Save: You have to have a document open to be able to save it. When you first open Fusion, this option will be disabled.

Cut: Allows you to cut (remove and place in the clipboard) an object or event, ready for pasting back into the Fusion application.

Copy: Makes a copy (doesn't remove the object or event but places an exact copy on the clipboard) ready for pasting back.

Paste: Pastes the object or event back into the Fusion application.

Undo: If you make a mistake or decide the change you just made was incorrect, you can revert to the previous version by using the Undo option.

Redo: If you use the Undo option and then decide that you didn't want to, you can reapply the changes.

Contents: This will launch the Help document, which provides further information on how to use Fusion.

The Workspace Toolbar

The Workspace toolbar shows the application and the frames (levels) that make up the game. This is a high-level view and is used to navigate between the levels of your game quickly. It is also used in conjunction with the Properties toolbar, so clicking on the application name or a frame will reveal its properties. An example of the Workspace toolbar in use is shown in Figure 5.5.

Within the Workspace toolbar, you can also see all of the game objects involved in the creation of your game (which you can see by clicking on the plus icon to expand the text). You can also create folders to contain a selection of the game objects, so you can place similar objects together for ease of use.

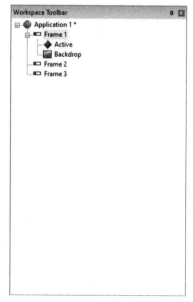

FIGURE 5.5 The Workspace toolbar, high-level game view.

The Properties Toolbar

When clicking on an application or frame within the Workspace toolbar, or clicking on an object in the Frame Editor, its associated properties will appear in the Properties toolbar. Properties of these items allow you to configure them for your game, which can change the look and the way they behave in your final executable. An example of the Properties toolbar can be seen in Figure 5.6.

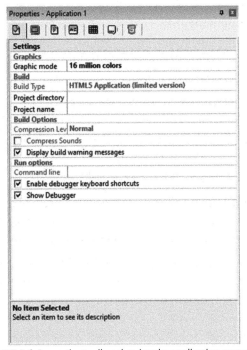

FIGURE 5.6 Properties toolbar showing the application properties.

The Navigate Toolbar

The Navigate toolbar is used to move between the Storyboard, Frame, and Event Editors, and to move between game levels (known as frames) (see Figure 5.7).

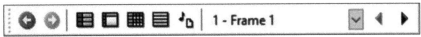

FIGURE 5.7 The Navigate toolbar.

Back and forward: If you move from one frame to another and want to quickly go back or forward between screens, press the red arrowed buttons. Think of this as a Web browser, where you can move between Web pages, except in Fusion, you are moving between screens.

Storyboard editor: Clicking on the Storyboard icon will display the Storyboard Editor, which is a high-level view of all of the levels within your game.

Frame editor: The Frame Editor allows you place all of your images and game objects within each of your levels.

Event editor: The Event Editor is the area in which to code your game. You will use actions, events, and conditions in a simple mouse-clicking environment to build your games.

Event list editor: When you create actions, you apply them to a condition line one at a time in a left-to-right order. The Event List editor will show a more tailored top-down list of these actions so you can move their order precisely. This is extremely important, as the order in which actions happen can have a massive effect on the working of your game.

Data elements: These are elements such as sound, music, and external files that have been added to your game. This allows you to view, play, add, or replace particular files globally through the application.

Frame navigator: Using a drop-down box, you can select a specific level of your game to go to, which is identified by its frame name.

Previous frame: Go back to the previous frame if one is available.

Next frame: Go to the next frame if one is available.

The Run Toolbar

When you want to test your games, you use the Run toolbar. Five options are available, as shown in Figure 5.8.

FIGURE 5.8 The Run toolbar

Run project: A project file contains multiple application files; you use the Run Project button to launch the first application file.

Run application: This option will start the game and run it from the beginning as if the end user were running the final executable on his PC, so you can test each part of your game as a final running program.

Run frame: The Run frame will run only the frame you are currently editing. Use this to test a particular frame; any exits to other frames will automatically close the running game.

Stop: This option will be grayed out until you select either Run Application or Run Frame, after which you can stop the game from running by pressing this button.

Build and run: This will allow you to build the current application and generate its executable. This will depend on the version of Fusion you have and what executable setting you have selected; in the Free version this will be HTML5.

 If you have multiple applications loaded into Fusion, the Run Project button will launch the first application file in the Workspace toolbar.

The Editor Toolbar – Storyboard Editor

When working in the Storyboard Editor, there are a number of buttons in the toolbar you can choose from (as shown in Figure 5.9).

FIGURE 5.9 The editor toolbar for the Storyboard.

Zoom bar: The zoom option is a small bar that you can drag either left or right to increase or decrease the amount of zooming. This will make the Storyboard Editor increase or decrease in size.

Zoom entry: You can enter a specific numeric amount to zoom in or out the Storyboard Editor. The default is set at 100; anything below 100 will make the Storyboard area smaller, and anything above 100 will make it larger.

Show headers: This is turned on by default, and clicking it will turn the column headers off (the headers detail what is shown below them). You can turn them back on by clicking the button again.

Show comments: The comments column in the Storyboard Editor can be turned on and off by clicking on this button (comments are turned on by default). To turn them back on, click on the button again.

The Editor Toolbar – Frame Editor

When doing any work within the Frame Editor (as shown in Figure 5.10), you will have a number of options to choose from, but not all will be available at all times. You will only have access to certain features when using specific options (e.g., editing text).

FIGURE 5.10 The Editor toolbar.

Zoom: You can zoom the Frame Editor in or out using a drop-down box to select the percentage you need. You can choose from 25%, 50%, 100% (normal size), 200%, and 400%.

Free move: Allows you to drag around the play area (where your game contents are); this will allow you to see objects that are off-screen or reposition the area for access to particular positioned objects.

Paint mode: Allows you to use the cursor to paint an object onto the play area multiple times (like using a paint brush). Once you have added a single object, click on the paint icon and then select the object you wish to paint in the object list.

Grid setup: Clicking on the Grid Setup button will display a dialog box to allow you to configure a grid. This grid can then be placed on the Frame Editor to help you place your game objects and images using the Show Grid button.

Show grid: Once you are happy with the grid configuration, you can display it on the Frame Editor by clicking this button. You can turn off the grid by clicking the Show Grid button a second time. The grid appears as a set of dots across the playfield.

Snap to grid: By clicking the Snap to Grid button, you can precisely position any objects on the playfield using the grid dots.

Font: If editing text, you can select the font you want to use by clicking on this button.

Bold: As with the Font button, if you are editing text, you can apply the bold option.

Italic: You can apply the italic option to any text you are currently editing.

Underline: A line will appear under any text you are editing.

Text color: If you are not happy with the default text color (black), you can select a different color. As with the other text options, you must be editing a text object to have these options available.

Align left: Moves the text to the left in the edit box.

Center: Centers the text in the edit box.

Align right: Moves the text to the right in the edit box.

Center frame: This will force the display to center the current frame you are editing, which is very useful if you are editing a very large playfield and want to go back to its center.

The Library Toolbar

With the full version of Fusion, you receive a number of graphic images and animations that can be accessed via the Library toolbar. When creating the games in this book, you will use this toolbar. The Library toolbar allows you quick access to a folder on your hard drive that contains images, animations, or library files from previous versions of your product. The Library toolbar can be seen in Figure 5.11.

FIGURE 5.11 An example library loaded and ready to use.

 If you cannot see the full Library toolbar, you will need to move your mouse cursor to the tab at the bottom of Fusion; the window will appear, then click on the pin icon on the bottom right-hand corner to pin the window into place.

The Layers Toolbar

Layer is a term usually used in graphics packages to describe various layers in which an image or color might be positioned (think of a stack of books, and each book is a layer). You can position forward or backward, display, and hide each layer if need be. Layers are a great way to make images disappear behind other images or produce a scrolling technique called parallax scrolling. Parallax scrolling was a popular type of scrolling used on many older game creations. The Layers toolbar allows you to create your various game layers, turn them on or off, and configure the scrolling settings. The Layers toolbar can be seen in Figure 5.12.

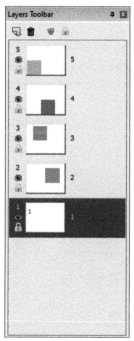

FIGURE 5.12 The Layers toolbar with two layers configured.

There are additional icons at the top of the Layers toolbar which can be categorized as:

New layer: Create a new layer.

Delete layer: Will delete the currently selected layer.

Hide unselected layers: Any layers not currently selected will be hidden, which is very useful when you are working on one particular graphics layer and don't want other images to clutter the play area.

Lock layer: This will prevent any changes (movement/deletion) of objects in the locked layer.

The Editors

When making games within Fusion, you will use a number of editors. These editors are the core components for putting all of the various aspects of your game together or for viewing its current state.

Storyboard Editor

To understand what the Storyboard Editor is, you need to understand how games are created. Each game can be made with a number of frames that generally relate to a level or story within your game. Consider a frame as a blank piece of paper on which you will design your game and then place a number of other pages under it to create your levels. The Storyboard Editor can be described as the top-level layout of your game creation. From here, you will be able to see all of your game's levels and screens and be able to select a specific frame to go into more detail. Figure 5.13 is an example of what the Storyboard Editor looks like.

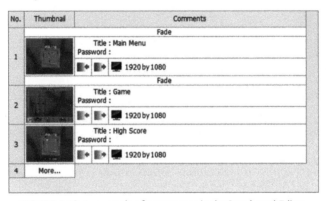

FIGURE 5.13 An example of a game seen in the Storyboard Editor.

Within the Storyboard Editor, you have a number of options that you can configure:

Frame picture: Each game frame is represented by a picture. This is a zoomed-out picture and is not meant to show the full game screen, just a representation so you know what the frame is about.

Frame title: Each frame can also be identified by the frame title. This is the name you give to each frame; by default, it takes the form of frame 1, frame 2, and so on.

Password: You can assign a password to each frame by entering a combination of letters and numbers.

Transition: A transition can be applied to the start and end of a frame. Transitions are very common in games, and you can put one for the start or end of a frame. In Figure 5.13, you can see a number of fade transitions, which means as it ends and starts particular frames it will fade in and out without you needing to code a thing. Each frame will have a screen size. There can be different screen sizes for each frame and for the application.

The Frame Editor

The Frame Editor is where you place all of your game objects on-screen to create your levels. You can have multiple frames but can only work on one frame at a time. Frames can contain many types of objects, which are the building blocks of your game creation. The Frame Editor is very visual, and you can use drag and drop to move and place items on the screen. An example of the Frame Editor can be seen in Figure 5.14.

On the left side of the Frame Editor is the object list bar, which displays all of the objects that are placed on the play area. You can display the items as small or large icons or sort them by name or object type. It is possible to reduce or increase the size of the object list bar by holding down the left mouse button on the edge of the window and moving it smaller or bigger.

The right side of the Frame Editor is called the play area, which is where the game will be shown when the program is run. By default, the area that will be displayed is shown as a white box, but this can be configured to

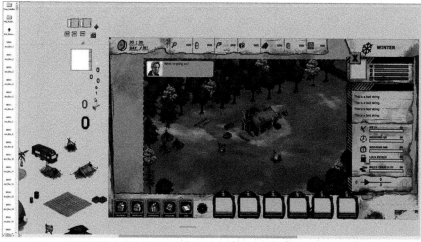

FIGURE 5.14 The Frame Editor with a frame setup for Dead of Day.

another color if required. Any objects within the white box will appear in the game. If you are making complex games, you will place a number of objects out of view (outside the white box) and introduce them when they are needed.

The Event Editor

Once all game graphics and objects have been placed on the frame, it is time to make them interact, and you do this by coding in the Event Editor. The coding in Fusion is not the same as a traditional scripting program, but consists of creating events, conditions, and actions using the right mouse button. An example of the Event Editor with some code programmed into it can be seen in Figure 5.15.

- Each number represents an event line.

- Text on a white background (in this example) are comment lines or group titles.

- The first seven icons across the top are called System objects and are always present. All objects after the initial seven are objects that have been added to the program by the developer.

- Each event is made up of conditions.

- A checkmark indicates that an action (or actions) has been applied to that object (above) to the condition on the left.

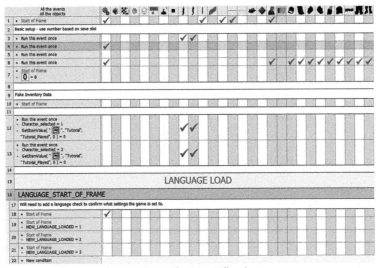

FIGURE 5.15 The Event Editor in use.

The Picture Editor

The Picture Editor is used when you are making changes to the appearance of any graphical image or creating a new image from scratch. This image might be an active object or another object that has graphic properties. It is also used to edit the Application icon (the icon that is displayed when the game is run in an Application window). An example of the Picture Editor in use can be seen in Figure 5.16.

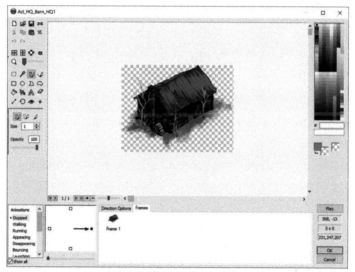

FIGURE 5.16 The Picture Editor.

 In the free version of Fusion you will not be able to export graphics, so it would be better to create them in an external graphics package.

The Picture Editor contains many options that you might find in a graphics package. The benefit of using the one included in Fusion is that you can save some time, as you are making changes directly within Fusion rather than in another program and then importing them. Some of the options you can find in the Editor are (starting from the top line and working to the right):

Clear: This will remove any images that are currently being displayed.

Import: You can import a number of pre-created graphic formats into Fusion, including TGA, PNG, JPEG, GIF, BMP, and PCX. Browse for the image, highlight it, and then click Open to complete the import.

Export: If you have created or amended an image, you may want to export it to a file. The same image file formats are available for import that you can use when saving for export. When exporting, you will need to specify a format and its name.

Options: The Options button allows you to configure how the right mouse button is used in the Picture Editor. The default setting when pressing the right mouse button in the Picture Editor is set to draw the selected background color. If this option is amended, it will pick the color under the mouse cursor when pressing the mouse button.

Cut: Takes the selected area of the image and places it on the clipboard, ready for pasting into this or any other package.

Copy: Copy the selected area and place it on the clipboard for pasting.

Paste: Take the contents of the clipboard and paste it into the Picture Editor.

Delete: This will take the selected area on the graphic and delete it.

Undo: Undo what you just did. For example, you may have deleted something or drawn on a part of the picture that you didn't mean to; selecting Undo allows you to go back a step and start again.

Redo: If you have just pressed Undo and feel that the change you made was actually okay, you can put that change back by clicking on the Redo button.

Flip horizontally: This will flip the image horizontally (left to right).

Flip vertically: This will flip the image vertically (top to bottom).

Crop: If you have an image that has a lot of white space, and you want to resize the canvas to the size of the graphic image, you can use Crop. Select the area of the image you want to keep, and then click on Crop to remove the rest of the graphic area. The canvas will automatically be resized.

Transparency: This allows you to assign varying levels of transparency to an image (how much you can see through an object).

Zoom: The Zoom bar allows you to zoom in or out of the object (making the image bigger or smaller).

Selection tool: Using the Selection tool, you can pick an area of the image ready for cropping, deleting, copying, and so forth. The selected area will be shown as a dotted box.

Color picker: The Color Picker allows you to click anywhere on an image and get a specific color, which can then be applied to the drawing tools.

Brush tool: If you want to draw freely (like a brush on a painting), you can use the Brush tool. Keeping your finger on the left mouse button will activate the drawing effect.

Line tool: If you want to draw straight lines on the images, you can use the Line tool.

Rectangle tool: If you need a Rectangle shape within your image, you can use the Rectangle tool rather than trying to draw it with individual lines.

Ellipse tool: If you want to apply an ellipse shape (circular-based shapes), you can quickly create one using this button.

Polygon tool: You can quickly and easily create a polygon shape by using this icon. When using it, you will have a line-type object where you will draw a line and then continue to draw another line from the last point of the previous line.

Shape tool: Using the Shape tool, anything you draw will become an enclosed shape. You can then apply fill and line size options to this.

Fill tool: If you want to apply a specific color to an area of an image, you can use the Fill tool to do this.

Spray tool: Exactly like a spray can, you can draw color on your image in various sizes.

Text tool: If you wanted to write some text on your image, you would select the Text tool and then apply the font, size, and color properties.

Eraser tool: The Eraser tool allows you to delete parts of your image using a small square. You can change the size of the Eraser by increasing the size number.

Size: If you want to increase or decrease the size of an image, you can use the Size tool. You also have the option to redraw proportionally, stretch, or resample the image.

Rotate: You can rotate an image on its axis to change its orientation.

View hot spot: A hot spot is an invisible location on your images that is used as an image reference point. You can reference this hot spot within the Event Editor.

View action points: An action point is the location at which something can happen. For example, if you have a spaceship that will fire bullets, you could state the location of the action point so the bullets appear from a certain location. You can move the action point by clicking on the View button and then left clicking on the image to relocate it.

On the right side of the Picture Editor is the color grid, which is where you would select the specific color with which you want to draw. You can use the left and right mouse buttons to apply a different color to the clicking of each button. The bottom half of the Picture Editor includes the ability to create animation frames. You could create an image of a spaceship, and then create an animation frame for it moving upward, being destroyed, and appearing on screen. You would then access these animation frames from code within the Event Editor.

 You can find out what an icon is called using the Tools Tip. Keep the mouse over the icon, and a text name will appear.

The Expression Evaluator

The Expression Evaluator looks very much like a large scientific calculator (see Figure 5.17). The Expression Evaluator's appearance will change depending on where you use it. The Evaluator is used to create mathematic calculations, text and number comparisons, text manipulation, and a number of other things.

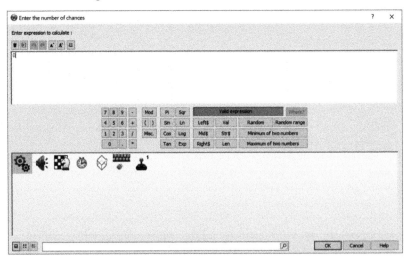

FIGURE 5.17 The Expression Evaluator.

The Expression Evaluator may look complicated at first, but once you have used it a few times, you will find it an extremely powerful tool. Some areas of the Expression Evaluator include:

Number keypad: Here you can press a number or mathematical sign (plus, minus, etc.) to insert it into the expression. Alternatively, you can use the number pad on your keyboard, as this is a much quicker method.

Mod: Mod is used to find the remainder of an integer that's been divided from two numbers. For example, if you typed "100 mod 15," the answer would be 10. If you find how much 15 can go into 100 the amount would be 90. Therefore, from this calculation the answer is 10.

(: Left parenthesis. When creating some expressions, you will need to separate certain items (usually numeric calculations) with a set of parentheses. This inserts a left parenthesis. You can also use the keyboard to enter this.

) : Right parenthesis. When you want to close an expression that uses a left parenthesis, you must use a right closing parenthesis.

Misc: When you click on the Misc button, you will be given four options: Power, Bitwise AND, Bitwise OR, and Bitwise XOR. It is a way to compare bitwise operators and find if they are true. Power takes the form of "Number Pow Number"; for example, "2 Pow 5 = 32," which is the first number times itself up to the second number. Therefore, the number 2 is multiplied by 2 five times, to make the calculation look like "2 * 2 * 2 * 2 * 2." Consult the program's help file if you require more information on this subject.

Pi: Pi is a word that is used to represent a mathematical equation that is displayed in Fusion as 3.141592654.

Sqr: Sqr stands for Square Root; the result is the reverse of squaring a number. The number that gives the square root is when the result is multiplied by itself; for example, the square root of 9 is 3, as 3 * 3 = 9, and the sqr of 100 =10, because 10 * 10 = 100.

Sin: Sin (also known as sine) is a basic mathematical function used in trigonometry.

Ln: Returns the Neperian logarithm of the given value.

Cos: Cos (also known as cosine) is a basic mathematical function used in trigonometry.

Log: Returns the decimal logarithm of the given value.

Tan: Tan (also known as tangent) is a basic mathematical function used in trigonometry.

Exp: Returns the value of e power to the given value.

Left$: Takes a number of characters from a piece of text from the left-hand side. For example, Left$("Hello this is a piece of text",5) would return the word "Hello."

Val: Converts a string to a number. An example of this would be Val("5").

Mid$: Allows you to remove a number of letters from the left and right of a string. For example, Mid$ ("Hello again",7,5) would return "again." The first number (in this example, 7) tells Fusion how many characters to remove from the left, and the second number (5) tells Fusion how many characters to keep.

Str$: Converts a number to text. For example, Str$ (5) will convert the number 5 to a string so it can be displayed in a text object.

Right$: Removes a number of characters from the left side of a string. For example, Right$("Hello",1) would return "ello."

Len: This returns the number of characters in a string. For example, Len("Hello") would return the number 5.

Random: Will generate a random number based on the parameters the programmer provides.

Random range: Will generate a random number from within a range of numbers.

Minimum of two numbers: Will return the minimum value of two numbers.

Maximum of two numbers: Will return the maximum value of two numbers.

Valid expression: Shows if the expression within the Expression Evaluator is correct; if the expression is correct it will display in green, if not it will show up as red.

Where?: If there is an error in the Expression Evaluator, it identifies where it believes the expression is wrong.

Retrieve data from an object: You can obtain data from another object, compare it, and read it into the Expression Evaluator. You could, for example, read the number of lives from the lives object and display it in a string object. You can see all of the objects at the bottom of the Expression Evaluator from which you can retrieve data.

 You cannot mix numbers with text when doing calculations; they can only contain one or the other. You can, however, convert a number or a string to another format using the Val( ) and Str$( ) commands. You will use these a lot when programming in Fusion.

Making More Space

With all of the Properties toolbars in use, the Fusion screen can get very busy, especially if you are running a screen resolution less than 1920 x 1080 (or a resolution for a game bigger than your screen size). You can create more space by minimizing areas of the screen that you are currently not using, or alternatively hide them from view until you need them. There are a couple of ways to make more space:

Toolbar buttons: Right-click anywhere on the button toolbar area to bring up the "Toolbar" pop-up menu. Click on any of the checked options to hide them from the screen; additionally, if you want to bring an option back, you can click on an unchecked option.

Window edge: Move the mouse cursor to the edge of a toolbar window; a double pointed arrow will appear. Hold down the left mouse button and then drag in the direction you desire to increase or decrease the size.

Close window: On the corner of each toolbar is a small "x"; click on this to remove the toolbar from the screen. Use the Toolbar pop-up menu to bring it back.

Dragging toolbar: Drag the Toolbar buttons so some are on the same line.

Dragging window: Drag the windows to where you want them. When you left click and hold a window a set of icons will appear, and by moving the mouse cursor onto an icon you can move a window. The icons are shown in Figure 5.18.

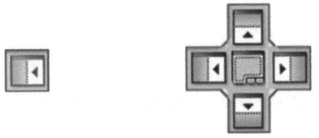

FIGURE 5.18 The icons that allow moving a window.

Summary

You should now have installed Fusion and have a basic understanding of its screens and editors. In the rest of the book, we will start drilling down into the editors and programs of Fusion in more detail, so you can make amazing games. The program is extremely powerful and can feel a little complicated initially; however, once you have made a couple of games, you will find it straightforward. In the following chapters, you will begin to learn about objects and properties, a very important aspect of configuring how your graphics and screens react.

CHAPTER **6**

WORKING WITH OBJECTS

In This Chapter

- What Are Objects?
- Object Manager
- Object Instances

In this chapter, we discuss what objects are and how they are used in games. Within your game you will use a group of objects which are the cornerstone to your creation, and you cannot create a game without them. We will look at what you can do with them and what specific objects are available in Fusion.

What Are Objects?

A game is comprised of various components, for example, a simple alien spaceship graphic, a noise sample when bullets are fired, background graphics, and in-game video, all of which will be put into your game using objects. Fusion comes with a number of built-in objects that will help you generate many different game types.

The free version of Fusion has fewer objects available to it than the full version; we have broken the list into free and paid so that you have an idea of what is available in the full version and what version you may need if you are making different games.

Adding an Object

To view the objects, you must be in the process of adding an object. To add an object, you must be at the Frame Editor screen (where you can see the playfield of where you will make your game).

1. Start Fusion. Select File | New from the menu.

2. Double-click on the text "Frame 1" in the Workspace toolbar (this will load the Frame Editor and display the play area).

3. From the menu, select Insert | New Object. You will now see a list of all the objects you can use in your game (see Figure 6.1). In Figure 6.2, you can see the list of objects available in the full version of Fusion.

 You can also add a new object by double-clicking with the left mouse button anywhere on a clear bit of the play area (i.e., where there is no current object).

FIGURE 6.1 The Create New Object dialog box in the free version of Fusion.

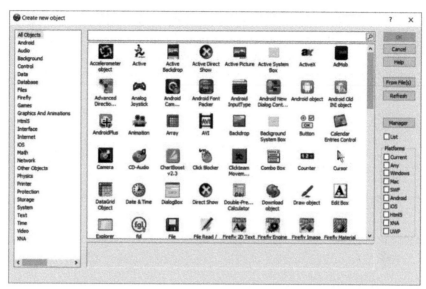

FIGURE 6.2 The Create New Object dialog box in the full version of Fusion.

Browse through the list and select the object you want to use by clicking on the object image once and then clicking the OK button, or you can double-click on the icon. Your mouse cursor will then change to a crosshair over the playfield frame; click the left mouse button anywhere on the playfield to place the object. Once you have placed the object, you will be able to configure its properties and use it within your game. Don't worry where you place it within the play area, as you can move its position once it's been added.

Objects in Fusion

It is very useful to understand how each of the default objects included with Fusion can be used within your game and, more importantly, when you need to use them. Each object has its advantages, and some may seem similar but are used for different reasons. Some objects can only play a single role within your game creation; for example, the "High Score" object.

The following objects are included in the free version of Fusion:

Active: Any object that will move and interact within Fusion; a perfect example of this would be a player's ship or a set of planes. The object may also have animation assigned to it.

Backdrop: A backdrop is a static image and is perfect for background images and pictures that do not need to move.

Button: You will see buttons in use in standard Windows dialog boxes and programs. Within Fusion, you have the ability to apply a number of button types to your games, including pushbuttons, bitmap buttons, checkboxes, and radio buttons.

Combo box: The Combo Box is another standard Window control, and it allows you to create simple lists and drop-down menus.

Counter: Used as a counting mechanism, this can be visible to the player as a graphical representation or hidden behind the scenes to keep track of data values.

Edit box: The Edit object is another standard Windows control that allows simple text editing features such as data entry and the cutting and pasting of text.

FGL: An object that allows the creation of in-game advertisements and monetization for HTML5.

Hi-score: Many games have the capability for users to enter a high score if they beat a specific score. Fusion allows you to set up a hi-score table to record the score and the name of the player. You can specify the number of scores the game will display and some default names.

HTML5: Specific functions that relate to HTML5 and JavaScript, such as Opening a URL (Website address), adding parameters, and writing to cookies (tracking data files).

List: A simple yet effective way of creating lists in Fusion using the standard list box, with configurable options.

Lives: A special object that can be used to track, add, and reduce player lives.

Physics-engine: Core physics engine that allows you to add real-world effects to objects, such as gravity, force, density, and friction.

Physics-fan: Creates a physics effect that mimics a fan which can push an object.

Physics-magnet: Creates a physics effect that mimics a magnet.

Physics-particles: Create particles within your game (graphical effects).

Physics-rope and chain: Creates a physics effect that mimics ropes and chains to allow you to create swinging/jumping effects.

Question & answer: This object allows you to set up simple question and answer games and applications. For example, you could ask the users if they like a certain color, and then make the program react to the answer.

Quick backdrop: Creates a simple yet effective background picture, which can also be a gradient (selection of colors).

Score: An object to keep track of the player's score.

Screen zoom: Allows you to scale and rotate the application and its graphical layers.

String: An object that allows you to place text on-screen.

Sub application: Allows you to insert another Fusion file into an area on the current loaded file.

The following additional objects are included in the full version of Fusion:

Active backdrop: Graphical object that is in the background (always at the back) but may have some animation.

Active direct show/direct show: Plays video or sound files using Windows DirectShow. This will allow you to play from a range of media such as MP3, MPEG, AVI, and WAV.

Active picture: Allows the import of various picture file formats including BMP, GIF, JPG, and PCX onto the playfield. You can then move, rotate, and resize the object in real time. You can import the image when configuring the object properties or when using the Event Editor.

Active system box: If you want to create a button or background that can use the local computer's system colors, you can use the Active Box. The Active Box also allows it to be used as a checkbox or hyperlink.

ActiveX: Allows Fusion to access and make use of ActiveX controls installed on the computer, thereby increasing the functionality of the program. It is possible to write ActiveX programs within other languages such as C++ or to use those that are installed locally.

Analog joystick: Although many users these days are used to playing games via the keyboard, there is a joystick option where you can configure the buttons to specific actions within the game.

Animation: Using file formats such as FLI, FLC, and JPEG, you can import a number of still images and play them as a single animation, which will create the illusion of smooth, animated movies.

Array: We discussed the concepts behind arrays in Chapter 3, "Basic Programming Concepts." If you want to store game data or configuration information, the Array object is a great way to do so. You have the option of selecting a one-, two-, or three-dimensional array, which allows more power and flexibility in storing data.

AVI: AVI is a popular video format that allows you to play Windows movie files in Fusion. You can use video clips to enhance your games by making them more exciting or as a way to separate levels. You have standard video controls available to you, so you can pause, play, stop, and move forward and back any AVI file you have within your program.

Background system box: Used as a background object that can have a tooltip (text appears when the mouse is over it) or an image.

CD audio: If you want to play audio tracks from within your program off a CD, the CD Audio object is the way to do it. It will allow you to play, pause, skip, and stop tracks. This is a very useful object if you want to make your game play high-quality CD music tracks off your CD-ROMs.

Click blocker: This object can prevent (block) mouse clicks.

Clickteam movement: Allows access to additional movement options above and beyond the default installed items.

Cursor: Change the Windows cursor graphic with your own or in-built ones of the operating system.

Date & time: The Clock object allows you to put a clock in your productions. You can insert either an analog or digital-looking clock onto the playfield. The Clock object is also useful for setting a time or creating a countdown or stopwatch effect (you may want to limit the amount of time a player has to complete a task on a specific level).

Download object: An object that allows you to download a file from the Internet.

Draw object: Using the Draw object, you can paint directly onto the playfield while the game is running. You can do this passively (where you set the shape in the code), or you can do it interactively (where you use the mouse or other control to draw directly to the screen).

File: The File object allows you to create standard disk operations such as creating a file and appending to a file as well as allowing you to run external files or applications.

Formatted text: If you wanted to insert text onto the screen and apply formatting to it (font, size, bold, color, etc.), you would use this object.

FTP: File Transfer Protocol is a standard method of transferring files up to (or down from) a Web server.

Get object: Allows you to retrieve data from a URL via HTTP GET or Post.

InAndOut movement: Is a movement type that mimics the moving in and out of screen of objects, very much like you might create in an online presentation. You can also use it to create effects in your game such as scrolling text.

INI: An INI file is a specially formatted text file contained on the end user's hard disk. The file contents can be written to and read from.

Layer object: Allows you to precisely control the object layers within your game.

MCI: MCI stands for Media Control Interface and is a format for controlling multimedia devices that are connected to your computer. It is useful for playing sound and video files.

Mixer: If you wanted to control the volume of samples and music files, you would use the Mixer object. The Mixer object also allows you to specify which speaker you want sound to be played in (so you could configure certain sounds to go through the left or right speaker only).

MPEG: MPEG stands for Motion Picture Expert Group, and the object allows movies saved in this format to be played with Fusion. You will need to have a software MPEG driver already installed to use this within your games (so will the client computers that you want to distribute your programs to).

Multiple touch: Handles gestures and touch screen interaction like those needed for mobile, tablet, or touch screen monitors.

Network: Allows you to create games that use a local area network.

Object mover: This is an invisible zone which can be moved in real time that will also move objects that fall into its area of control. Imagine you have a UI element that has a number of component parts; when you move the core element, you may want the other elements to move at the same time to the same location.

ODBC: Handles basic database communication (Open Database Connectivity System).

Physics – ground: Allows you to define the floor (ground) of the game for your physics objects.

Physics – joint: Allows you to create movable joints between objects.

Physics – treadmill: Allows you to create a treadmill effect that can move objects in a particular direction at a specific speed.

Picture: The Picture object is very similar to the Active Picture object in that you can import a picture in various formats (BMP, PCX, JPG, GIF, and others) for showing in your game. You cannot rotate and re-size the object in real time, though; this is for simply showing a picture as a background. You can get the user to select an image or import one before the game starts.

Pop-up menu: Allows you to generate pop-up menus. This is more likely to be useful in applications than it is in games.

Print: If you want to allow the player to print a specific part of the screen or perhaps the in-game instructions, you will need to use the Print object.

QuickTime: You are able to place QuickTime videos within your games.

Quiz object: Generate complex quizzes or question-based systems.

Registry2: Allows you to read and write to the player's Windows registry.

Rich edit object: Allows for more complex text effects to be used in your games, above and beyond basic string objects.

Screen capture: Allows you to capture parts of the screen and save them to the hard disk.

Search: Allows searches to be completed of text-based files on the user's hard disk.

Shared data: Ability to share data between two Fusion programs.

Static text: Basic text-to-screen object.

ToolTip object: Tooltips are used to provide information about a particular button or object within your game. This will display text in a pop-up of a chosen color and time frame, for example when you move the mouse cursor over a button.

Tree control: Allows you to create a tree file or folder system within your games. This is probably more common in applications than it is in games, but it allows you to create structures of data which could be used for inventory, upgrade, or help systems.

Vitalize plug-in: The Plug-in object allows you to connect to an external URL (Web page) and download a file. This object is pretty much depreciated and should not be used.

Window control: The Window Control object allows you to change the visibility, size, and location of your game window on the screen, which is very useful if you want to display multiple windows in specific positions on the screen.

Window shape: Allows you to change the shape of a displayed window. For example, you could create an application in the shape of a face, rather than the traditional rectangle. Mainly used for applications but could be used for themed games.

Xbox gamepad: The Xbox Gamepad is a common controller for playing games on a PC. This object will allow you to configure and access the Xbox Gamepad device.

 Additional objects will be available for additional exporters such as IOS, Android, and UWP.

Object Manager

We've already discussed earlier in this chapter that objects are the most important aspect of Fusion in terms of adding functionality and features to your games. The object manager allows you to look at what objects you have installed, reinstall them (if you have issues running them), and download new ones. When you use the free version of Fusion, you will not be able to download and install additional objects, but as they are so important, so it would be good to just give you a quick look at the Extension Manager. You can access this when adding a new object; click on the Manager button on the Create New Object dialog box, and this will bring up the Extension Manager dialog as shown in Figure 6.3.

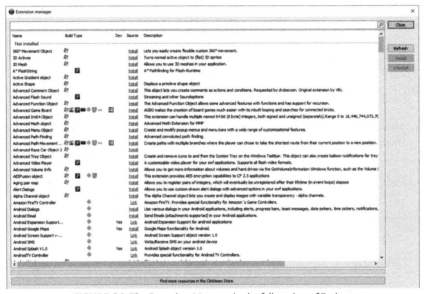

FIGURE 6.3 The Extension Manager in the full version of Fusion.

The most important thing to take into account with the objects is what build type they are available for; for example, Windows, MAC, Android, and so on. If you are building a game for a particular platform, you must ensure that you use objects that are supported on that build. If you are considering making a game that will run on multiple platforms, such as Windows and Mac, you must ensure all objects that you use will work on both platforms. Working out what platform you intend to make your game on before you start work can save you lots of time once development has started, because if you use an object that is not supported, you will have to change the object and most likely have to recode your game.

Object Instances

When you add new objects (of the same type) onto a Frame in Fusion, these are handled by Fusion as individual objects. For example, if you add five active objects onto your frame (using Insert Object), they will be called Active through Active4. These will appear in the Event Editor as separate objects, and each can be individually tailored to have their own look and code that only affects them. If you want to have an event affect all of them, then you would use Qualifiers.

If you copy and paste an object, this will create an instance of the copied object. This means it will have all of the same settings as the object it was copied from. It will have the same name, and you will not see any additional objects in the Event Editor. This is because any code that you create is affecting all instances of that object. So, if you create five copied (instances) of Active and then in the Event Editor "Destroy" after 5 seconds that object, all five objects will be destroyed. If you replace the image or resize any instance, it will also change any other instances of that object. You might be thinking, what's the point of instances if they are all the same and creating an action will affect all of them? The good news is that you can create conditions and actions that only affect a particular instance. It depends on the particular event but, for example, if you were to check if a bullet has collided with an object and then destroy it, the code will know which specific object to remove (it won't remove all of them).

Instances save memory and reduce the number of elements in the Event Editor. This in turn makes the amount of code to write smaller, as you won't need to write the same code for each individual object that is the same. You will see this in Amazing Fighter Pilot in Chapter 14, where you have a number of aircraft in a wave of the same color and will only destroy a single instance when a bullet hits it. You can also store different values in instances, which means you can also create different health or difficulty values for the same instances.

Summary

Objects are a key component in making games in Fusion and allow you to create many possible game types (different game types were discussed in Chapter 1, "Video Games"). Take a good long look through the objects available in Fusion before starting any major projects and make a note of which ones you will use. This will make the process of creation much quicker, rather than trying to find an object to suit your needs when you are already in the process of making your game.

CHAPTER 7

CONFIGURING PROPERTIES

In This Chapter

- Properties Explained
- Application Properties in Depth
- Frame Properties in Depth
- Object Properties in Depth

I n this chapter, we look at how to configure our games. To do this, we use the Property window. We will be able to configure our games at various levels, from the entire game, to each level, and each object added on the playfield. We will also look at properties that only apply to objects, and some useful shortcuts that will allow you to set the same configuration for any number of objects.

Properties Explained

Within Fusion, each application, frame, and object you create will have its own set of properties, which in turn will affect its appearance and behavior. Properties for each of these items will appear in the Properties toolbar. An example of the Properties sheet can be seen in Figure 7.1.

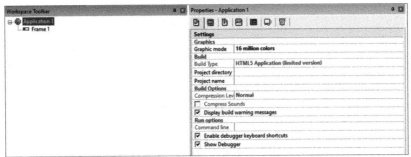

FIGURE 7.1 The Properties toolbar showing application properties.

Every time you select a different frame, application, or object, the Properties toolbar will display the relevant options that can be configured. Three property sheets will appear when using the product:

Application properties: The Application properties apply to the entire game. The configuration of these properties are generally high-level settings for the game you are making, which include properties such as the filename or the type of program it will be exported as (e.g., screen saver or executable).

Frame properties: Within each game you create, you can have multiple frames, and each frame has its own configurable properties, allowing you to tailor each section of your game to your specific needs.

Object properties: Each object you place on the frame can have its own set of properties. The individual object properties can be quite in-depth and allow configuration of things such as text type and size, movement and position, and many other options. You can also set object behavior and qualifiers using the property sheet (discussed later in this chapter).

A frame can be thought of as a level within a game, and you can have multiple frames within a game, each representing different aspects. In the games we will be making, a frame will be configured as a main menu, the game itself, and the area to add high scores. We discuss frames in more detail in the next chapter.

Property Tabs

Each property sheet (Application, Frame, and Object) has all of its properties categorized and grouped into tabs, which allow you to easily find a specific set of properties you want to change (see Figure 7.2). The property tabs for each object you can add onto the frame may have a different set of tabs depending on what type of object it is. For example, a text-based object will have text formatting configurable options, whereas an active object would not.

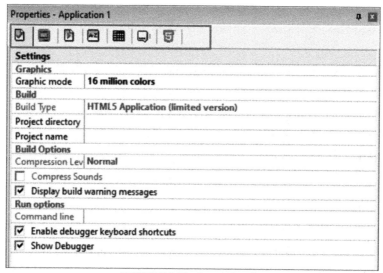

FIGURE 7.2 The Properties tabs.

You can find out what a tab is supposed to do by highlighting the tab image with your mouse cursor; a text description of the tab will then appear.

Application Properties

To see what properties are available at the application level, you will need to click on the Application name text within the Workspace toolbar (the topmost icon and text within the workspace area). Upon clicking it, the configuration details for the entire application will appear in the Properties window. The tabs within the Application properties are shown in Figure 7.3.

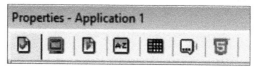

FIGURE 7.3 The Application Properties tabs.

The tabs are from left to right as follows:

Settings: Options for building the game and how much compression should be used.

Window: Details what size the game should be and has options for how the window should behave once the program has been built.

Runtime options: Options for when the game is running, including graphics and sound options.

Values: The application's global options that allow you to set up global values and global strings.

Events: The setting up of any events that will apply to the entire application (global events).

About: All about the application; this includes information that will appear once the game has been built as well as the option of including help files and documentation.

Html5 options: Various build options for HTML5.

 If you have the full version of Fusion and have selected a different export option, this will replace the HTML5 Options tab.

Frame Properties

The Frame properties can be accessed by clicking on the Frame icon, which is located below the Application icon in the Workspace toolbar. As there can be multiple frames within each game, you will need to select the relevant frame for which you want to change the properties. Any changes you make on one frame will not change the properties on any of the others. The tabs within the Application Properties are shown in Figure 7.4.

FIGURE 7.4 The Frame properties tabs.

The tabs are from left to right as follows:

Settings: Basic screen settings for each frame.

Runtime options: Configuration of each frame when the game is running; includes options for background colors and frame size.

About: Contains just the name of the frame and no other settings.

HTML5 options: Specific options relating to the frame and HTML5.

Object Properties

The Object properties can be accessed by clicking on any object on the frame. Once you have left-clicked on any object, the Properties sheet will then appear in the Workspace toolbar. An example of the Object properties tabs can be seen in Figure 7.5.

FIGURE 7.5 The Object properties tabs.

 Remember that different objects may have different property tabs.

Tabs that might appear include:

Settings: These are object settings that will be different on each object, as they are the configuration of that particular object.

Display options: Will the object be visible on the playfield, and will it use any transparency or ink effects?

Values: You can assign up to twenty-six alterable values against each object. This allows you to store numerical data against a particular object rather than using other objects to achieve the same effect. Flags are a new feature of Fusion and allow you to create multiple on/off flags per object.

Size/position: The size of the object and where will it be placed on the screen (using screen coordinates).

Text options: Setting the text display object, font types, sizes, and color.

Movement: Will the objects move? If so, which type of movement, in what direction, and at what speed?

Runtime options: Allows the object to follow the frame or be destroyed if it goes off the playfield. Includes options that will allow you to reduce memory allocation to your program by tidying up the use of the objects.

Events: The setting up of behaviors and qualifiers in an event(s) that will apply to the object when running the program.

About: This will contain the name of the object and display the object's icon (which you can modify).

Now that you understand how the Properties tabs work, we will now look at them in more depth, so you will know when to use them when putting together your game and be able to use this book as a reference for finding the right options to amend.

 The properties shown in this chapter are based on the free version of Fusion; additional tabs and information may be supplied if you own the full version or other add-on exporters.

Application Properties in Depth

As mentioned previously, amending the Application properties affects the entire game, so it is important to understand that any changes here might override any set in each frame. If your game is not displaying the way you want it to, there might be a conflict between these two groups of properties.

The Settings Tab
An example of the options in the Settings tab can be seen in Figure 7.6.

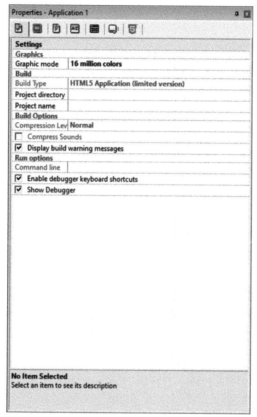

FIGURE 7.6 The settings tab with its properties displayed.

The following options are available:

Graphics mode: Allows you to specify the number of colors to use within your game; the default is sixteen million, but you could make a game that is 256 colors if you want to go for a certain retro/old school graphical effect.

Build type: This will be the final outputted file format; for the free version of Fusion this will be set to HTML5 Application (limited version). This option is grayed out and you are not able to change it.

Project directory: Where you want the project (files) for your game to be generated.

Project name: That is the name of the game file that you want when your game is generated.

Compression level: The compression level will allow you to try and reduce the overall size of your game. For the HTML5 build type, this is set to Normal and cannot be changed.

Compress sounds: This will try to reduce the size of any sound files added to your game. In the free version of Fusion, this is not selected and is locked so that you cannot change it. This option in the full version will only compress WAV-formatted sound files, and compressing them does reduce the quality (although it may not be that noticeable to the end user). Always test any settings to make sure you are happy with the results before distributing your game.

Display build warning messages: Having this selected will display a message when there are objects or events incompatible with the currently selected build type. This is particularly useful when you are building a game for a particular operating system and you use an object that isn't supported.

Command line: If you want to force your Fusion-created program to use a certain system resource, typing in a specific command achieves this.

Enable debugger keyboard shortcuts: This is used to avoid conflicts between the game keyboard shortcuts and the debugger shortcuts.

Show debugger: When you launch the game in test mode (i.e., you use the Run application option rather than the Build and run option), the debugger will also appear. The debugger provides information about your game, such as how many objects it is using and the amount of memory it's using.

 Be aware that changing the number of colors will downscale your graphic images, and if you decide to go back up a level you may lose color quality on your graphics and have to re-import them to make them look as you expected.

The Window Tab

The Window tab can be seen in Figure 7.7, and it shows the configuration options available.

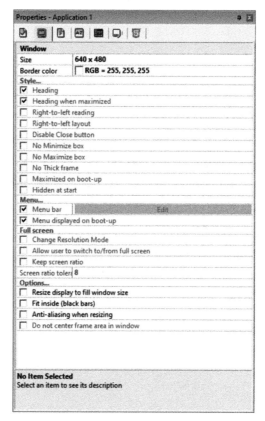

FIGURE 7.7 The Window tab settings sheet.

Many of the options available on this screen are locked out, as they relate to desktop applications rather than a HTML5 application. A number of options will appear in the Run application stage, such as heading and menu bar, but won't appear when you have built the game in HTML5. We will still mention them here for completeness so that you know what they are when you come to use them.

Size: This is the size of the application window, which is the area the user can see when running the game.

Border color: Allows you to change the border color of the application.

Heading: The heading is switched on by default, displays the name of the program, and presents the user with a text menu for selecting options within the game (which can be configured). This will not appear in any HTML5 application and is an option for desktop-based applications and games.

Heading when maximized: If you click this option, the heading bar will still be on-screen if you maximize the game. If it is unchecked and you maximize the game, the heading bar will disappear.

Right to left reading: Some languages are read from right to left of the page/screen; if this is selected the title will be displayed as such. This will only work in those languages that support right to left reading.

Right to left layout: In Windows, games and applications with a menu bar, the close, minimize, and maximize buttons are on the left-hand side of the application; by selecting this option they will appear on the right.

Disable close button: If you don't want the user to close the program using the "x" button in the top right corner of the Application window, select this option. You will need to give the user an alternate method of closing the game window if you do this (either through a key combination or through a menu system).

No minimize box: If you don't want users to minimize your game (put the game on the taskbar and hide it from the Windows desktop), check this option. They will be able to expand it again by clicking on the item on the taskbar.

No maximize box: If you want to prevent the user from maximizing the game, check this option. This is a good option to select if you want to restrict the user to a certain window size.

No thick frame: In many games and applications, you can put your mouse cursor on the edge of a window and drag it to make it bigger. Clicking this option removes the dragging/resizing option. Again, this is a very useful option if you are keeping the game screen to a specific size.

Maximized on boot-up: This option will expand the application window size to the size of the monitor's resolution when the game is started.

Hidden at start: This will hide the application when it is started (so it will look like nothing is running). You can make it reappear again using code in the Event Editor.

Menu bar: You can include a menu bar on your game by leaving the option checked (it's on by default). This will allow you to include the standard menu system of File, Options, Help, which is already configured as standard. You can click on the Edit button to change the menu system more to your liking.

Menu displayed on boot-up: By default, when a game is started, the menu is displayed; if you wish to remove it, uncheck this option. You can, however, re-show it later by entering some code into the Event Editor.

Change resolution mode: Change the resolution of the monitor to the resolution in the game. Once you have quit the game, it returns the monitor to the original settings.

Allow user to switch to/from full screen: If you use the key combination Alt-Enter, you can change the size of the game window to full screen or back to its original size.

Keep screen ratio: When the game you are making is in full screen, it will try to match the screen resolution.

Screen ratio tolerance: When a game is being resized, setting a tolerance level (as a percentage) will ensure that it is not stretched to an unusual size and can reduce distortion. With the various different screen sizes available, it is recommended to read the Fusion help files for more information about this subject if you intend to make Windows full screen games.

Resize display to fill window size: This option stretches the playfield of the frame to fit the application screen size. The screen will appear zoomed but has been stretched to fit the screen.

Fit inside (black bars): This will scale the game as best it can to the computers resolution and will use black bars (borders) to cover any area where it is unable to maintain its aspect ratio.

Anti-aliasing when resizing: When the screen has been resized, add anti-aliasing. This will reduce jagged edges in your game that can make the game less attractive. Adding anti-aliasing does normally come with a performance impact.

Do not center frame area in window: Each frame can be bigger than the application size. With this option checked, it will not center in the middle of the frame, but at the top left instead.

The Runtime Options Tab

An example of the runtime options can be seen in Figure 7.8.

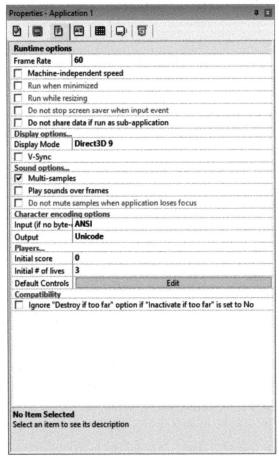

FIGURE 7.8 Default settings of the Runtime tab.

Frame rate: The default setting for Fusion is 60; you have the option to increase or decrease this amount to increase the speed of your game. Increasing the frame rate will cause Fusion to use more processor powerer (CPU) to make the game faster. Where possible your games should run at either 30 or 60 FPS (though in the new PS5 and XSX consoles as well as PCs, some games are now set to run at 120 FPS).

Machine-independent speed: If you want the game to run at the same speed regardless of the type of machine the user has, check this option. This is very useful for ensuring that a game doesn't run too fast on the latest leading-edge equipment.

Run while resizing: If you resize the game, does it continue to run or will it pause/black screen? Resizing while the game is running will have some impact on the performance of the game.

Do not stop screen saver upon input event: Screen savers usually will continue to run until the user moves the mouse or presses a key. Using this option, you can prevent that and configure a different way to exit from it (setting up the Escape key, for example). It is very important to let the user know how to exit the screen saver; otherwise, you may have some unhappy customers contacting you.

Do not share data if run as sub-application: A sub-application is a pop-up or window which is launched from the main application. If you select this option, the sub-application will not share any global values and strings with the main application.

Display mode: The display mode your game will use. You have three options in this version, Standard, Direct3D 9, and Direct3D 8. Selecting standard will use the default graphic drivers. Using Direct3D is faster, as it is hardware accelerated; most modern Windows PCs will work with this option, but it is dependent on their installed graphics card.

V-sync: This stands for vertical synchronization and is related to how often the screen refreshes. V-sync can prevent screen tearing, but having it switched on can affect performance.

Multi-samples: If you wish to play a number of samples (sounds) at the same time, you will need to check the Multi-samples box.

Play sounds over frames: Sometimes you may want to play the same music across multiple frames; if so, you will need to check this item. The main reason for selecting this is when you want continuity within your games sound-wise from one frame to another.

Do not mute samples when application loses focus: Losing focus means clicking away from the game onto another application or the desktop. This will allow the sound to continue uninterrupted while you are doing other things.

Input (if no byte-order mark): Choose the character encoding for any text documents that your game uses; you have the choice between

ANSI and UTF-8. Ensure the application matches your file type format, or it may fail to read them correctly.

Output: Select the character encoding of the files that your game exports (saves to).

Initial score: You can set an initial score using this entry box. Most games start from zero and don't require you to change this, but you may decide that your game starts from another number and counts down.

Initial # of lives: The number of lives with which the player starts. This is an easy way to set the default number of lives whenever a user starts the game.

Default controls: You can configure the game to be controlled by a joystick or via the keyboard. You can configure up to four players by pressing the Edit button. The default options can be changed at runtime by the player if you wish.

Ignore "destroy if too far" option if "inactive if too far" is set to no: Compatibility option for games built in an earlier version of Fusion where this option previously didn't work.

The Values Tab

Next is the Values tab, which can be seen in Figure 7.9.

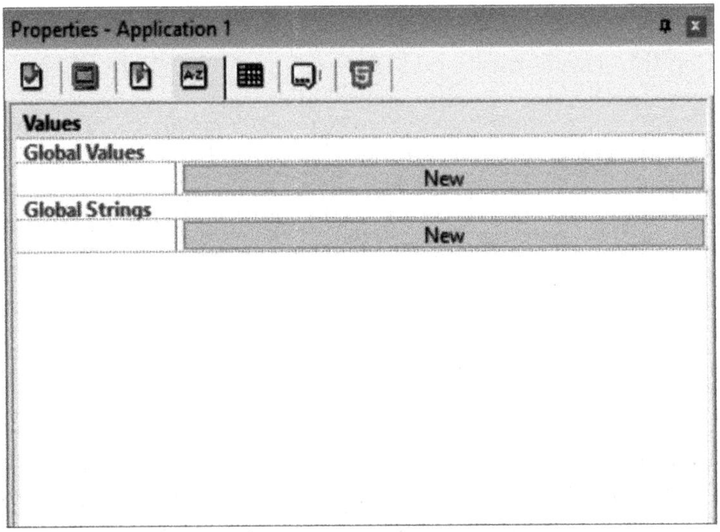

FIGURE 7.9 The Values tab in the Properties sheet window.

Global values: If you want to transfer values between frames, you can create a global value. You can define a large number of global values by clicking the New button. Using global values is a fast way to move values between frames, and it takes up less memory space than using a specific object to do the same thing.

Global strings: If you want to transfer text between frames, you can create a global string. You can define a large number of global strings by clicking the New button. Using global strings is a fast way to move text between frames, and it takes up less memory space than using a specific object to do the same thing.

The Events Tab

The second from last tab is the Events tab, which can be seen in Figure 7.10.

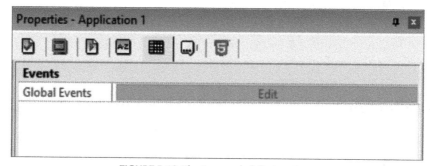

FIGURE 7.10 The Events tab default options.

Global events: Global events look like normal events configured in the Event Editor but will run from when the application is started to when it is closed, regardless of what frame the game is on. This makes them independent of any frame and useful for code that needs to run through the life of the program. Click the Edit button to enter the Global Events screen.

 Global Events are not available in the free version of Fusion.

The About Tab

The last tab for the Application properties sheet is the About Properties sheet. The settings within that tab can be seen in Figure 7.11.

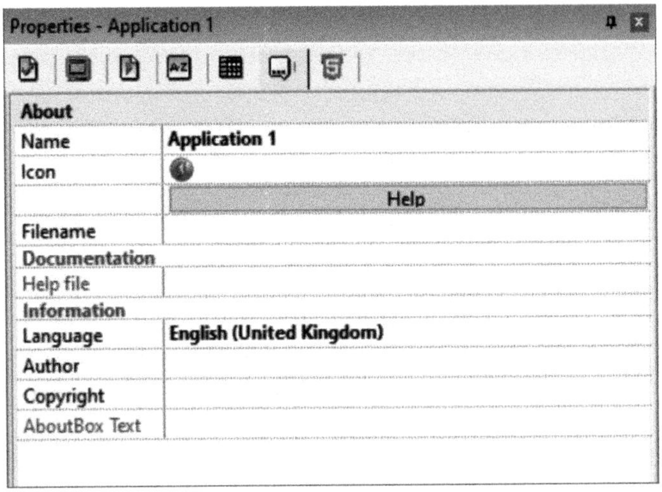

FIGURE 7.11 The About tab Properties sheet.

Name: This is the name of the game you have created, and it will appear on any menu bars or in the About box (the About box is an informational dialog, which can be seen by running your game and then selecting Help/About).

Icon: Icons appear at various stages when your game is running. You will see an icon in the top left corner when you are running your game, and you will see one if you click on the Help/About menu option and the icon for the actual executable. If you click on the Edit box, you can amend the different icons in your game to a picture more suited to their function.

Filename: Filename displays the folder path to where the Fusion game has been saved and its saved filename.

Help file: With your games, you can have a help file that the user can open by pressing the F1 key. The help file can contain product information, where to get help, and perhaps hints and tips on playing. Create your help file in Hlp, Txt, Doc, or Wri format and then select it using the file Browser button. If you are not sure how to create certain help formats, start with Txt (using Notepad) and then move to a more complex format if necessary.

Language: This will convert non-Unicode text and retrieve it from non-Unicode-created extension objects (mainly third party). If you set the language to Language Neutral, it will take the language defined in the Windows operating system.

Author: Who created the game; put your name in here (or your company or team name).

Copyright: If you want to enter a copyright to your game, enter your name in the copyright box.

AboutBox text: When the user clicks on the File menu Help | About, the text entered here will be placed in an About box.

The HTML5 Tab

The final tab of the application properties is the HTML5 tab, as shown in Figure 7.12. This relates to the export build type, which is the format in which you can create your game. This will allow you to run it on other computers.

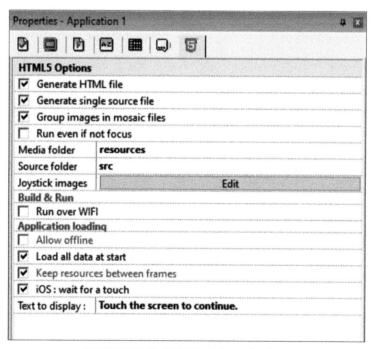

FIGURE 7.12 The HTML5 tab Properties sheet.

Generate HTML file: This will create an HTML file along with your game; the added benefit of this is that you can upload this file along with your game, which serves as the landing page to access your game. If you want to insert your game into another Webpage or site, you can uncheck this option.

Generate single source file: This will generate a single source file, which can help avoid problems when using multiple HTML5 applications within the same Webpage.

Group images in mosaic files: If selected this will place images into large image files (think of a roman mosaic). This allows the game to be loaded faster into memory than if each graphic file was a separate entry. You may have heard of similar techniques such as Sprite Sheet. A mosaic will make the build process take longer, so you may want to only do this toward the end of development if you have a lot of graphical images.

Run even if not in focus: If you are on another Webpage or application, this option will define if the game will continue running.

Media folder: The folder location for the images, sounds, and data for your game.

Source folder: The folder location of the JavaScript files.

Joystick images: These are the default images that are used when running a HTML5 game on a mobile device which only has a touch screen controller. You can edit these images by clicking on the Edit button.

Run over WIFI: Allows you to build the application and then run it on any device connected to the local network.

Allow offline: This will allow your app to run offline, so even when you are not connected to the Internet it will still be available. It does this by generating an .appcache file when first connecting to the server.

Load all data at start: This option will load all of the games graphics and sounds before the game starts. This means when you move between frames in your game, there will be no pause for loading. You may need to weigh up the benefit of no loading between frames and a long load once at the start of the game.

Keep resources between frames: This will keep resources (graphics, sounds, etc.) stored in memory. If you use objects between frames, this will increase frame loading time.

iOS wait for a touch: The game will pause at the start of the game once all data has been loaded and await a press from the user.

Text to display: This will display a particular text string advising the user to click the screen to continue. This is related to the iOS wait for touch option also being enabled.

 In the full version of Fusion, you will have additional export options available to you.

Frame Properties in Depth

You can have multiple frames within one game; in fact, it is generally assumed you will have more than one. Each frame can be configured with its own properties, which means you can have different frames taking different roles within your program. Any configuration you do on one frame does not pass over to any other frames, so if you want something to be global (available to the entire application), you will need to configure it in the Application properties.

The Settings Tab

The first tab for the Frame properties is the Settings tab as shown in Figure 7.13.

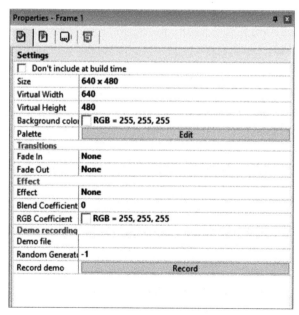

FIGURE 7.13 The Settings tab.

Don't include at build time: You are able to remove frames when you build the game into a final HTML5 format. Perhaps you have a frame for testing data or a frame for a level that you haven't finished. Removing these frames will ensure that your final game size is also reduced.

Size: Enter the size of the frame; remember, frame size can be different from the application size. To make scrolling games, you would make the frame size bigger than the application settings size.

Virtual width: You can set a virtual width (and height) for your game, which is very useful when creating scrolling-based games.

Virtual height: See Virtual Width.

Background color: Select the background color you wish to use for the frame. You can have different background colors for each frame, but you would in most instances create a graphic image that covers the frame background.

Palette: Using this option, you will be able to select an image and use the colors contained within it as the game palette. Perhaps you have a certain image you want to keep at the same range of colors throughout the frame or game. Clicking Edit will show you the different colors used in the palette, and from there you can import an image.

Fade in: When the frame starts, you can insert a fade-in transition, which is a special wiping effect that moves across the screen to reveal your game.

Fade out: At the end of the frame, you can insert a fade-out transition, which is a special wiping effect that moves across your screen to make your game (frame) disappear.

Effect: Apply a graphical effect to all objects on that frame. For example, you could set a semi-transparent or grayscale effect on the frame. Not all effects work with all exporter types.

Blend coefficient: You can set the level of transparency with the slider; 0 is not transparent, 255 is fully transparent.

RGB coefficient: Set a blend between the objects and an RGB color.

Demo file: You are able to record key or joystick presses so that you can create recorded events. Enter the filename that you want to save the demo (data) to.

Random generator seed: Random numbers are not as random as they may seem, and if you don't use this option when you generate a random number it will generate the same sequence.

Record demo: Press the button to record a demo of your game. You can reload this saved file (.mfd) into your game using events.

The Runtime Options Tab

The second tab for the Frame properties is the Runtime Options tab, as shown in Figure 7.14.

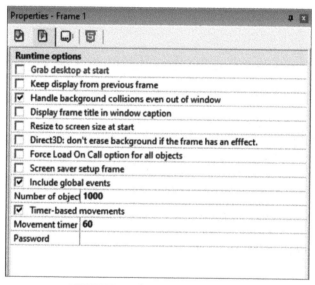

FIGURE 7.14 The Runtime Options tab.

Grab desktop at start: Grabbing a user's desktop at the start of the frame will paste the contents of the current screen into your game. If a user has other programs open on the desktop that overlap the frame area, they will be copied and then pasted into the game. If you want to create a game or screen saver that would take advantage of the user's desktop, check this option.

Keep display from previous frame: If, when changing frames, you would like to keep the graphics from the previous frame, you will need to select this option.

Handle background collisions even when out of window: If objects collide outside of the window area, selecting this option will mean that any code written to deal with any collisions will still be handled. With this selection enabled, Fusion will still test to see if collisions are happening.

Display frame title in window caption: The name of the frame (each frame has its own name to distinguish it) will be displayed in the window caption (also known as the title bar).

Resize to screen size at start: This option will maximize your game window to the same size as the screen resolution.

Direct3D don't erase background if the frame has an effect: If using any graphical effects, this will keep the background graphic intact rather than overwriting it.

Force load on call option for all objects: This will only load the objects into memory when they are required. This will reduce the overall memory utilization of your game, but it may slow your program if many objects need to be loaded into memory per frame.

Screen saver setup frame: If you are creating a screen saver and wish to have a configuration screen (where you select the screen saver options, for example), check this option to make this frame the screen that appears first when launching a screen saver.

Include global events: The ability to enable or disable global events within a frame. This may be used to prevent specific code being run that you may have placed in other frames.

Number of objects: The number of objects option lets you define how many objects each frame will contain. Fusion uses this figure to generate the memory space to run the program. The default setting is 1000, but if you have more than this in a frame, increase this figure or you may get strange results (certain objects may not work). Setting this number too high will have a negative effect and reduce the performance of your game.

Timer-based movements: The movement of objects is based on frame time rather than machine independent speed. If this option were unselected, you could find that faster computers would run the level quicker (i.e., the speed of movement would be faster).

Movement timer: Default is set to 60. This means you can specify the frames per second for objects separately from the frame/application frames per second.

Password: A password will allow users to navigate to a specific frame within your game if they know the password. You can set a separate password for each different frame, and the user will then enter it using the menu option when the game is running by selecting File | Password. A pop-up dialog box will appear asking the user for a password. A password is very useful if you want the player to be able to come back to a specific level in the game at another time. It is probably better to do this via code (make it yourself) than it is to use the inbuilt function, as this feature isn't particularly useful in full-screen games.

The About Tab

The About tab has only one configurable bit of information, as shown in Figure 7.15.

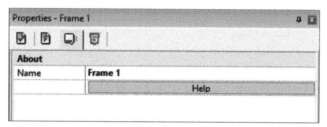

FIGURE 7.15 The About tab Properties sheet.

Name: You can change the current frame name to something more appropriate by clicking on the text area. The default names are frame1, frame2, frame3, and so on, but it is useful to change these to something more descriptive; for example, main screen, high-scores, game frame, and so forth.

Help: Will launch the help file and display the Frame Properties help page.

Object Properties in Depth

A number of different objects come standard with Fusion, and each object you place within a frame may have a different set of properties. This will depend on the type of object you select; for example, the Hi-Score object is different from the Active object. Some objects will have Settings or Properties tabs, and others will not. The wide range of object configurations available makes it impossible to list them all here. Some tabs and properties are common to all or most objects and are discussed next. If you need to see an object's properties, click on the object in the Frame Editor.

The Settings Properties Tab

The Settings Properties tab is different for each object and defines how that object can be configured and used within your game. For example, if you are using the Counter object, you would be able to specify an initial value, a minimum and maximum value. If you were using the Hi-score object, you would be able to specify the number of scores and length of names to display. It is very important to check the Settings tab of every object you place within your game, as there may be some important configuration you will need to amend. An example of the Settings tab for the Hi-score object can be seen in Figure 7.16.

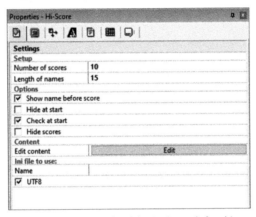

FIGURE 7.16 An example of the Settings tab for objects.

The Size/Position Tab

Using the Size/Position tab on the object's Properties sheet, you can specify the screen location, the object's actual size, and if it should be rotated. An example of the Properties tab for this is shown in Figure 7.17.

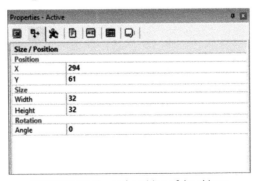

FIGURE 7.17 Size and position of the objects.

X (position): The X position on the screen (left to right).

Y (position): The Y position on the screen (its location top to bottom).

Width: The width of the object.

Height: The height of the object.

Angle: The angle the object is displayed at (zero is the default where there is no rotation).

The Display Options Tab

The Display Options configuration is for setting up how the object will appear on the playfield when the game is running. An example set of options is shown in Figure 7.18.

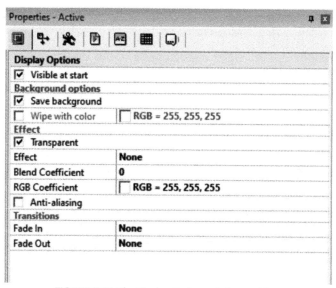

FIGURE 7.18 The Display Options tab for an object.

 Remember that not all objects will contain the same set of display (or any other tab) options. Each will be different depending on the role of the object.

Visible at start: Is the object visible when the frame starts? You can make it invisible (by not checking the checkbox) and then show it using code at an appropriate time.

Save background: This option is enabled by default, and for most games should be left checked. This option saves the background, so once the object has moved away from it, it will then paste the original image back, so you get a smooth-scrolling object. If you uncheck this option, the object image will be pasted across the screen, as it doesn't have information on what other image should be stored on-screen. If you want to make some interesting screen savers, this is an option worth trying.

Wipe with color: If you uncheck Save Background, you will be able to select Wipe with Color and select and choose an RGB color (this is a number that represents a color). You do not have to enter its RGB number, because when you click on it, you will be able to pick the color you want from a drop-down box. If you do this rather than just uncheck Save Background, it will paste the selected color over the background where the object has been.

Transparent: All images when created are drawn in a square. When you create any images, you can "paint" a transparency around the image that creates a perfect shape. Without transparency, your image (e.g., a ball) will have a square around it. With transparency, the area around the ball will be transparent, which means it will be invisible to the user.

Effect: Add a graphical effect to the object, such as transparency or grayscale.

Blend coefficient: Transparency of the object against the play area. 0 is fully visible while 255 is invisible.

RGB coefficient: Using an RBG-assigned color to blend with the object.

Anti-aliasing: Select anti-aliasing if you want your object's appearance to look smoother.

The Event Properties Tab

The Events tab for objects contains two very important options for your game creations, Qualifiers and Behaviors. The Qualifier property allows you to place like-minded objects into named groups. A set of groups has already been defined by default (e.g., Good, Bad, Player, Friends, Bullets, Arms, Collectible, etc.). Once you have assigned an object to a particular Qualifier, you can then go into the Event Editor and program code for that particular group. This allows you to code efficiently (as you can assign code to multiple objects using just one object column in the Event Editor), and it is very useful when you are making games, because you can assign your object to game types. For example, you could create an enemy group or obstacle grouping and then create code specifically for how they would react within your game.

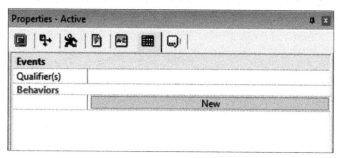

FIGURE 7.19 The Events Properties tab for an object.

To assign an object to a Qualifier:

1. When you click on the Qualifiers button, you will be presented with an Edit box. Click on the Edit box to bring up the Object Qualifiers dialog box.

2. Click on the Add button to bring up a list of predefined types; these are just examples and are there to help you place the object. When you have chosen one, select it and then click OK.

3. Notice that the group you selected is now visible in the Object Qualifiers dialog box. You can click on Add again if you want to add it to other groups or click OK to get back to the Properties sheet.

4. The Qualifier icon image now appears on the Properties tab.

Adding a qualifier to an object will not have any effect until you create code for it within the Event Editor. If you don't like the initial object types, you can select one of the others, which are numbered 1 to 99. The initial groups are only suggestions, so you do not have to use them if you do not want to.

In Fusion 2.5+, you are able to create your own icons for qualifiers. This can be found in the Events tab in the Application properties.

The Behavior option within the Events Properties tab allows you to open the Event Editor and set up specific code events to each object. The benefit of this is that if you want a single object to work in a certain way, you can code it to do so. The only downside is that you must remember that you have put events on the object. When testing the game, you may find it acting strangely. If you look at the main code and cannot find the reason why, it could be object assigned code. This problem aside, it is a very useful way to reduce your main code list size, and you can copy and paste code between objects, so you only need to code an event once.

The About Properties Tab

Figure 7.20 shows an example of the About Properties tab for an object. This tab details general information about each object (also called an extension), including creator and copyright text. You can also change the information here, which will amend its appearance on the Frame Editor and be easier to work with if you have many of the same objects on the screen.

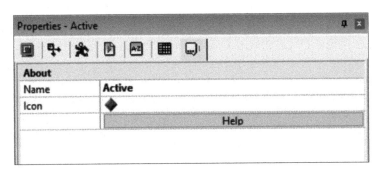

FIGURE 7.20 The About Properties tab.

Name: The name of the object, which you can amend to something more useful; for example, from animation to player1 animation. Click on the text to amend the name, which will then be updated on the Frame Editor and within the Event Editor.

Icon: The icon image that will appear on the Frame Editor and within the Event Editor. You can amend this to something more memorable if you wish, but it will not appear in the game; it is for programming identification only.

Help: This will launch the help file for the object.

Some objects will have more options available; some of the additional items you may see in the About properties tab could be:

Extension name: The name of the extension (object).

Extension filename: The filename to the extension (object).

Author: The person who wrote the extension; the majority of the time this will be Clickteam, but it could be another author.

Copyright: Copyright text for the object.

Comment: Any comments about the object will appear here.

Website: Any Website of the object author will appear here.

Summary

Properties are a very important aspect of configuring your games, and you need to know how to make them work to your benefit. It may seem a little daunting at first that so many properties can be changed. The defaults will be sufficient in many cases, and you only need to change them if you want the game, frame, or object to perform differently. Some of the properties will only need to be changed at the beginning of your game creation, and you can ignore them for the rest of that project's development. Take the time to look over each object's Properties sheet to see what you can do with each object and the power Fusion has. We cannot list every property of every object here (as that would be a book in itself), so make sure you review the help files that come with the product if you require more information on a specific object.

CHAPTER 8

FUSION CODING BASICS

In This Chapter

- Introduction to the Event Editor
- Coding Concepts
- Code Comments
- Code Groups
- Loops
- Runtime Order
- Qualifiers and Behaviors

In this chapter, we discuss basic coding techniques and concepts that you will be using later in this book. Using the Event Editor, you can make your games extremely powerful using mouse clicks and selecting items from menu pop-ups.

Introduction to the Event Editor

The Event Editor screen (as shown in Figure 8.1) is the primary screen for pulling all the game content together and creating the game's playability. Any coding (programming) that needs to be done will be done from this screen, so it is very important to understand how the Event Editor works; although easy to use, it can be slightly confusing at first. The Event Editor has a spreadsheet appearance (albeit with a graphical top column) with a selection of blank rows. As you create your code the columns/rows begin to have checkmarks within them; this is stating that there is code for a particular event line and object.

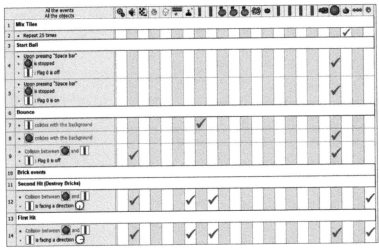

FIGURE 8.1 An example of game code in the Event Editor.

Using Figure 8.1 as an example, the naming of each of the items can be detailed as such:

- The numbers down the left side represent the event line number.

- Next to each event line number is an attached box, within which can be a single or group of conditions. You can have multiple line numbers (events).

- Across the top of the Event Editor are a number of graphical icons. The first seven icons will always be present in every game you make and are called System Objects. Any objects after the seventh will be ones you add manually to the game.

- Within each of the blank boxes to the right of the events and below the objects is where you can insert an action (these are called action boxes). Once you have added an action, it will then be represented by a large checkmark icon. If you hover the mouse over the checkmark, you can read the action in that location. You can have multiple actions in each box by right-clicking on the same action box and adding a second (or third, etc.) action.

When you add a condition to an event line (a line will appear after a number) and then add an action (so a checkmark appears), you will end up with a system very much like a treasure map grid. The action will correspond to the relevant condition on the left and the corresponding object above it.

 A more detailed description of what each of these items means and how it can be used is discussed shortly.

Coding Concepts

The Event Editor uses a simple yet powerful point-and-click programming language to allow anyone to program a game, even if that person has little or no previous programming experience. Clickteam came up with an ingenious way to achieve this simplicity using coding logic and presenting it in an easily comprehensible manner. Within Fusion are a number of elements that can be assigned to an object:

- Events
- Conditions
- Actions
- Functions

The great thing about Fusion and previous versions of these products that use the Event Editor is that all of these elements can be explained and understood using simple logic. This makes programming a breeze, and it means that you can complete games faster.

Events

An event is when Fusion is waiting for something to happen in its lines of code. An event is only created in Fusion once a condition or group of conditions has been added to it. Each event waits until any conditions placed within it are "true" before running any actions. Each event is given a line number, which is displayed down the left side of the Event Editor screen. Figure 8.2 shows a blank Event Editor where nothing has been programmed. The number 1 on the left side is the event number, which is awaiting some conditions to be assigned to it before it creates a line numbered 2.

FIGURE 8.2 A blank event with no conditions programmed in.

Conditions

Conditions are the test criteria within your games to allow the program to understand when to do "something." Examples of conditions include:

- Left mouse button is clicked
- Ball hits bat
- Score reaches 200
- Player lives = 0
- Arrow key is pressed
- 15 seconds have passed

You could place one or all of these conditions within a single event. An example of single and multiple conditions in a number of events can be seen in Figure 8.3. By adding more conditions to the same event, you can create very complex programming logic that is easy to read and create.

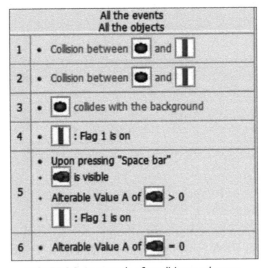

FIGURE 8.3 An example of conditions and events.

To create a single condition and event, first ensure you have launched Fusion and created a new application.

1. Open Fusion.

2. Click on the New button, which will create a game file with a single frame.

3. Double-click on the text Frame 1 in the Workspace Editor to bring up the Frame Editor.

4. In the button toolbar click on the Event Editor button (or use the shortcut key of CTRL & E).

You will now be in the Event Editor for Frame 1, and you should see a single event line numbered 1 with the text New Condition.

5. Click on the text New Condition in the Event Editor.

6. A New Condition dialog box will appear as shown in Figure 8.4.

7. You then need to select the object you want to test; for this example we will select the knight chess piece and chessboard icon. You can do this by left-clicking or right-clicking on the icon of the chosen object. A pop-up menu will appear as shown in Figure 8.5 with a list of conditions that Fusion can test for that object. Then select the pop-up menu item Start of Frame. This will now create a single event condition called Start of Frame.

To create another condition in the same event line (make sure you have at least one condition in an event line before attempting to do this):

8. Right-click on the condition in the event line to which you want to add another condition. A pop-up box will appear. Select Insert, and a New Condition dialog box will appear; select the object you want to test.

9. From the pop-up menu, right-click on the New Objects icon, which looks like a 3D cube, and from the pop-up select Pick an object at random.

You will now have two conditions within one event as shown in Figure 8.6. This means that both conditions will need to be true before any action will take place; in this case it needs to be as the frame starts and there being an object available (if so, it will select one).

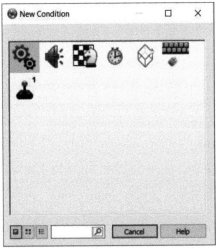

FIGURE 8.4 The New Condition selection dialog.

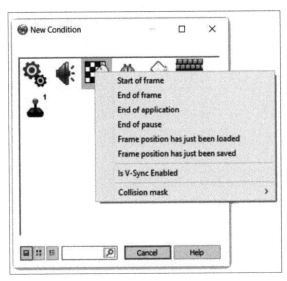

FIGURE 8.5 The New Condition menu pop-up.

 Though the condition in Figure 8.6 is set up to run at the start of the frame, it won't currently do anything in-game until you assign an action.

 You can have many conditions making up the event, and the event will only run if all conditions are true.

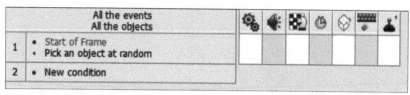

All the events All the objects									
1	• Start of Frame • Pick an object at random								
2	• New condition								

FIGURE 8.6 Two conditions within one event.

The Order of Conditions

It is very important to note that the order of conditions can impact the way your games react when running; the way the computer reads the code determines what happens. With regard to conditions (remember, you can have multiple conditions), they are read from the first to the last in each event. Using an example that is not computer related, perhaps you are mailing a letter to a relative. You wouldn't walk all the way to the post office and then decide to write the letter; you would write the letter first, then put it in the envelope, write the address, and then go to the post office to mail it. The same is true with Fusion and programming languages generally. You must be very careful in ordering your conditions, as you will be creating actions based on this order. Once you have written many lines of code, it can be easy to place code in the wrong order. If you are experiencing strange results in your code, check the order of your conditions. Another thing to note is that when creating multiple conditions, it is best to place a specific condition first before placing any other conditions below it. For example, if you have two conditions, the first being "when user presses left mouse button," the second being "when counter equals one," it is best to put the more "non-general" condition first. In your game, the user might press the left mouse button many times, but the counter may only equal 1 at a specific time in your program. If the mouse button condition is first, Fusion will begin to read that line of code and then see if the second condition is true every time the mouse button is clicked. You might be wondering why this is a problem, but the fewer events Fusion has to read (check), the more processing power it has to put over to the game. Therefore, ensuring that your conditions are in the correct order will make the code run correctly and make it more efficient, saving valuable processing time for more important things like graphic movements and animations.

Negating Conditions

You might want to create a condition that is the opposite of the one you just created. To do this, you can use the Negate option. For example, perhaps you created a condition to see if the player is pressing the spacebar key and you want another condition to see if they are not pressing the spacebar. The events would then be true if one or the other is correct, and then it would run the relevant action associated with it.

1. On the menu bar, click File | New; this will generate a brand-new game for you to work on. Double-click on the words "Frame 1" in the Work-space toolbar.

2. Click on the Event Editor button in the toolbar.

3. You will now be in the Event Editor. Click on the "New Condition" text to begin creating your events. Left-click on The Mouse Pointer and Keyboard object in the object list and then select The Keyboard | Upon pressing a key from the pop-up menu.

4. A dialog box appears asking you to press a key, so press the spacebar to assign that key to the event condition.

5. Create another event on Event Line 2 (by clicking on New Condition text) and then select the Mouse Pointer and Keyboard object and condition, then select The Keyboard | Upon pressing a key and then press the spacebar when asked.

 If you are using the Free version of Fusion, you can only have one game file loaded at a time. If you are creating a new file, ensure any other game file is closed.

Now, two events are checking to see if the spacebar is being pressed. What we want to do is change the second of these events to check to see if the spacebar isn't currently being pressed.

6. Right-click on the second event and from the pop-up menu select the option called "Negate." It will now make one of the conditions have a red cross next to it. This means that it is the opposite of the statement (negated), and so this event would run as soon as the game starts (assuming you are not pressing the spacebar). An example of a negated condition is shown in Figure 8.7.

All the events All the objects							
1	• Upon pressing "Space bar"						
2	• x Upon pressing "Space bar"						
3	• New condition						

FIGURE 8.7 A normal and negated condition.

Not all objects can be negated. If it is not possible on a specific object, the negate option will be grayed out.

 In the companion files, load and run the example file "negate. mfa" located in the \Examples folder to see how you can use negate to test to see if the opposite is true.

Actions

An action is run when the result of a condition has been found to be true. For example, you have an event condition that tests if the player's score is greater than 100. The action you want in this example, perhaps, is to add a life to the player. So, a condition is "What are you testing to be true" while an action is "What you want to do," and in the previous case it is adding a new life.

Once this condition has been met, any actions on that event line will be run. Each object that is added onto the play area has its own set of actions that can be used once the condition has been met. There can be many actions in each object box and spread across all of your objects on a single event line, so it is important to try and keep your code tidy and where possible create additional events to reduce the number of actions on an event line.

 When an object you have never used before is added to your game, it is a good idea to read the help file or examine what actions are available.

Examples of actions that can be applied to objects can include (depending on the object):

- Execute an external program
- Play a sample or sound
- End the application
- Set the timer
- Set, add, or reduce the score
- Make object invisible/visible
- Add or change text

- Animate an object

- Launch an object from another object

The Order of Actions

Just like the order of conditions, the order in which you add actions can have an effect on how your game will work. The order of actions has a bigger impact on what happens in your game than the order of conditions, because the decision by Fusion on which events to run will depend on which conditions are true, and a set of actions in the wrong order can make whole bits of your code run at the wrong time.

Imagine you are making a cake and you put it in the oven before adding some vital ingredients into the mix. The cake will most likely turn out incorrect. This is exactly what will happen in Fusion, but it may be subtler than just the cake doesn't rise or taste nice; you may find your code works in most cases, but you are struck by weird, unusual bugs that only happen now and again. This is most likely due to an order issue; the code is being read from top to bottom and is running the actions, and when it comes back around to read the conditions, at some point your values or checks are wrong and it runs the wrong set of events.

Probably the most common order issues that appear are when setting values within actions and within your events you have conditions to check for values or are resetting flags.

Functions

Functions play a very important part when using the Event Editor. A function allows you to retrieve data from one object to use in another object. There may be information in one object that you want to display, for example, or you may want to read in some data from an array that points to an image and then use this in the Picture object to display the image. Functions are classified in two groups:

- General functions

- Object functions

General functions retrieve data from the System objects, which are those you cannot add to the play area and always appear in the Event Editor. These functions are Special Conditions, Sound, Storyboard Controls, The Timer, Create New Objects, The Mouse Pointer and Keyboard, and Player 1. Object functions retrieve data from all objects other than those that are restricted (i.e., anything you can place on the play area using Insert | Object). To access these functions, you will need to click on the object icons at the bottom of the Expression Evaluator (you can also type it in if you know what you need to retrieve). An example of the Expression Evaluator is shown in Figure 8.8.

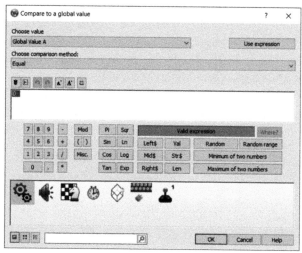

FIGURE 8.8 The icons allow you to retrieve information from other objects.

Code Comments

In every programming language, you can comment your code. Comments within your programs are very important for a number of reasons. When you have created many games (even those that are not finished), you might decide to go back and restart or update them. When you created the game, you were familiar with what you were writing at the time, but later it is easy to forget why you coded something a certain way. Commenting your code is a great way to put notes in to remind you why you were doing something. You can also use code commenting to put copyright messages into your programs, so if you allow a program to be used in the "game community," you can stamp the code with the copyright message so other programmers understand what is required of them if they take that code and use it in their own games. An example of a code comment in a traditional programming language might look something like Listing 8.1.

Listing 8.1 Traditional coding comments.

```
// Copyright Jason Darby
// Date Created : 14 November 2018
// Date Last Modified: 14 November 2018
// Program Name : The Lab
// If you wish to use this code email me at name@name.com
```

As you can see in Listing 8.1, traditional languages allow programmers to put in dates when the program was created and when it was last updated. It is also common to put in a date for the last change made (including a description to what has been changed), so if it stops working, you know exactly what was done, and you can check it to see if that was the cause. Fusion allows you to make comments in the Event Editor between event lines; you may do so as follows:

1. If you have the Event Editor already open, you are ready to enter a comment line. If you are not in the Event Editor and Fusion is not currently open, start Fusion, then click on the menu system, and select File | New. Double-click on the frame and then click on the Event Editor button in the toolbar.

2. Right-click on any number on the left of the events (if you have not added any previous events, this will be event 1) to bring up the pop-up menu. Select Insert | A comment. An example of the pop-up is shown in Figure 8.9.

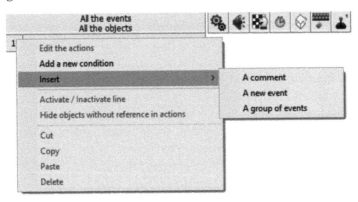

FIGURE 8.9 Example of the pop-up for adding a comment line.

3. The Edit Text dialog box appears (as shown in Figure 8.10). You can type text here to help you remember why you coded a specific part of your

game, a copyright message, and so forth. You have the option of changing the text size, amending its alignment, or changing the background color. Type the words "My Game Copyright" in the text box and then click OK.

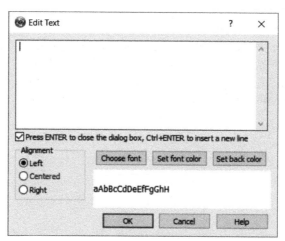

FIGURE 8.10 The Edit Text dialog box where you can put your comments.

4. You should now have a comment line in the Event Editor that looks like Figure 8.11.

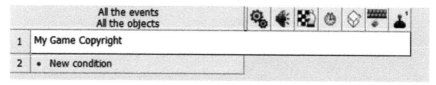

FIGURE 8.11 A comment line.

Code Groups

When programming, it is very easy to separate your game into logical steps and concepts. For example, a side-scrolling shoot-'em-up game might consist of ship movement, enemy ships appearing from the right side of the screen, scores, and explosions when a bullet hits an enemy. In a scripted programming language, you would create a selection of code to handle some of these items independently from the main code. Doing so makes your code more structured and makes it very easy to make changes to a specific part of your game. It is also easier to find any bugs related to a specific issue, as it will be contained in a group. Fusion uses groups as well, but the benefit, of course, is that it is graphical in its approach. There are two main reasons for using code groups in Fusion: first, to organize specific aspects of your code so you can keep it tidy, as you can store code within them and then hide the code until you need to see it. Second, with code groups you can enable and disable each group throughout the running of the game. This allows you to code specific events within your game that only happen at a certain point in time. Having groups of code disabled until you need them also makes your game more efficient, as it won't try to test those conditions every time the game logic loops around.

 Remember, Fusion reads the code line by line; if a set of conditions is true, it will then run any associated actions. It does this extremely fast, but the more events the more work Fusion has to do to confirm if a condition is true or false.

To create a code group:

1. Start Fusion, and from the menu bar click on File and then New. This will load Fusion with a blank game.

2. Double-click on the Frame 1 text in the Workspace toolbar to open the Frame Editor. Then, click on the Event Editor icon in the menu bar, which will take you to the coding screen, which is currently empty.

3. To insert a group, you need to right-click on an event line number (in this case, starting from a new program, you will only have line one available). From the pop-up menu, select Insert | A group of events. A New Group dialog box will appear (as shown in Figure 8.12); enter the group name "First Group."

4. Click OK. You will now have an entry in the Event Editor that will look like Figure 8.13.

The Group Events dialog also allows you to password protect a group, which allows you to distribute source code by only allowing users to open specific areas. When you create a group, by default it is active when the frame starts, which means that Fusion will read the code within the group and run it. If you disable this option (by unchecking it), the program will ignore it until you enable it again within the code. This is particularly useful when you only want the group to run at a specific time.

FIGURE 8.12 Group dialog box.

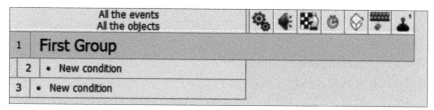

FIGURE 8.13 Group in the Event Editor.

Groups within Groups

Groups within groups allows you to place multiple groups under another group and enable and disable them when needed. You may be wondering why you might want to do this, and it has a lot to do with code redirection. As mentioned previously, you can have a group disabled when the program is first run, which means you can go to a specific selection of code at a certain time and enable it (run it). If you have more groups under this, you can enable them when a specific condition is true. This allows you to make very powerful programs that only run code when you need them to, which makes your games easier to write. To make several groups within a group:

1. Start Fusion, and from the menu bar, click on File and then New. This will load Fusion with a blank game.

2. Double-click on the Frame 1 text in the Workspace toolbar to open the Frame Editor. Then, click on the Event Editor icon in the menu bar, which will take you to the coding screen, which is currently empty.

3. Insert the first group by right-clicking on an event line number (in this case, starting from a new program you will only have line one available). From the pop-up menu, select Insert |A group of events. A New Group dialog box will appear.

4. Enter the group name "First Group" and then click OK. You will now have the first group entry within the Event Editor.

5. On event line number 2, below the First Group, right-click again and insert another group, this time called "A."

6. On event line number 4, right-click and insert another group; call this one "B."

You will now have two groups within a group as shown in Figure 8.14.

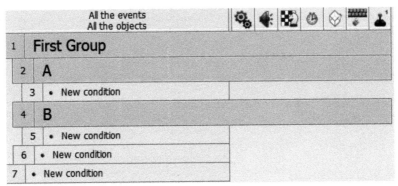

FIGURE 8.14 Groups within groups.

 Although this example shows all three groups being enabled (disabled groups are shown as grayed out), it is best to disable groups by default and use conditions to enable each group.

Loops

A loop is something that happens repeatedly a number of times. When programs begin to get more repetitive in nature (where you have to do something more than once), you can code it over a number of lines of code or use a loop. Take as an example the drawing of a crossword puzzle. If you had a 17x17 grid, you could code each line of boxes or write a loop that would generate the 17 lines of boxes for you. The obvious benefit of a loop is that you have less code to write, and it is a more efficient way to write your programs. To create the basic loop structure, you will require two lines of code: one event which will detail what you want to happen when your loop is running and a second event to call the loop, which will also contain information on how many times it should run that loop.

An example of a very basic loop is shown in Figure 8.15. The first event in our example is the code of what will happen when the loop is run. You need to name your loops (as you can have many loops in Fusion). In this example, we have called our loop "Start." You can see to the right of this event that we have a single action, which is to Add 1 to Counter.

Now that we have our loop, we want to call it, so we need an event to trigger it; in this example we have created a simple "Run this event once" condition, which will run automatically. As an action to this event, we state that we want to run a loop called "Start" 5 times. So, when this loop is run, it will run 5 times and each time will add 1 to the counter, so the final counter number is 5. It runs too fast to see this happen, and it will just display the number 5. You can use logic and more complex situations to call the loop in your own games, but hopefully this example has shown you how to generate a simple loop.

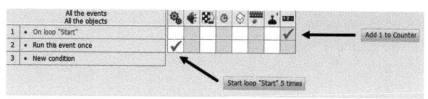

FIGURE 8.15 A loop example.

 In Figure 8.15, we have the first event line as the setup for the loop, and the second event is calling the loop; these could be created the other way around.

 We have only used the counter to display the number of loops; you don't need to add a counter.

 A basic loop example as shown in Figure 8.15 is stored in the companion files folder \Examples and is called SimpleLoop.mfa.

Runtime Order

When you run a game created with Fusion, it will read the events, conditions, and actions in a specific order. We have already detailed the order of conditions and actions, so you should have a good idea of how to structure your code to reduce any problems when you are bug finding. When a game is run, Fusion reads the first event line; if the condition is true, it will then run the actions to the right of it. If it is not true, it will continue to the next event line, and so on. Additionally, if there is a comment line, it will also ignore that, as there is no code for it to run.

Qualifiers and Behaviors

Qualifiers and behaviors are two ways to improve how you code within Fusion and can be configured in the Object Properties Workspace toolbar. Learning how to use both of these options well will allow you to write better code and make it easier to read, so when you go back to a program at a later stage, you will understand it faster.

Qualifiers

When you want to logically group your objects, you can place them in a group. This qualifier group then allows you to code events and actions specifically for that group of objects, rather than one at a time. This makes it easy to put in specific logical types (e.g., enemy, bullets, doors, collectibles, etc.), but it also means that you can significantly reduce the amount of coding needed in the Event Editor to do specific actions. A simple example of a qualifier in use can be seen as follows:

1. Start Fusion, and from the menu bar click on File and then New. This will load Fusion with a blank game.

2. Double-click on the Frame 1 text in the Workspace toolbar to open the Frame Editor.

3. Insert three Active objects by using the Insert | New Object menu option. Place them across the bottom of the frame, all at the same height.

4. Click on one of the three Active objects (which will appear as green triangles) to reveal that object's properties. Click on the Events tab in the Properties toolbar. You will now see text that says "Qualifier(s)." Click on the right of this in the blank empty box (as pointed out in Figure 8.16) to

bring up an Edit box. Click on the Edit box to bring up the Object Qualifiers dialog box, as shown in Figure 8.17.

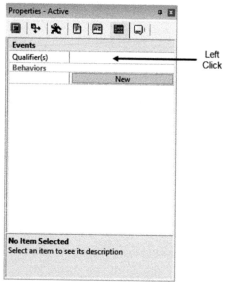

FIGURE 8.16 To access the Qualifier Edit button.

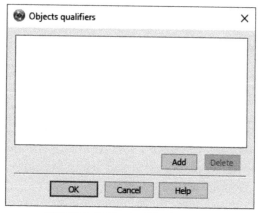

FIGURE 8.17 The Qualifier dialog box.

5. If you click the Add button, you will get a list of possible groupings to which this object can belong, as shown in Figure 8.18. Fusion provides a list of default qualifier names; if they do not suit your purpose, you can always select one of the numbered group names. For this example, select the Good group (which looks like an apple). Then, in the dialog box, click

the OK button to save the configuration. On the Qualifier(s) in the Properties toolbar, you will see a small red apple. Do the same for the other two Active objects.

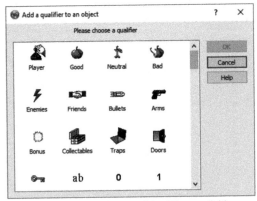

FIGURE 8.18 A selection of Qualifiers available.

 You can select multiple objects and change a property on all objects at the same time. So, you could select the other two active objects and add a qualifier group to both.

6. Click on the Event Editor icon to begin to code your new Good group. In the Event Editor, you will now see a group called "Good" in the object listing.

7. Click on New Condition, select the Timer option (which looks like a stopwatch) by left-clicking on it, and then select Is the Time Equal to a Certain Value from the pop-up menu. Move the second bar until it is 5 seconds, and then click OK.

8. Move across to the right until you are directly under the Good group icon on event line 1. Right-click and select Position | Set Y Coordinate. In the Expression Evaluator, type in the number 20 and click on the OK button.

If you now run this example, you will notice that the Active objects start at the bottom of the frame, and then after 5 seconds, all three move to the top end of the frame. If you were to do this coding without qualifier groups, you would have had to program in three actions to make the Active objects move. When your programs become more complex, you will save a lot of programming effort and time simply by using qualifiers.

You can assign the same qualifier to multiple objects at the same time by left-clicking (and then holding down the left mouse button) and dragging a box around the objects that you want to edit. You'll notice in the Object properties window that it now states multiselection.

Behavior

A behavior is a set of events that are applied to a specific object. So, rather than write code in the main Event Editor for a particular object, you specify rules for an object within the object itself (the object has its own special event editor code list). A good example of using behaviors would be for enemy objects; perhaps you have some code which defines how an enemy spaceship moves and have a variable that sets the speed of the spaceship. When you create another enemy spaceship using original enemy, it will also include this original code where you can then just amend the speed variable to create a new enemy behavior type.

Keeping this object-specific code away from the main event editor is much more efficient and, when your program code becomes extremely long, will make editing and updating your game much easier. This is also true when using the same objects over multiple frames, rather than having to code an object for every frame; the code follows the object, reducing overhead significantly.

Behaviors are not available in the Free version of Fusion, but information is detailed as follows if you have upgraded.

1. To use object behaviors, click on the object in question and then select the Events tab in the Properties toolbar.

2. You will now see some text that says "Behaviors," and under this is a button labeled "New." Click on the New button to create a new event behavior.

3. A set of dotted lines will appear; click on them to bring up an Edit button, and click this button to go to the Event Editor for this object.

An example of a behavior applied to a single Active object can be found in the companion files. The file is located in the \Examples folder and is called "behavior." Open this file and you'll see three Actives from the qualifier example, but one of the Actives now has a behavior to flash separately.

If you try to load the behavior file in the Examples folder into the free version of Fusion, you will get an error message; you will need the full version to run this example.

Summary

You should now have a good idea of how to use the Event Editor and some of the terminology used throughout this book. Later in the book, we will be spending a lot of time entering code within this screen, so if you are unsure of any concepts, come back here and review the details.

CHAPTER 9

BACKING UP YOUR GAMES

In This Chapter

- Why Back Up?
- What Systems Are Available?

O ne of the most important things you can do when making your games is to ensure that you have a good set of backups. Many programmers use support forums when they have had a hard disk failure or have been infected by a computer virus and want to know if they can recover from it. You can understand their frustration when they are told that nothing can be done, and the program they have been working on for the last 12 months is lost. They relied too much on technology and became complacent about making sure their work was safe and secure. So, let's explore one of the most important areas you need to consider before taking on any major project.

Why Back Up?

Before we get into the details of what solutions and systems are available, let's take a step back for a moment and think about why we might need to back up our programs. Let's ask a simple question:

Do you want to lose any game you are in the middle of, or have completed?

The answer to this is probably "no"—you do not want to lose your game(s). Don't take anything for granted when it comes to backing up your programs.

There are many reasons why you will lose data, some of which are detailed here:

Viruses: Viruses have become a serious problem for PC users over the years, with more appearing each month. The generic meaning of a computer virus is something that replicates itself. Generally, they are more than that; some are just irritating, and many will cause data loss or open your computer to hackers (who might steal your data). Many people will get a virus from downloading a program from the Internet or opening an email attachment. If you are careful about what you download from the Internet, you are generally safe, but remember, even what you consider safe could distribute a virus to you. An attachment from a friend in email or chat programs could be from a hacked account. Therefore, you can never be too sure of any file, wherever you are downloading it from.

Power loss or spikes: These are much more common than people realize (even more so in older houses where power cables are old). Power spikes occur when the current of the electricity suddenly goes higher, which doesn't sound too serious, but it can cause data loss and hardware failure. Power loss can cause the same problems as power spikes, increasing the risk of damaging opened files.

Hard disk failures: This is a very common reason for data loss; many people take disks for granted and think their data is okay because it is stored on disk. A total disk failure can happen very quickly with little or no warning.

Theft: This is something we hope will never happen, but in the world in which we live, it is a possibility. Not only is your data taken from you, which means others have access to it, but many people store multiple copies of their data on the same machine. Consequently, once their base unit is taken, they won't have any way to get their files back. One indie studio had much of their equipment stolen in a break-in but were fortunate to have backups of their work; unlucky for them that it was more than a few weeks old, so they had to redo the work.

Accident: We are all prone to making mistakes, especially after long hours at work or just general tiredness. You may decide to clean up your hard disk or move some folders, and suddenly you've deleted all your work and emptied the Recycle Bin.

Hackers: Hackers are always trying to find new ways of getting into your machine, and with today's Internet speeds, this makes it easier for hackers to copy files, run scripts, steal data, crash or delete data, and even take control of your machine. They are unlikely to want to steal your Fusion files, but they will probably try to delete much of your data indiscriminately. The most common hack is locking out your machine and trying to get you to pay a ransom to unlock it (ransomware).

Act of God: This is a term used by insurance companies, but it generally means an act that is not caused by a human, such as extreme weather events or earthquakes. On a Christmas Eve in 2013 an indie studio called Hello Games had a flood where their office was located. The water ended up going to waist height and destroyed many documents and, more importantly, computers. Fortunately, the latest game they were working on, "No Man's Sky," was backed up, and so they could continue to work on the game. They spent most of their Christmas holiday, trying to get the studio back into a reasonable state. Had they not it would have likely been the end of the company and a product that achieved much success a few years later.

Flooding is getting more frequent, and even if you don't live in an area where there are risks of flash floods from heavy rains, there is still the risk of a burst water pipe.

Time and Effort

It takes time and effort to make any program, and you certainly don't want to have to start from scratch. Most people would probably want to give up if six months of work were lost.

Many creators like to work on something and then go back to it either to continue it or to take some work (code) from it to put into their latest creation. Game creating with Fusion is very much like any other form of programming; you can write your code and then import it into other games. You may even want to update it and re-release it. Consequently, making sure that even your old code is backed up and stored somewhere safe is very useful and something to consider.

What Systems Are Available?

A number of possible solutions are available to us that we need to explore:

- Backing up using Fusion

- Media backups—CD-R, DVD-/+R, thumb drives, Websites

- Software Solutions – cloud storage and online backups

- Other hardware considerations—UPS, spike-protected power unit

When the first edition of the book was written, there were technologies available that could ensure your data was secure, but costs were high; fortunately in today's Internet- and technology-led age you now have many possible solutions to back up your work, and some are free or of minimal cost. So, there is no excuse to not having backups of your work.

Backing Up Using Fusion

Fusion's system for game and application recovery is straightforward. First, you will need to configure it, as it is not turned on by default. Go to the menu options and select Tools/Preferences, which will bring up the Preferences dialog box mentioned in Chapter 4, "Fusion Basics." Click on the General tab; a number of options will appear. From here, you will see the General Options section, which is shown in Figure 9.1.

As you can see in Figure 9.1, the Autobackup option is checked by default but set to back up a single copy; you can change this by using the up and down arrows. The number you specify in the "Number of backup copies to keep" box represents how many times your file will be backed up. For example, if you put the number 5 in the box, every time you save your game it will save an additional copy up to the maximum number you entered (in this example, 5 more copies). You will be able to identify these versions, as the filename is followed by the save copy number. If your game is called game1, it will save copies called game1001, game1002, game1003, game1004, and game1005. Once it has reached the maximum number, it will then begin to overwrite those files starting from game1001. The system is not complex, but it will allow you to rescue an earlier version of the program if you run into problems. It is recommended that you set the number of copies to no fewer than 20, as anything less could mean that you may have a problem but not notice it, and all 5 backups could, in theory, have the same issue, rendering all the files useless. This option is not the only method you can use to secure your files, and it should only be used as an extra way of covering

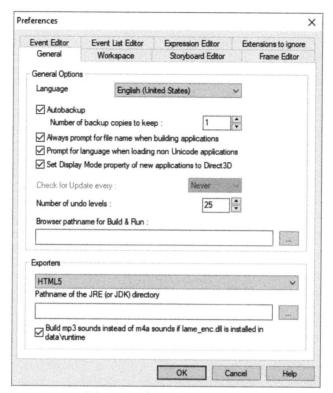

FIGURE 9.1 The Autobackup feature.

yourself. Always make regular backups to other media or, when you save the program, change the name of the file you are working on. You will then get a new set of backup files, and you can archive the others. There are two downsides to this backup feature; first is that as your game grows so does the backup, which could take up a lot of hard disk space. Second, the file is kept local with your core game file, so any hard disk failure could mean a loss of all files, rendering the backup system obsolete. If you use this system, it is recommended you copy the backup files elsewhere onto different media to prevent a single point of failure.

Media Backups

There are quite a few different options available to you if you want to back up to something other than just a folder on your hard drive. One benefit of using different media to back up is that you can store backups off-site, or away from your computer, so if anything happens at the place your computer is located, you can go and retrieve the backup.

Let's go through a few of the options you have to ensure you have backups of your files:

CD-R/DVD+/–: CD and DVD writers allow you to save your data to removable disk-based systems. Though useful for backing up, they have fallen out of favor over the last few years and have been replaced by the more versatile USB. If you order a PC these days, they may not even ship with a drive as a default. If you decide to purchase a drive, media for these devices are relatively cheap to purchase (in 25- or 50-pack sizes). With the rise in screen resolutions and graphic complexity in games, CD drives become even less useful, as a CD can only contain approximately 700MB of data. Media can get damaged or scratched, leading to it being unreadable. Unless you already have a device in your PC and some spare disks, this should be used as a last resort for a quick backup only. Disks were once a widely used source to store and backup files. Over the course of time, however, CD and DVD disks can deteriorate with age as well as become easily damaged in storage thus rendering them unusable, so disks are all right strictly for short term backups but overall it is certainly not what would be recommended over something like buying multiple memory sticks, for example.

Memory Stick: One of the easiest ways of moving data between machines is the USB thumb drive (memory stick). Thumb drives are about the size of a key ring and can store GBs of data (size ranges from 2GB and can currently go up to 128GB). USB is a common computer connection type, and all modern computers have at least one USB 2.0 port (3.0 is now becoming more common). When you plug the USB thumb drive into your PC, it shows up as a removable hard disk, which allows you to copy, delete, and use it like a normal disk. It is not recommended to use the thumb drive as a long-term backup device, but it is handy for moving data between machines and storing short-term data copies. Thumb drives are very small and can be damaged if you are not careful; the other downside is that as they are easy to pick up and put in your pocket, so they can easily be lost or stolen.

SSD Hard Disks: Slowly but surely the traditional hard disk with its moving parts is being replaced by the Solid-State Disk. This is like a big memory stick; with no moving parts they are less liable to failure. The cost of these drives is starting to drop quickly, and you can easily purchase a 500GB to 1TB drive for less than $150. An even better solution is buying an external SSD which, after working for the day on your game, you can disconnect from your computer and take with you or put somewhere else for safekeeping.

External Hard Disks (USB): External hard disks that are connected to your PC using USB are very common these days and relatively cheap. These are very useful if you want to store multiple copies of your games on a separate disk that isn't stored internally in the PC. They are much cheaper than the SSD drives but you are less likely to move these around, so with any issues around your desktop, such as flooding, etc., the disk could be impacted. You might find external hard disks still to be prone to failure and have mostly moved to NAS or SSD these days.

Network Attached Storage (NAS): NAS systems used to be quite expensive, but for a little more than $100 you can now buy a hard disk that also has an ethernet or wireless connection. These offer the added advantage of being able to be accessed from any PC in your network as well as externally over the Internet while you travel. For a few hundred dollars you can buy a NAS device that has slots for multiple hard drives and will allow you to configure them in different ways to protect your data. For example, you can get a two-drive bay NAS and configure it to be mirrored. This will use half the storage space (you'll effectively lose one disk in space, so if you put in two 4TB disks you'll only have 4TB of space available), but all data copied to one drive will be copied to the other, so in the case of a disk failure you can still rescue your data.

Cloud Storage: If you own your own Website or have an Internet account, then it most likely comes with an amount of online storage space. This allows you to copy files and store them on the Internet. It's quite easy to get 500GB–1TB of storage with your ISP these days. Unfortunately, there is a downside to this type of storage: many ISPs will not back up your data, so if they have a server problem, you could lose everything you uploaded. The benefit of this system is that as you have files locally and online, if one system does go down then you can easily and quickly copy to another location. You can also sign up to cloud storage services such as Dropbox, which provide additional ways of getting your local data backed up online. The one added benefit of Dropbox that is something to take into account is the benefit of version control. When you save your file locally it is automatically updated to the cloud, and so the latest version is always available.

There are many ways to ensure your data is safe and secure these days, and even with a computer failure your game data can still be safe (even if it means getting a new PC or reinstalling the operating system). Find a system that suits your working methods, but make sure you have a system that is easy to implement and doesn't take much thought. It's quite easy to forget to back up, and that will be the day when you'll have the problem. You can store things locally but will also have it uploaded straightaway to an online cloud storage system; this should give you peace of mind that if a problem exists locally, you can still access my files quickly from any other device.

Other Considerations

There are a few other areas to consider to help protect and secure your data, some of which require some investment, and others that are free. Feel free to choose what items you feel would add the most benefit to you and what you can afford.

UPS: A UPS (uninterruptible power supply) is used to prevent power surges and power loss so you can close your work and then shut down your computer safely (using the UPS's battery power). If you live in a house or an area in which there are power fluctuations, buying a UPS is a sound investment. UPSs were, in the past, used solely for businesses, but in the last couple of years they have become a piece of hardware that is now cheap enough for hobbyists and semi-professional developers to invest in.

Surge protectors: If you feel a UPS is overkill with regard to protecting your files (you may be in a situation in which you have a system that is backed up regularly), investing in a surge protector might be the next best thing. The surge protector is a standard power block (where you can put in multiple power sockets from all your devices), but it has built-in power spike/surge protection. It will not protect you from power loss, but it will regulate the power so a surge doesn't damage your equipment or open files.

BIOS password: When your PC boots up, it first has to run the motherboard's BIOS. You can create a password that needs to be entered before the operating system takes over and loads. The benefit of a BIOS password is that it can prevent unauthorized access to your PC. Of course, you need to ensure that the password is something you can remember so you can get into your own PC. The BIOS password is not a fully secure system, and it can only be used to prevent people within the same location from accessing the machine. It isn't a secure method if your machine is stolen, as the BIOS password option can be reset by using jumpers located on the motherboard. Users who just want general access would not take your PC apart to get access, as it would be too much hassle.

Laptops and desktops: Computers have become much cheaper over the last few years, leading to many households having more than one PC or PC-based device (e.g., a tablet). Using networking technology or USB, it is very easy to transfer data between machines for backup purposes. It is a useful way of storing files away from your main machine so that you have a backup that can be recovered in the event of hardware failure.

Computer Locks: If you have devices that could be easily moved, such as laptops, you can buy a lock for them. These resemble locks used for bicycles and are attached to your machine. It may not prevent your device being stolen but may reduce the likelihood in the event of a break-in.

Anti-Virus: Viruses are still a big issue around the world, and it's important to ensure you are protected against them. There are a number of well-known virus protection products out on the market, some paid and some free. If you are downloading files from the Internet, you should definitely have an AV product installed.

Summary

Unfortunately, developers don't consider the consequences of data loss until it's too late. It doesn't have to cost a lot of money or effort to provide a reasonable level of protection these days, so there is no reason not to invest now rather than after disaster strikes. The only issue when making multiple backups on hard disks, CDs, and cloud storage is ensuring that you know what and where the latest revisions of your changes are so you can go back to an earlier version if necessary. Even larger game development companies with the equipment and investment can lose work through hardware failure or illegal activities.

CHAPTER 10

MOVEMENT

In This Chapter

- Movement Basics
- Movement Type Examples

B efore creating your first game, you need to understand how movement works within Fusion. In the games you are making in this book, all of the movements have been predefined, so it is essential to understand how these concepts work, as you may have to refer to them in your own game making.

Movement Basics

A large number of games that you will create will need some form of movement applied to the Active objects you are using. For example, in a side-scrolling shoot-'em-up game, you would require movement for the Player object, the Enemy objects, and any bullets or missiles that are fired against them. Fusion comes with a number of prebuilt movement engines that allow you to configure your game quickly without the need to program a large number of events. These movements are separated into three categories, Non-physical movements, Physical movements, and Movement extensions. Non-physical movements are the standard set of Fusion movements that don't have any real-world physics applied to them. Physical movements are movements with real-world type physics applied and should be used when you want to get a more realistic depth of movement. Finally, movement extensions are movement types that cover other types that mimic a specific task.

Static: This is the default option for any Active object inserted onto the frame. This means the object will not move unless you specify it within the Event Editor.

Bouncing Ball: This gives the object ball-like movement. You can set options for speed, deceleration, number of angles, randomizer (how random the bounce), and security (to prevent getting stuck). Bouncing ball movement is very useful in bat-and-ball-type games, and is used in the first game example in this book called "The Lab."

Path Movement: If you want to make your game use path movements (whereby objects follow a specific route), you can use this option. You might consider using path movement in maze-type games.

Mouse Controlled: This allows an object to be directly controlled by the movement of the mouse. When creating this type of movement, a box will appear on-screen that can be increased or decreased in size. You can also move it to a specific area to limit its use to a particular portion of the screen.

Eight Directions: You can configure an object to have eight possible directions using this movement type, and can set speed, acceleration, deceleration, direction of movement, and the initial direction in which it should move. This is a good option if you only want a basic movement type, as you can easily preconfigure a group of options quickly.

Race Car: This allows you to preconfigure speed, acceleration, deceleration, rotation angles, and initial speed. This is a useful movement configuration if you are trying to replicate a racing car game.

Platform: If you want to create a platform-based game, this movement type sets up the basic requirements for creating one, including speed, acceleration, deceleration, gravity, jump strength, jump control, and initial direction of the object.

There are additional physical movement types for Eight Directions, Bouncing Ball, Platform, Race Car, and Static that are the same as those previously specified but which contain further configuration options. Some additional physical movement types are:

Background: Objects that do not move by themselves but are moved or rotated by other objects.

Spaceship: Create movement on an object that acts like a spaceship with options such as acceleration, deceleration, rotating speed, and gravity.

Spring: Create movement on an object so that it acts like a spring.

 In this book, we will only be using the non-physics-based movement types, but if you do intend to use any of the physics-based objects, as soon as you select this for an object it will ask you to also add a physics engine object to your frame.

There are three movement extensions, as follows:

Circular: Create a movement using a circular radius.

Invaders: Create a movement that works similar to the old Space Invaders video game, where enemies move in a left, down, right, down motion.

Pinball movement: Creates movement that will mimic the ball on a pinball table.

 Fusion allows you to create movement based on one of the preprogrammed options, but you can create your own movements using code if you feel you need to do something that is not a standard feature of the program.

 The movement groups are labeled for a specific type of game; for example, bouncing ball movement. While you would expect to use this movement for bat-and-ball-type games such as "The Lab" in this book, you can also use it in many other types of games that are not of the bat-and-ball type. For example, we could have used bouncing ball movement in our second game, "Amazing Fighter Pilot," for moving the enemy planes. Therefore, don't think that you have to use the race car movement for racing cars or the platform movement for platform-only games; each has a particular feature that you may be able to apply to the movement of an object within your games.

Applying Movement

The movement types previously mentioned are only applied to specific types of objects, so you will not find the Movement tab on all objects available within Fusion. You can apply movement as follows (in this example, we are using an Active object, but it could be any of the other objects that have the Movement tab properties assigned to them):

1. Start Fusion, click on the File menu option, and select New.

2. Double left-click on the frame labeled "Frame 1" in the Workspace toolbar.

3. Select New Object from the Insert menu option, and when the Create New Object dialog box appears, double-click on the Active object and then click anywhere on the play area. The Active object will now be visible on the play area; click on it with the left mouse button once to reveal the properties of the item within the Object Properties toolbar.

4. Click on the Movement tab in the Object Properties toolbar. You will see a screen as shown in Figure 10.1.

5. Notice that within the Properties dialog is a movement number and a movement type. You can apply multiple types of movement to the same object, which allows you to change the object's direction and movement response depending on a specific condition. The Type is a drop-down box containing the movement groups discussed earlier. Selecting any of the types from the drop-down box will reveal more properties specific to that movement type.

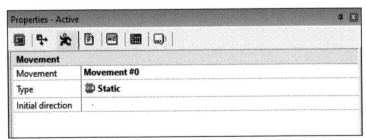

FIGURE 10.1 The Active object's Movement Properties.

 By default, there is always a single movement type already created called "Movement #0" with the type of "Static" defined.

Movement Type Examples

Now that you know where to find the movement properties for an object, we will now go through a number of examples to show them working and introduce you to any specific dialog they might have.

For each of the movement types, a basic Fusion file was created and is available within the companion files. These files were created to speed up the process of going through the examples by having the objects already inserted onto the play area. No movement has been applied to any of the objects, and they only have the default settings configured (it would be exactly the same settings as inserting a new object onto the frame). All example files can be found in the folder \Movement.

For each movement type a completed version was created. All final examples can be found in the folder \Movement.

Bouncing Ball

A good example of where you might use the Bouncing Ball movement is the game featured in this book called "The Lab." The Lab is a bat-and-ball game where you try to keep the ball in play and destroy all of the blocks. The Ball object has been given a movement of Bouncing Ball and is made to bounce off the walls around the screen, with the exception of the right side, where it will disappear and the player will lose a life. We will now make an object bounce around the screen, which will require us to apply the Bouncing Ball movement to the object and create one line of code to keep it on the screen at all times.

A final version of the example (called "Bouncing Ball Final. mfa") can be found in the companion files in the Movement folder.

1. Start Fusion, and then click on the File | Open option from the menu. When the Open dialog box appears, browse for the book's companion files and locate the file "Bounce Basic.mfa," which is stored in the Movement folder. Choose this file and then click OK to open the file.

2. Double-click on the text "Frame 1" in the Workspace toolbar to open the Frame Editor.

3. Click on the Active object that is located within the frame (it will look like a green diamond shape). The properties for the object will appear in the Properties toolbar.

4. Click on the Movement tab within the Properties toolbar.

5. You will now see three options: Movement, Type, and Initial Direction. Click on Type, and a drop-down list will appear; select Bouncing Ball. A set of new properties for this object will now be shown (as seen in Figure 10.2), allowing you to fine-tune the object to react in a specific way. Also notice the Try Movement button, which allows you to run the frame and see how the object reacts to its new movement.

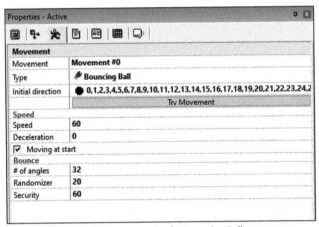

FIGURE 10.2 Object properties for Bouncing Ball movement.

6. If you click on the Try Movement button, you will notice that the object flies off to the right and then disappears. This is because the initial direction is set to go to the right, and there is no code to prevent it from leaving the frame.

7. Click on the Event Editor button in the toolbar, and then click on New Condition to create a new event.

8. When the New Condition dialog box appears, left-click on the Active object (this will look like a green diamond shaped object) and then select Position, Test Position of Active from the pop-up menu.

9. A Test Position of Active dialog box will appear. Click on all of the outward pointing arrows on the edge of the white box (four in total), and then click OK.

10. Move to the right of the event until you are directly under the Active object. Right-click and add the action Movement, Bounce.

If you now run the program, you will see the Active object bouncing around the screen. From within the properties, you can vary the speed, number of angles in which it bounces, the Randomizer (how random is each bounce), and the security (to prevent it getting stuck).

Path Movement

Path Movement allows you to set a specified route of an object around the screen. You create this route by placing a number of markers for which you can set the speed or allow the object to be paused at each point.

 You will find the basic working file "Path Basic.mfa" for this walkthrough in the Movement folder.

1. Start Fusion and click on the File | Open option from the menu. When the Open dialog box appears, browse the companion files and locate the file "Path Basic.mfa," which is stored in the Movement folder. Choose this file and then click Open to open the file.

2. Double-click on the text "Frame 1" in the Workspace toolbar to open the Frame Editor.

3. Click on the Active object that is located within the frame (it will look like a green diamond shape). The properties for the object will appear in the Properties toolbar. Click on the Movement tab within the Properties toolbar. Click on Type and a drop-down list will appear; select Path. An Edit box will then appear that allows you to configure the movement of this object. The Properties sheet for the object is shown in Figure 10.3.

4. Click on the Edit box to begin editing the path movement using the dialog box, which is shown in Figure 10.4.

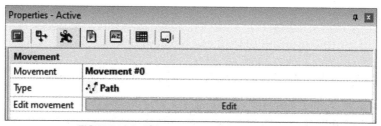

FIGURE 10.3 Object properties for path movement.

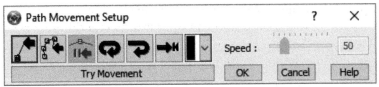

FIGURE 10.4 Path movement.

There are a number of options you can apply to your path movement:

New Line: Creates a line that can be moved to any point on the screen. The first line that was created when using the Path dialog will be attached to the inserted object. On each end of the line will be a small black square (these are called nodes) where you can configure pauses or the speed of the movement between points. Using this option, you will place a single line; you can then create a second line that originates from the last square from the last new line.

Tape Mouse: This option allows you to create multiple points quickly using a single mouse click, rather than placing them individually. Hold down the left mouse key and then move the mouse cursor to create the path.

Set a Pause: If you want to pause the object at a specific point on the screen (making the object wait), you can set a pause.

Loop the Movement: This will allow you to make a movement repeat continuously. Once the object has reached the end of the movement path (the last square), it will disappear and reappear at the start, and then begin moving again. If you are using this for an object, you may need to make the start and end points out of view of the player, so you do not allow the player to see the object disappear on screen.

Reverse at End: If you want an object to go to a certain end point and then retrace its steps along the same path it was just on, you can select this option.

Reposition Object at End: This will place the object back to its original starting location when it has reached the last node.

Try Movement: If you want to test the movement you just created, click on Try Movement, which in turn will run the movement for the specified object. You can quit out of it at any time using the ESC (escape) key or alternatively wait until the movement is complete.

Speed: You can change the speed of the object between each node by clicking on the node where you want it to have a different speed. The line where the speed change will be applied will flash to give you a visualization of where this will take place.

If you hold your mouse cursor over the items on the Path Movement Setup dialog, a small help text will appear, advising you what each option is.

If you load and run the Path Final.mfa in the movements folder, you will see the active object, which has a Tape Mouse applied to the frame and has Reverse at End and Loop (you will need to click on the Path Movement Edit button to see this information).

Mouse Controlled

If you want an object to be controlled by the mouse cursor, select the Mouse Controlled movement type.

To follow along with the next example, you can use a basic starting file that places an object on screen, ready to be configured for mouse movement. The file can be found in the Movement folder of the companion files and is called "Mouse Basic. mfa."

1. Start Fusion and then click on the File | Open option from the menu. When the Open dialog box appears, browse the Movements folder and locate the "Mouse Basic.mfa" file. Choose this file and then click OK to open the file.

2. Double-click on the text "Frame 1" in the Workspace toolbar to open the Frame Editor.

3. Click on the Active object that is located within the frame (it will look like a green diamond shape). The properties for the object will appear in the Properties toolbar.

4. Click on the Movement tab within the Properties toolbar. You will now see three options: Movement, Type, and Initial Direction. Click on Type and a drop-down list will appear; select Mouse Controlled.

5. A set of new properties for this object will now be displayed, as shown in Figure 10.5.

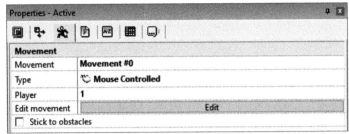

FIGURE 10.5 Object Properties sheet for Mouse Controlled movement.

6. You will notice a player item with the number "1" assigned next to it, and an Edit button to configure the movement options.

7. To create the area where you want the object to be moved by the mouse, click on the Edit button. Once you have clicked on this button, you will see Figure 10.6.

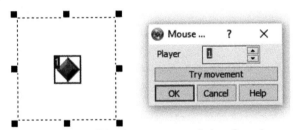

FIGURE 10.6 Editing the mouse-controlled configuration.

8. Using the mouse, expand or decrease the size of the box area where you want the object to be moved by the mouse. Once you are happy with the area you have specified, you can then click on Try Movement to test the movement and see if you might need to make some changes to the box area. You will now be able to move the object using the mouse, but only within the area you selected.

9. Press the Escape key to exit the example.

If you Run the example rather than just testing the movement, you will find that you are unable to close the application, as your mouse control is now the green active object. Even though this is a simple example, it's useful remembering that in some circumstances you may have to give the player alternative ways of closing or backing out of a screen. To close the running app, hold down the ALT key and press F4.

In the movement folder you will find the final version of the mouse movement, where the mouse has been set to move the green active object on the left-hand side of the screen only.

Eight Directions

Eight Directions is a good starting point for movement of an object, and it is frequently used in (but not exclusively) player movement in a platform or side-shooting game.

 To follow along with the next example, you can use a basic starting file, which places an object on screen ready to be configured for Eight Directions movement. The file can be found in the Movement folder and is called "Eight Basic.mfa."

1. Start Fusion, and then click on the File | Open option from the menu. When the Open dialog box appears, locate the file "Eight Basic," which is stored in the Movement folder. Choose this file and then click OK to open the file.

2. Double-click on the text "Frame 1" in the Workspace toolbar to open the Frame Editor.

3. Click on the Active object that is located within the frame (it will look like a green diamond shape). The properties for the object will appear in the Properties toolbar.

4. Click on the Movement tab within the Properties toolbar. You will now see three options: Movement, Type, and Initial Direction. Click on Type and a drop-down list will appear; select Eight Directions.

5. You will now see a number of new object properties as shown in Figure 10.7.

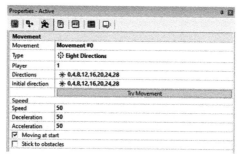

FIGURE 10.7 Object properties sheet for Eight Directions movement.

6. We will leave the movement to player 1.

7. You can specify the directions in which the object can travel (which are represented by direction numbers), and its initial starting angle, which is useful for objects that move without player intervention. By clicking on any of the directions, a dialog appears, which can be seen in Figure 10.8. Ensure that Directions are just up, down, left, and right (you can remove all directions by clicking the dotted circle in the bottom left of the Directions dialog). By clicking on a direction, you can add a direction so that it will work with the keyboard controls. So, click on the up, down, left, and right directions.

▪ You can see how this should be configured in Figure 10.9.

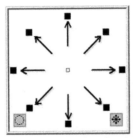

FIGURE 10.8 Direction dialog with Eight Directions selected.

8. You can also specify the speed, acceleration, deceleration, and if the object is starting when the frame is first loaded. Click on the Try Movement button to load a test frame and test the object's movement. Use the arrow keys to move the object around the screen.

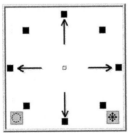

FIGURE 10.9 Direction set to up, down, left, and right.

 You can find the completed basic eight directions movement in the "Eight Final.mfa" file.

Race Car Movement

Another option that can be chosen as a type of movement is Race Car. By selecting this option, you can mimic the movement of a race car without any additional programming. This allows you to make the object respond in a specific way via the arrow keys, including acceleration, reversing, and cornering (rotating speed).

 The file used to follow this example is located under the Movement folder; the file is called "Racing Car Basic."

1. Start Fusion, and then click on the File | Open option from the menu. When the Open dialog box appears, browse to the file "Racing Car Basic. mfa," which is stored in the Movement folder. Choose this file and then click Open to open the file.

2. Double-click on the text "Frame 1" in the Workspace toolbar to open the Frame Editor.

3. Click on the Active object that is located within the frame (it will look like a green diamond shape). The properties for the object will appear in the Properties toolbar.

4. Click on the Movement tab within the Properties toolbar. You will now see three options: Movement, Type, and Initial Direction. Click on Type and a drop-down list will appear; select Race Car.

5. You will now see a number of new object properties as shown in Figure 10.10.

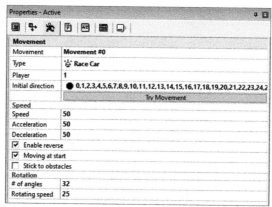

FIGURE 10.10 Race Car movement initial properties.

To get the race car moving, you do not need to amend any of the options. Click on the Try Movement button to test the race car with the arrow keys on your keyboard.

You'll notice that it's quite difficult to control the car when it is set as a basic shape, so to show you how adding in graphics makes it easier to understand and see how it works, in the movement folder you'll find "Racing Car Final.mfa," which contains a racing car graphic.

Platform Movement

The final type of movement available within Fusion is Platform Movement. If you want to create a platform game, you will apply this type of movement to your main character as well as the platforms and ladders.

The file used to follow this example is in the Movement folder; the file is called "Platform Basic." The file provides you with a single frame with all of the graphic items in their correct positions, ready to be configured.

To enable the game to play in Platform Movement, we first need to apply Platform Movement to our active object character. In the file Platform Basic we have an animated character object called Player_Robin (who strangely enough looks like a Robin Hood type of character).

1. Start Fusion and then click on the File | Open option from the menu. When the Open dialog box appears, browse to the file "Platform Basic. mfa," which is stored in the Movement folder. Choose this file and then click Open to open the file.

2. Double-click on the text "Frame 1" in the Workspace toolbar to display the pre-created level in the Frame Editor.

3. Single-click on the Player_Robin object to display its properties in the Properties toolbar, and then click on the Movement tab. Click on the Type box to reveal a number of options; click on the Platform option.

You can see the Platform options in Figure 10.11.

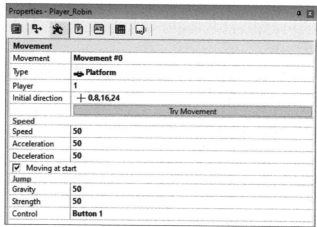

FIGURE 10.11 The Platform options.

4. Change the gravity to 35 and the strength to 100. This will define how the character jumps within the world.

You have now configured Robin to make him move with a platform configuration; the only problem with this is that there are no platforms. If you run the frame at this point, you will see Robin fall through the floor; as far as Fusion is concerned, there are no platforms available for him to land on. Therefore, we need to configure the floor and raised areas that Robin will walk on as "platforms."

5. Click on one of the Floor objects (any under Player_Robin will be fine), and then in the Object Properties window, click on the Runtime Options tab. Click on the blank space next to Obstacle type, and from the drop-down menu choose Platform.

6. You will also need to set Floor_Left and Floor_Right as a Platform.

Lastly, we have a ladder on the frame, which we need to configure as a "ladder" obstacle type.

7. Click on one of the Ladder objects; the object Properties will then appear. Click on the Runtime Options tab and then click the white space next to the Obstacle Type option. From the drop-down menu, choose Ladder.

There are a number of instances of the same object in the example file, so if you change the settings for one Floor instance it will change it for all, so making changes to the platform type can be very quick.

If you now run the frame, you will see that your character can walk, jump, and climb up the ladder (use the left and right arrow keys to move and the Shift key to jump).

 The final version of this platform example can be found in the Movements folder and is called "Platform Final.mfa."

Summary

In this chapter, you learned how to create movement of your objects. You are now ready to tackle the two final concepts that are important when making your games: importing graphics and creating animations. As with the movements, all the graphics of our games are predefined, so it is useful to know how to make your own for your games.

CHAPTER 11

GRAPHICS AND ANIMATION

In This Chapter

- Graphics Creation
- Animations

This chapter shows you how to import your own graphics using images created in a third-party graphics product, create your own using Fusion's built-in Picture Editor, and animate your images into moving graphics.

Graphics Creation

You may want to create your own graphic images for your games or import ones that have already been created in another graphics package; this is possible using Fusion's Picture Editor. To access the Picture Editor, you need to have inserted onto the play area a graphic-based object—for example, an active, picture, or backdrop object. Once you have placed it, double-click on it to enter the Picture Editor and begin the process of making your own images or importing one.

Importing Graphics

In the following example, we will import a single PNG-formatted file that was created in another graphics program into Fusion.

 The image called "Import_1.png" has been created for you and can be found in the Graphics folder in the companion files.

1. Start Fusion, and then click on the File | New option from the menu to create a new program file.

2. Double-click on the text "Frame 1" in the Workspace toolbar to open the Frame Editor.

3. From the File menu, select Insert | New Object. When the Create New Object dialog box appears (you can also double-click on the play area), double-click on the Active object. Place the object somewhere on the playfield by left-clicking on the frame.

4. A green diamond-shaped object will now appear within the frame; to enter the Picture Editor, double-click on the object.

5. Click on the Import button (the second in from the top left) to open the Import dialog box. A dialog box will now appear, and you will need to navigate to the location of the file you want to import. In this example, it is "Graphics\Import_1.png." Select the file and then click on the Open button. An Import dialog box will appear, as shown in Figure 11.1. Click on the OK button to import the image.

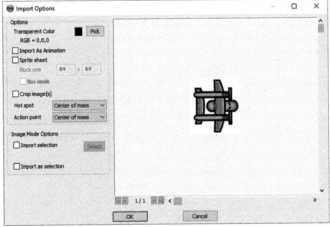

FIGURE 11.1 The Import dialog box.

The image of the yellow plane will now replace the green diamond shape; click on the OK button to save this to the object.

Drawing Graphics in Fusion

Perhaps you don't have access to another drawing package, or you would prefer to make your images from within Fusion's own powerful Picture Editor. In the following example, we are going to create a simple graphic image to give you a flavor of the Picture Editor, because it uses many common drawing tools (lines, fill, erase); we won't be going into detail on those aspects.

 An example of the final output from this walkthrough is contained in the Graphics folder; the file is called "Draw Final. mfa."

 You can make your own drawing creation in the following example if you want to practice drawing in the picture editor. Get creative with it.

As we are experimenting with the drawing tool, the exact image you create will not be exactly like the picture in the Fusion "Draw Final.mfa" file.

1. Start Fusion, and then click on the File | New option from the menu to create a new program file.

2. Double-click on the text "Frame 1" in the Workspace toolbar to open the Frame Editor.

3. From the File menu, select Insert | New Object. When the Create New Object dialog box appears, double-click on the Active object. Place the object somewhere on the playfield by left-clicking on the frame.

4. A green diamond-shaped object will now appear in the frame; to enter the Picture Editor, double-click on the object.

5. First, we need to delete the current image that is occupying the Active object. You can do this using either the Clear command or the Erase tool. The Clear tool deletes the entire area, and the Erase tool allows you to select a certain area of the image to delete. We want to remove the entire image, so click on the Clear button, which is the first icon at the top left of the Picture Editor (it looks like a blank piece of paper). The image will now be removed from the Active object.

6. The image is too small for the drawing we want to do, so to resize we need to use the Size button, which is the bottom-left button on the tool-bar (it resembles a line with an arrowhead on each end). On clicking the Size button, a dialog box will appear allowing you to configure certain sizing aspects of your image, as shown in Figure 11.2.

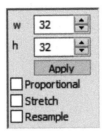

FIGURE 11.2 Resizing Tool dialog box.

7. Now we need to amend the image size, so type in "200" for the width and "160" for the height, and then click on the Apply button to make the change to the image.

8. Now, select the Line tool (which looks like an image of a straight line and a pencil), select a dark color from the color palette on the right-hand side by left-clicking, and then make a number of crisscrossing images on the image canvas. You will now have an image that should look similar to Figure 11.3.

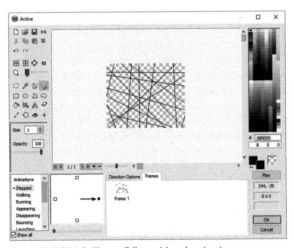

FIGURE 11.3 Picture Editor with a drawing in progress.

9. We now need to fill in some of the areas of the image with different colors, so choose the Fill tool in the toolbar (it looks like a paint pot being tipped over), and then click on any color from the selection of colors on the right of the Picture Editor. Click within some of the blank areas on the image to fill them with the selected color. Do this a few times and then choose another color, and then continue to fill more of the white gaps. Do this a number of times until you are happy with the image.

10. Click on the OK button to save the work to the Active object.

 If you have trouble seeing some of the gaps, you can use the Zoom function within the Picture Editor to increase the size of the image temporarily.

 Do not click on the "X" in the corner of the Active Picture dialog box or on Cancel if you want to save your image, as this will revert the object to its original image.

Animations

Animations are important in games, making the images look like they are moving (this could be the movement of the main character, an item in the background, or an enemy player). In addition, animations make the game look more interesting and more realistic. All animations used within Fusion are created within the Picture Editor, and use the same process as importing a single image.

1. Start Fusion, and then click on the File | New option from the menu to create a new program file.

2. Double-click on the text "Frame 1" in the Workspace toolbar to open the Frame Editor.

3. From the File menu, select Insert | New Object; when the Create New Object dialog box appears, double-click on the Active object. Place the object somewhere on the playfield by left-clicking on the frame.

4. A green diamond-shaped object will appear in the frame; to enter the Picture Editor, double-click on the object.

5. Click on the Import icon to open the Import dialog box. Browse for the graphics folder and select the image called "anim_1.png," and then click on Open. You will see the Import Options dialog. Rather than importing a single image, we want to import a set that represents the aircraft being destroyed. Ensure that "Import as Animation" is selected, and as we have numbered the images with _1 to _13 (all with the same starting name), Fusion will know they are part of an animation set. You know if an import has worked correctly when you see the From Frame and To Frame specify the number of images as shown in Figure 11.4.

6. Click on the OK button to complete the import.

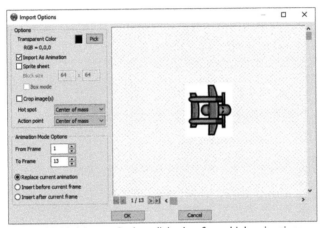

FIGURE 11.4 Import Options dialog box for multiple animations.

If you click on the Picture Editor OK button, this will save this animation to the active object. If you run the frame, you'll notice that the animation will run as soon as the frame starts and will run very fast, in fact so fast that you hardly see it.

 We have created a slightly amended version of this animation in a file called "Anim Final.mfa," which can be found in the Graphics folder.

To make this run at a more reasonable speed, we have reduced the animation speed to 25. To see the animation speed, double-click on the active object representing the aircraft, and you will see next to a tab called Frames one called Direction Options.

In the Event Editor we have also added two events, the first that stops the aircraft animation from playing and the second which will activate it when pressing the spacebar.

Summary

In this chapter, you learned two of the most important aspects of making your games with Fusion: how to import or draw your own images, and how to animate them. You are now ready to tackle the first game in this book, "The Lab," where we will use some of the features and functionality of Fusion with which you are now familiar.

CHAPTER 12

CREATING A BAT-AND-BALL GAME

In This Chapter

- About the Lab
- The Lab – Initial Setup
- The Lab – Main Menu
- The Lab – The Game Screen
- The Lab – High Score
- The Lab – Programming
- Bat and Ball Retro

In this chapter, we will create our very first game, which will be an exciting and fun Bat-and-Ball-style game. We will learn the basic concepts of Fusion and the best way to structure your games using the product. We will take the game idea from a set of graphics to a fully playable one-level game with its own high-score table.

About the Lab

The first game we are going to make is called "The Lab." Although it is a traditional Bat-and-Ball type of game (details of this type of game can be found in Chapter 1, "Video Games"), by putting in some nice graphics and an interesting story, you can make it an excellent game for people to play. It is very important to remember that although this type of game has been done many times, you can make it different using an interesting concept. "The Lab" is an interesting take on the Bat-and-Ball type of game; the story goes something like this:

You are a lab technician working on a new experiment. There is an accident in the lab and your chemicals have been mixed up, creating a force field so you are unable to escape. You must destroy all the items on the shelf, which will reveal new ingredients to help you free yourself.

You will need to separate this game into three easily manageable sections:

The Main screen: Also known as the title screen or loading screen. This is where you introduce the game to the game players, provide options to start the game, see the high scores, and quit the game.

The Game screen: This is where the user starts to play the game and tries to beat the current high score.

The High-Score screen: This is where players can see all of the current high scores so they can think about what they have to do to get onto the leaderboard.

To make things easier, all the graphics have been premade, and the objects used within this game are preconfigured, again to make things easier. We covered these configurations in Chapter 6, "Working with Objects," and Chapter 7, "Configuring Properties." Before we begin, we need to break the game down into more detail of what will happen in each stage.

 This first game is documented in detail at each stage; the other two main games have less detailed instructions, as you should then be familiar with how to do certain aspects of the programming.

When the game starts, the main menu graphic appears, which displays the title of the game and three options: Start Game, High Scores, and Quit. Clicking on any of the options makes the program go to another frame. Start Game takes the program to Frame 2 for the player to play the game, High Scores takes the game to Frame 3 to see the current highest scores, and Quit exits the program.

When the player clicks on the Start Game button, he will be taken to the game screen. The blocks will be placed on-screen, and the user will need to press the Space bar to begin playing the game. Each block will take two hits to be destroyed, and then will be removed from the play area. There will be four special blocks that release a bottle or a chemical shape, so if the bat hits them, the player will get a special bonus. The bat will be moved using the Up and Down arrow keys. Once all three lives have been lost (the ball will need to disappear behind the bat on the right-hand side of the screen), a box will appear asking the player to enter his or her name.

After entering your name, you will be taken to the High Scores screen (Frame 3), where the current scores will be listed. Clicking on the Leave button will take you back to the main screen (Frame 1).

Before you begin to create the game, check out the final creation in the companion files. The executable file is located in \ Game_1, and the file to run it is called "TheLab.exe." This will show you all the sections of the game and how it plays.

Graphics Library – The Lab

All of the graphics and objects used in this book have been placed in library files to make the game development easier. A library is a Fusion .mfa file into which I've already imported the graphics and associated objects you need for the games. The major benefit of this is that if you have a number of similar game concepts, you can place them all in the same folder, and then drag and drop items from them onto your new game when required. This means you could save common objects, and their properties could already be preconfigured, ready to drop into your next game.

To use our ready-made graphics and objects, we need to point the library to the files in the folder \Game_1\Lib.

If you cannot see the Library toolbar, use the text menu View | Toolbars | Library Window to make it visible.

1. Right-click on the left-hand pane of the Library toolbar to reveal a pop-up menu.

2. Click on the New option. A dialog box will appear, allowing you to browse your computer and any attached devices. Find the folder \Game_1\Lib

in the companion files, and then click on the OK button. You will then need to enter a library folder name; for this game we will call it "The Lab," so type that in the box that appears in the toolbar.

3. Click on "The Lab" folder name in the Library toolbar; a small graphic will appear in the right windowpane. Double-click on this item to browse down into the library. You will then see more items in the right windowpane, which separates the graphics and objects into relevant level (frame) groups. You can double-click on any of the three available groups to see some of the game items. Depending on your screen resolution, you may need to use the scroll bar to view all of the available items you can use in your game. Remember, you can increase the size of the Library toolbar if you have the room to do so by moving the mouse over the edges of the Toolbar box and dragging the window. You will then see all the items needed in the game as shown in Figure 12.1.

To add an item to your game, simply drag the item onto the Frame Editor.

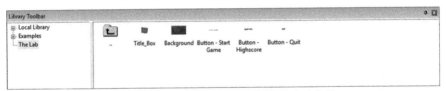

FIGURE 12.1 Some of the objects available in the Lab library.

The Lab – Initial Setup

First, we need to set up all the frames we will work with for this game. We will need three frames: one for the Main Menu, one for the Game, and one for the High Score screen.

Creating the Frames

The first thing we need to do is create the Fusion file and then create our initial three frames.

1. Start Fusion, and then click on File | New option on the menu. This will create the initial game program and its first frame.

2. Highlight the text "Application 1," which is the top item in the Workspace toolbar. You can then either right-click and select New Frame or select Insert | New Frame from the menu. This will create a second frame called "Frame 2"; type in the name "Game." Press Enter to accept the frame name.

3. Insert another frame using the same method as before and call it "High Score."

4. We now need to change the name of the first of the frames, "Frame 1." Highlight it by clicking once on it with the left mouse button, and then right-click on it and select Rename. Call this frame "Main Menu," and then press the Enter key to accept the changes.

Changing Application Settings

The application settings are configuration options that affect the entire game. These could include the size of window, can it be maximized, minimized, what graphic mode does it run in, and so forth. You can see what the current setup of the Workspace toolbar should look like in Figure 12.2.

FIGURE 12.2 The current configuration of the Workspace.

1. First, we need to change the name of the game to something a little more interesting and descriptive than "Application 1." Click the left mouse button once on the word "Application 1" to highlight the text. Change the text to "The Lab."

2. You may see a small * next to the game name, which means that you haven't saved the game yet, and you have made a change since the last save. Try to get into the habit of saving your game regularly, so if you have any problems or your computer crashes, you hopefully will not lose any work.

3. We need to change the size of the game; currently it is 640 × 480, which is way too small, so click on the Application Name (The Lab), and in the Application Properties, click on the Window Tab (icon of a monitor) and change the size option to 1920 × 1080. As you are making this change at the application level, you will see a pop-up box asking you to change it for all frames; click on the Yes button. In the Storyboard editor it should show all frames as 1920 × 1080.

4. Save the game by clicking on File/Save on the menu or the Save button on the toolbar.

You could have changed the name of the game by left-clicking once on the word "Application 1" to highlight it. Then, right-click on the text to bring up the pop-up menu. Select Rename and then type in the game name.

If you are running the full version of Fusion and have Windows Executable as the build type, you'll notice that you can click on the Maximize button and the game will fill the entire screen. We don't want this to happen, as the game graphics are configured to play within a certain screen size (1920 x 1080), and you will have a border around the game if a user presses the Maximize button, which doesn't look very professional. You'll need to go into the Application Properties; you can do this by clicking on the game name "The Lab" in the Workspace toolbar. This will now load the Application Properties into the Properties toolbar. Click on the icon that looks like a monitor, which is the Window Properties tab. Find the No Maximize Box and check it. This will disable that option from being clicked when you next run the game. Figure 12.3 shows an example of how the properties will look when you have made that change.

FIGURE 12.3 Removing the maximize option for Windows Executables.

The Lab – Main Menu

If you run the game, it will display a white blank window on-screen. Nothing else will happen, so now you need to create the main menu screen. The main menu is used as an introduction screen to the players and allows them to play the game, view the high scores, or quit. We are keeping the main menu as simple as possible and very easy for the player to understand what each option does; this reduces the risk of making it too confusing and limits the amount of screens the player can navigate to.

1. Click on the words "The Lab" in the Library toolbar (the library link was created earlier; if you do not have it, see the "Graphics Library—The Lab" section for more details).

2. You will now see an icon and the words "The Lab" in the right-hand window; this is the library file containing all the objects and graphics we need. Double-click on the icon "The Lab" to drill down to the next level.

3. Within the Library toolbar, you will now see the icons Main Menu, Game, and High Score. To make this game easier, we have placed all the required objects in these three areas; for the main menu of our game, all of the items you need are stored under Main Menu. Double-click on the Main Menu to see the items we will use in the first frame of our game.

 If you want to back up at any time, click on the upward pointing arrow.

4. Before we can place any items on the playfield, we must be able to see the right frame on the screen. To do this, double-click on Main Menu in the Workspace toolbar to go to the correct frame. Your screen should now look something like Figure 12.4.

5. The first item you will need is a background graphic to make the screen look more interesting. You will see an image in the Library toolbar called "Background." Left-click on this graphic and continue to hold down the left mouse button while dragging the image across onto the playfield. Once it's in position, let go of the left mouse button and the background image will appear in the Frame Editor window. If the image doesn't cover the playfield precisely, you can move it with the mouse by dragging it into position; otherwise, right-click on the image and then select Align in

Frame | Horz | Center and Align in Frame | Vert | Center. The second method is preferred, as the graphic will be placed automatically in the center.

6. Next place the Title_Box on the screen, using the same method as the Background object.

7. Next, you need to place the three buttons on the playfield. In the middle of the Title_Box image, put the buttons in the order of "Button – Start Game," "Button – Highscore," and "Button – Quit." You may have to click and drag the objects once placed to get a more precise position that you are happy with.

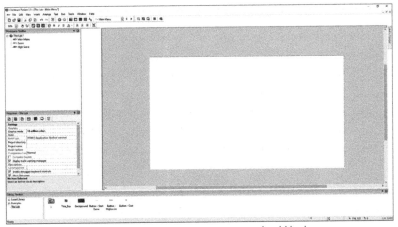

FIGURE 12.4 How your current screen should look.

There are a number of ways of creating buttons in Fusion; in this example we have used an active object and used its animation direction to specify a hover and unhover graphic. This means that with code we can change the button when you move the mouse over it and then change it back to its original state when the mouse isn't overlapping it. You could have also used the Button object to create a graphic button.

You now have all of the elements needed for the main menu on the screen. An example of this is shown in Figure 12.5. If the game is run at this stage, the game window will appear with a nicely drawn background and three buttons down the middle.

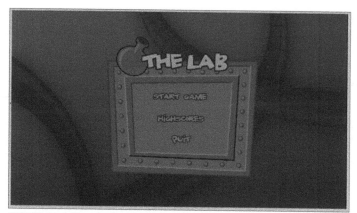

FIGURE 12.5 How the first frame should look once the items have been placed.

The Lab – The Game Screen

Now that the Main Menu screen is complete, it is sensible to put all of the graphical elements of the game screen together. This will be more work than the Main Menu screen because of the number of objects involved to represent all the blocks. There are a number of shortcuts we can use to make placing them much quicker:

1. Double left-click on the frame entitled "Game"; this will change the Frame Editor from the first frame to the second. The playfield will be blank because we have not put any objects on this frame.

2. In the Library toolbar, we are currently viewing the objects for the first frame; double-click on the up-pointing arrow to move up a level. Double-click on the library group called "Game." You will now see all the objects you need to use in this frame.

3. Drag the Background image from the Library toolbar and place it precisely onto the playfield. Now, drag the image called "Border" onto the playfield. This will place it on top of the Background image. You may need to center both images in the middle of the frame (using the right mouse button, click Align in Frame, discussed in the section "The Lab— Main Menu"; or you can click on the object, select its properties, and set its X and Y positions to 0).

4. You now need to place the first brick onto the play area. Drag the graphic object called "Brick" and put it anywhere on the screen. Left-click on the brick to bring up its properties in the Properties Workspace. We need to access the Size/Position tab to change its position on the screen. Click on the Size/Position tab to see the settings. Type "272" in the X position and "258" in the Y position. This will place the first brick in the correct position on the playfield, and it will be used as the placeholder for all the other bricks we need to add.

 Remember, the X position starts from the top left of the screen and goes to the far right, while the Y position value starts from the top left and goes to the bottom left. Using a combination of X and Y, you can place an object anywhere on the screen.

5. The bricks will be placed 8 down and 10 across. This could take a long time if you had to drag and drop each brick onto the screen; luckily, there is a way to do this in Fusion called "duplicating." Duplicating an object makes another copy of the object, and although it contains most of the aspects of the original object, you are allowed to specify some different object properties. Left-click on the brick so it is highlighted, and then right-click on it and select the Duplicate option. A Duplication dialog box will appear as shown in Figure 12.6.

 There are two ways to create replica objects on the playfield: Duplicate and Clone object. Although they will create what appears to be exactly the same thing, there is a difference between the two options. Duplicate creates all objects with the same appearance and name, and they will appear in the Event Editor as a single object. Any changes you make to a single object will change all the others. The benefit of duplicating objects is that you can work with them as a group, or you can access single objects using an internal value assigned to each. You could call duplicates "Instances." Cloning looks similar to duplication, but creates a separate object with different properties, and each has a unique name.

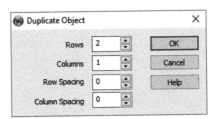

FIGURE 12.6 Duplication dialog box.

6. When duplicating an object, you have a number of options you can choose to make copies and place them on the playfield. "Rows" is how many copies of the object you will make going in a downward direction (the number includes the one that already exists). "Columns" is how many objects will appear to the right of the current object (again including the one you are duplicating). Then there are two options for spacing the objects on the screen: the higher the number, the bigger the gap between each object. "Row spacing" indicates the space between the objects going from top to bottom, and "Column spacing" will determine the space of each object left to right. You need to enter the following numbers to create the right number of bricks: 8 rows, 10 columns, 0 row spacing, and 50 column spacing. Once you click OK, you will see how the screen is starting to look more like a game. Delete four bricks from anywhere within the group of bricks and then replace them with the four special bricks from the Library toolbar (Brick_Large, Brick_Sticky, Brick_Shoot, and Brick_Double).

7. Place the Ball object onto the playfield. Click on the object to view its properties, and then click on the Size/Position tab. Set the X and Y settings as 1722 and 539, respectively.

8. Drag the Bat object onto the playfield. Then, click on it to highlight it and to display the Object Properties in the Properties Workspace area. Click on the Size/Position tab and set the X, Y settings to 1828 and 539, respectively.

9. Drag the Lives object onto the playfield and place it in the Lives box on the playfield. You don't need an exact position as long as you place it in the middle of the Lives box using the mouse (if you want to place it in the exact same place as the game, the X, Y settings are 396 and 992, respectively).

10. Find the Scores object, drag it onto the playfield, and place it in the Score box (on the right-hand side). You can place it manually or put it at the coordinates 1588, 1036.

11. Finally, you will need to drag the following objects onto the Frame Editor: Formula_Large, Formula_Sticky, Formula_Shoot, Double Ball, Gun, and Bullet. They need to be outside of the playfield, as we don't want them immediately to be seen by the player. These objects will be used in the game but are not to be shown when the frame runs. An example of how your game should look is shown in Figure 12.7. By placing them outside the play area, you can call on the graphics when you need them using code.

FIGURE 12.7 The setup of the game and how it should look.

The Lab – High Score

The High Score frame is the last frame within the game and is used to show the players if they achieved a good score.

1. Double left-click on the frame entitled "High Score"; this will change the Frame Editor from the second frame to the third. The playfield will be blank because we haven't put any objects onto this frame.

2. In the Library toolbar, we are currently viewing the objects for the second frame; double-click on the up-pointing arrow to move up a level. Double-click on the library group called "High Score." You will now see all of the objects you need to use in this frame.

3. Drag the Backdrop object onto the playfield. Once placed, you will need to drag it correctly into position or use the Align in Frame option from the pop-up menu (using the right mouse button).

4. Drag Score_Border and place in the middle of the frame.

5. Drag the Quit_String and place it below the Score_Border object at X and Y coordinates of 663 and 950.

6. Finally, drag the Hi-Score object onto the playfield and place it in the middle of the Score_Border. You can place it precisely using the co-

ordinates 762, 426. An example of what it should look like is shown in Figure 12.8.

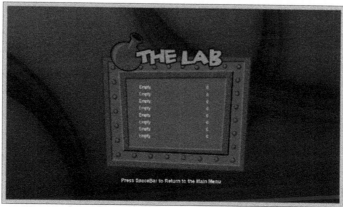

FIGURE 12.8 The look of the frame once all the game objects have been placed.

The Lab – Programming

All of the components are now in place, ready for you to program them into your game. We will start with the Main Menu, move on to the game, and finish with the final frame, the High Score frame. The first and third frames contain very little code and will be straightforward to code; the Game frame involves much more complexity. If you have trouble with any of the programming parts, you can examine the full source code that you can download.

 The source code for the games in this book are stored in the folders Game_1, Game_2, and Game_3, under a directory called "\Full_Source." "The Lab" is stored in Game_1.

Programming the Main Menu

As you may remember, the first frame (called the Main Menu) consists of active objects which are the navigational buttons, which when clicked with the left mouse button will take the player to various areas of the game. The first frame is straightforward to program and involves similar code for all three navigational items.

Run the game and you'll see that each of the three text graphic objects is yellow. This is because we have three animation frames; when the game starts it will run through these animation frames, and when it gets to the last one, if it's not set to loop, it will display that graphic all the time.

1. Make sure you are on the Main Menu frame and that it appears in the Frame Editor. If it currently is displaying a different frame or you are not sure, double-click on the words "Main Menu" in the Workspace toolbar. Click on the Event Editor toolbar button so you can begin to enter your code.

2. Click on the New Condition text and then a dialog box will appear as shown in Figure 12.9. The third icon in is of a chessboard and a knight; this object handles all of the key start-up, end, and navigational options of your game. From this object right-click on it to bring up the pop-up menu and select Start of Frame as shown in Figure 12.10.

FIGURE 12.9 The New Condition dialog box.

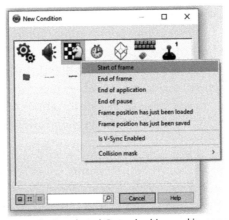

FIGURE 12.10 The Storyboard Controls object and its pop-up menu.

The Start of Frame condition will only run once, at the very start of the frame as it's created. The start of frame is useful for configuring any settings that you want to set before your game starts. Some settings can be set in the object properties, and you should set them there rather than in a Start Event, but in this case we need to do it using Events.

The first actions we need to configure involve animations for the three Button text objects. We need to tell Fusion to stop playing any animations at the start of the game; this will mean it will only display the first animation frame, rather than going to animation Frame 3 as it currently does.

3. Move to the right from Event line 1 until you are directly under the Button – Start Game object. If you are unsure which object that is (as the graphic icons can appear small—though you can enlarge them), you can hold the mouse cursor over an action box to reveal a tooltip that tells you which object you are currently under (as shown in Figure 12.11). Get under Button – Start Game and right-click to bring up the pop-up menu. Then select Animation | Stop.

4. We want to do this for the two other graphical buttons, so we can manually add them using the Animation | Stop actions or, as they are the same object type as Button – Start Game, we can drag and drop the single action from that action box to the other two.

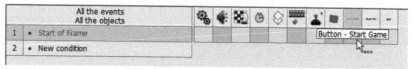

FIGURE 12.11 The object tooltip feature.

We will break up our code for the buttons using the comment lines, which we will use to explain what each set of events will achieve.

5. Right-click on the second blank event line and select Insert | A comment. Then in the dialog box that appears, type "Start Game Button" and then click on OK.

Now that we have a description, we need to program three different events. The first is changing the graphic when the mouse cursor is over the Button – Start Game object, the second event will reset the graphic when the mouse isn't over the object, and the third event will be taking into account when the player has clicked on the object. The first two events create a simple animation effect as you move the mouse over and off the object, while the third event will be used to navigate to the Game frame.

Let us now configure the first event, which will change the graphic status of the Button – Start Game object.

6. Click on the New Condition text on Event Line 3. Select the Mouse Pointer and Keyboard object, then select The Mouse | Check for mouse pointer over an object. You will then be asked for an object to check against; select the Button – Start Game object as shown in Figure 12.12 and then click on OK.

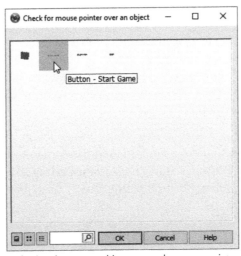

FIGURE 12.12 Selecting the correct object to test the mouse pointer over an object.

There will now be one line of code that says Mouse pointer is over and then a small graphic icon. If you hold the mouse over the graphic, it will bring up a help tip which will tell you what object this applies to. In this example it is for the Button – Start Game object. This means that Fusion will try to do something (an action) when the mouse cursor is over this object. You haven't programmed the action, so when mouse is over the object, nothing will happen. What we want to happen is the graphic of the Button – Start Game object to change.

7. Going across from Event Line 3, move your mouse until you are under the image of Button – Start Game. It may be difficult for you to tell which object this is, so hold the mouse over the empty box and it will advise you

which object is currently highlighted. You can see an example of this in Figure 12.12.

8. Once you are below the Button – Start Game object, right-click on it to bring up the pop-up menu, then select Animation | Change | Animation Frame. The Expression Evaluator appears, asking you to enter the frame number as shown in Figure 12.13. You'll notice that it warns you that frames use a 0-based index; that means it starts from 0. We have three animations in each of the text buttons: we have the first, which is the unselected button; the second, which is the graphic for when the mouse cursor is over the text; and the third, which is a graphic for if the object was clicked (which we won't program in this example, but it's common to have a clicked animation). So, we will enter 0 for the first animation, 1 for the second, and 2 for the third. Enter the number 1 into the Expression Evaluator and then click on OK.

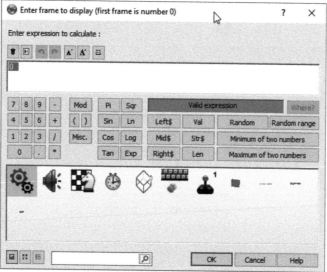

FIGURE 12.13 The animation frame number in the Expression Evaluator.

If you run the game now, you'll notice that if you move the mouse cursor over the Start text, it will change color (it will change to a different animation frame), but now we have found a problem; when you move the mouse away from the object, it doesn't return back to its original graphic.

We will need to create a new event that does the opposite of Event line 3 when the mouse pointer isn't over the object. We can do things quicker in Fusion without needing to start from scratch. There are two ways: we can drag and drop the text for the condition and put it in the new condition, or we can copy and paste a whole line and its actions and make the necessary changes. First, for this example, we are going to use drag and drop.

9. Drag the text of Mouse pointer is over Button – Start Game (left-click and then hold the left mouse button) and drag and drop it into the New condition text on Event line 4.

10. We now need to make it that the opposite is true, so right-click on the condition text event in line 4 and select Negate.

We need the action to be setting the animation frame to 0.

11. Right-click on the empty action box on line 4 that is directly under the Button – Start Game and select Animation | Change | Animation Frame. In the Expression Evaluator it already has a default value of 0, so click on OK.

The final event that we need for the Start text is that when the user clicks on it, we move to the Game frame.

12. Click on the New condition text on Event line 5, select the mouse pointer and keyboard object, then at the pop-up menu choose The mouse | User clicks on an object. A mouse interaction dialog box appears, as shown in Figure 12.14, where you can configure the type of mouse interaction. In this case we want to use the defaults, so click on OK.

FIGURE 12.14 The mouse click on an object dialog options.

13. Now you'll need to specify which object is being clicked on; in this case it's the Button – Start Game object. Select it and then click on OK.

For the action associated with Event Line 5, we want to move between frames, moving from the Main Menu to the Game frame; to do this we would use the Storyboard controls object, which is shown as the chessboard and knight piece.

14. Move across from Event Line 5 until you are directly under the Storyboard Controls object. Right-click and select Jump to Frame.

15. The Jump to Frame dialog box appears, showing you all frames within your game, as shown in Figure 12.15. When the player clicks the Start Game text on the main menu, it goes to Frame 2, which is the Game frame. So, click on Frame 2 – Game and then click on OK.

FIGURE 12.15 Selecting the frame to which to jump to.

If you run the game now, you'll notice when you move the mouse over the Start Game text it will animate, and when you click on it, it will take you to the Game frame.

Now we need to create the code for the High scores and Quit text. Create the following events (rather than type in all conditions in great detail, we have given you a brief overview of each of the conditions; if you get lost then consult how we did the previous ones. Adding a comment is right-clicking on the line number, while adding a condition is clicking on the New condition text):

 In most cases, you will be using a shortened way of explaining what code you need in the event editor by specifying the Event line and whether it's a condition or an action. This reduces the amount of text and makes programming easier to read.

- Event Line 6: Insert | A Comment | "High Scores Button" | OK.

- Event Line 7: Condition: the mouse pointer and keyboard | The mouse | Check for mouse pointer over an object | "Button – Highscore" | OK.

- Event Line 8: Condition: the mouse pointer and keyboard | The mouse | Check for mouse pointer over an object | "Button – Highscore" | OK. Negate.

- Event Line 9: Condition: the mouse pointer and keyboard | The mouse | User clicks on an object | OK | "Button – Highscore" | OK.

- Event Line 10: Insert | A Comment: "Quit Button" | OK.

- Event Line 11: Condition: the mouse pointer and keyboard | The mouse | Check for mouse pointer over an object | "Button – Quit" | OK.

- Event Line 12: Condition: the mouse pointer and keyboard | The mouse | Check for mouse pointer over an object | "Button – Quit" | OK. Negate.

- Event Line 13: Condition: the mouse pointer and keyboard | The mouse | User clicks on an object | OK | "Button – Quit" | OK.

Now that we have the base conditions done, we are ready for our actions; Figure 12.16 shows how your event code should look right now.

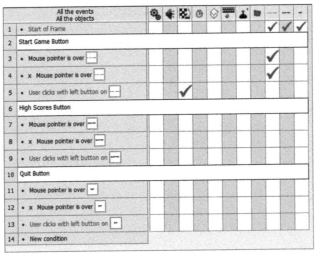

FIGURE 12.16 All of the conditions needed for the Main Menu screen.

Now we need to configure the actions; you could drag and drop the check-marks from the previous start game button events and then change them. The following is an abbreviated list of the events, with Event Line, Object (which one to right click on), and the associated action. For the actions, we have named the objects that you should right-click on to select the menu item.

- Event Line 7: Action: Button – Highscore: Animation | Change | Animation Frame | 1 | OK.

- Event Line 8: Action: Button – Highscore: Animation | Change | Animation Frame | 0 | OK.

- Event Line 9: Action: Storyboard Controls: Jump to frame "High Score (3)" | OK.

- Event Line 11: Action: Button – Quit: Animation | Change | Animation Frame | 1 | OK.

- Event Line 12: Action: Button – Quit: Animation | Change | Animation Frame | 0 | OK.

- Event Line 13: Action: Storyboard Controls | End the application.

You should now have your event editor looking like Figure 12.17. Congratulations, you have completed the code for the Main Menu. If you now test this frame, you should be able to navigate between the Game and High Score frames, though as we haven't programmed them yet, you won't be able to move away from them (and will have to close the app to test any further).

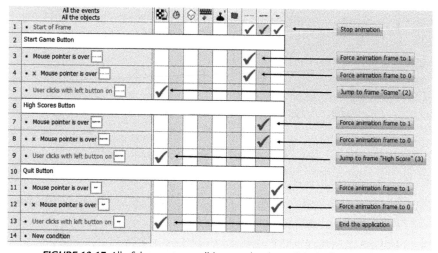

FIGURE 12.17 All of the events, conditions, and actions of the Main Menu frame.

Be careful not to get confused between Run Application and Run Frame. If you accidentally Run Frame, it will not activate any code that calls another frame, and so it will look like the game isn't working as intended (as you won't move between the Main Menu and Game/High Score frames).

If it doesn't work as expected, compare your code to the completed source code for "The Lab" in the \game_1\Full_Source\ folder in the companion files.

Programming the Game

It is now time to complete the programming for the game section and, compared to Frames 1 and 3, there is much more work involved, as this is where you will need to program all the movements and what happens when the graphics hit each other. There are many more lines of code, but much of it is replicated and just points to a different object. Therefore, even though it looks like a lot of work, the speed of development is very quick.

The Bat already has Eight Direction movement applied to it, but only movements up and down (so you can use the arrow keys to move the bat), and the ball has Ball movement applied to it but has Moving at start unchecked in the object properties, so it doesn't move when the frame is started. The bonus objects for making the bat larger, sticky, gun, and double bar have been set to have ball movement with a single going right movement (but not moving at start enabled).

Confirm you are on the correct frame by double-clicking on the text "Game" in the Workspace toolbar. The game frame should appear. Then, click on the Event Editor button on the Button toolbar to see the blank Event Editor for this frame.

Before we start programming the game, it is recommended that you play The Lab.exe that is included within the downloaded files so that you are fully acquainted with how the game works.

You can find the full game called TheLab.exe in the companion files, located in the \Game_1 folder.

You have the following items:

- A bat object that only moves up and down and will stop when it hits the border graphic.

- A ball object that will bounce around the screen but bounces off the bat and the sides of the screen.

- There are a number of standard bricks that take two hits to destroy them.

- When you hit a brick, you will score points.

- There are four special bricks that launch objects that when the bat collides with them grant special powers.

- If the ball goes off-screen you lose a life (if there is only a single ball in play). The graphical object that represents the lives will reduce by one.

- When you are out of lives, the game ends and you will be taken to the High Score frame.

- Various sound effects happen when you hit a brick, hit a special object, or when a special object goes off-screen.

- When you have destroyed all the bricks, the level will restart, and you will continue with all bricks back on-screen.

- All bricks have been assigned to the "Good" qualifier group; this means we can apply conditions and actions to that which will affect all bricks, rather than having to do it against each set individually.

There are quite a few events for your first game, and it may seem a little confusing at times, but hopefully by the end of coding the level you should have a reasonable idea of why you've done the events, conditions, and actions this way. If you get confused, you can always open up the completed version of the game and view the code (though remember if you are using the Free version of Fusion you cannot have two applications open at the same time).

So, let's start off with a comment line to remind us what the first bit of code will do.

- Event Line 1: Insert | A comment | "Mix Tiles" | OK.

The first bit of code we need to do is to mix up all of the bricks. Currently, there are four special bricks located within the standard bricks, and if the ball hits those, a bonus bottle or multi-ball graphic item will appear. This obviously is a little too predictable if they are always in the same place (it is also not much fun for the players if they know where they are). We will run this event to repeat 25 times so that the action will happen 25 times, which should give us some randomization in where the tiles will end up.

- Event Line 2: Condition: Special: Limit Conditions | Repeat | 25 | OK.

Move across to the right of this event until you are under an object that looks like an apple. This is the Behavior group Good. Each of the bricks, including the special ones, have been assigned to this group already, so applying any action will affect all bricks (unless you were dealing with a specific instance of one brick).

Add the following action, which will swap the positions of all the bricks (and it will happen 25 times).

- Event Line 2: Action: Good.Group: Position | Swap position with another object.

If you were to run the game now, nothing would work and nothing would have seemingly changed, but the special bricks would now be randomly swapped with the other brick objects.

Making the Ball Move

The first part of the game that we want to program that we will visually see is the movement of the ball. At the start of the game and when you have lost a life, it will be stationary on screen until the player has pressed the space bar. There is a second time when we will need to start the ball, and that is when you have activated the sticky powerup, and it will be attached to the bat but will not be moving.

Let's start with a simple comment line telling us what this section of code will be doing.

- Event Line 3: Insert | A Comment | "Start Ball"

Now let's move onto Event line 4, which will handle the movement of the ball when it's the start of the game or when the player has lost a life. We don't need to specify either in our code, as the conditions of checking when the ball is stopped is enough for this to work. We will need three conditions for this event.

- Event Line 4: Condition: the mouse pointer and keyboard | The keyboard | Upon Pressing a Key | Space bar.
- Event Line 4: Condition: Ball | Movement | Is Ball Stopped?

- Event Line 4: Condition: Bat | Alterable Values | Flags | Is Flag off? | Flag 0 | OK.

For the last condition on Event Line 4, we added a flag set to off on the bat. There can be multiple flags on a single object, and these can be either on or off. Flags are really good for doing simple checks on objects; in this case when the bat's flag 0 is off, this means that sticky mode isn't activated. For this game we have the following flags:

- Flag 0 = Sticky mode

- Flag 1 = Shoot mode

- Flag 2 = Large Mode

There are two actions for this event. First, to set the direction, the ball should move initially; second, the ball should start moving.

- Event Line 4: Action: Ball: Direction | Select Direction | 12 to 20 | OK.

When the direction box appears (as shown completed in Figure 12.18), choose left-leaning directions (if you hold the mouse over them, you'll see their numbers)—we need 12 to 20, as it would be bad gameplay if the ball were to move to the right when first starting (as this would make it very difficult for the player).

Now we need to tell Fusion to start the movement for the ball object.

- Event Line 4: Action: Ball | Movement | Start.

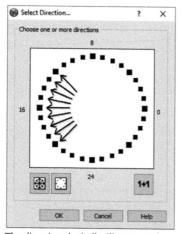

FIGURE 12.18 The direction the ball will move at the start of the game.

We need three conditions for the next event; the first two conditions are the same as the previous event (pressing space bar and ball is not moving), and the third condition is checking if the bat flag is on (the bat is in sticky mode).

- Event Line 5: Condition: the mouse pointer and keyboard: The keyboard | Upon Pressing a Key | Space bar.

- Event Line 5: Condition: Ball | Movement | Is Ball Stopped?

- Event Line 5: Condition: Bat | Alterable Values | Flags | Is Flag On | Select Flag 0 | OK.

For the actions we want the direction of the ball to just be to the left (so it just moves in a straight line) and then to start the movement.

- Event Line 5: Action: Ball | Direction | Select Direction | 16 | OK.

- Event Line 5: Action: Ball | Movement | Start.

Your events will look like Figure 12.19.

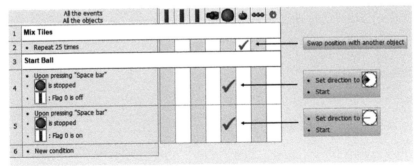

FIGURE 12.19 The Events so far.

Bat and Ball Off-Screen

If you run the game, you will notice that the ball goes off the screen and the bat can be moved up and down (using the up and down arrow keys) out of the play area. The bat needs to stay within the playfield and not go any higher or lower than the game border. The ball should only be able to leave the playfield on the right side of the screen (at which point, the player would lose a life).

The bat, ball, and objects all have their movements predefined. This is because we programmed them into the Object library to lessen the work you need to do. To learn more about movement, refer to Chapter 10, "Movement."

First, we'll create a comment line that tells us what this group of events will be doing.

- Event Line 6: Insert | A Comment | "Bounce" | OK.

There are three event collisions we need to worry about: when the bat is colliding with the top and the bottom of the screen, when the ball collides with the side of the screen, and finally when the ball collides with the bat and sticky mode isn't enabled. All three should have the ball bounce back into play.

 We'll be checking for collision with a backdrop object called Border, which has also been preconfigured as an obstacle type "Obstacle." If you were checking if the ball were going outside of the frame, you would use a different event.

The Events:

- Event Line 7: Condition: Bat | Collisions | Backdrop.

- Event Line 8: Condition: Ball | Collisions | Backdrop.

- Event Line 9: Condition: Ball | Collisions | Another object | Bat.

- Event Line 9: Condition: Bat | Alterable values | Flags | Is Flag off? | Flag 0 | OK.

The Actions:

- Event Line 7: Action: Bat | Movement | Stop.

- Event Line 8: Action: Ball | Movement | Bounce.

- Event Line 9: Action: Ball | Movement | Bounce.

- Event Line 9: Action: Sound: Samples | Play Sample | From a file (Browse) | Bounce lo | Open.

 For playing a sample you will need to browse to the game's sound files; these are stored in the \Game_1\Audio folder.

You can see the Play Sample dialog box in Figure 12.20. As you add any audio files to your game, they'll appear in the list, making it easier to use the same sample in different situations.

If you run the game now, you should be able to start the ball by pressing the space bar; the ball will bounce around the screen and will bounce off the bat (as well as making a sound when hitting it). The only direction the ball can disappear is on the right-hand side, where the background object border doesn't exist. You can see the code for the Bounce section in Figure 12.21.

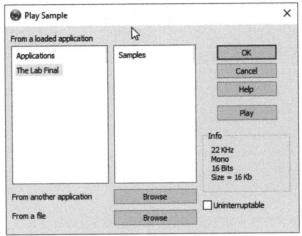

FIGURE 12.20 The Play Sample dialog.

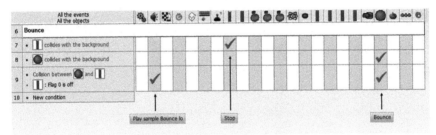

FIGURE 12.21 The Bounce code.

Destruction of Bricks

Next, we need to destroy the bricks once the ball has hit them. Each brick will be hit twice before it is destroyed (unless it's one of the four special bricks, which only take a single hit to destroy). When the brick is hit the first time, the color of the brick changes to show that it only needs one more hit to be destroyed.

For this group of events we need three comment lines and two events; these events check for a collision between the ball and a brick but also check the brick's animation direction. We use two different directions; one that is assigned when the brick is first hit, and a second when it has already been hit and should be destroyed.

- Event Line 10: Insert | A comment | "Brick Events" | OK.

- Event Line 11: Insert | A comment | "Second Hit (Destroy Bricks)" | OK.

- Event Line 12: Condition: Ball | Collisions | Another Object | Brick | OK.

- Event Line 12: Condition: Brick | Direction | Compare direction of Brick | 24.

- Event Line 13: Insert | A comment | "First Hit" | OK.

- Event Line 14: Condition: Ball | Collisions | Another Object | Brick | OK.

- Event Line 14: Condition: Brick | Direction | Compare direction of Brick | 0 | OK.

You may be wondering why Event Lines 12 and 14 are not the other way around (i.e., that the first hit isn't first). If the Events were the other way around, then when the ball hit the brick, it would change the direction to down and then automatically run the next event, as it would then be true to destroy the brick. Fusion runs very quickly through events, and the collision condition would be true for both objects, so changing the direction on the prior event means that the next event is only true if the object is collided with a second time.

So, for the actions on Event Line 12 when the ball hits a brick that has been hit before, we want to:

- Destroy the brick.

- Add 25 to the score.

- Play a sample sound.

- Set the current score to the on-screen graphic.

You might be wondering why we don't just set the score and that should be displayed, right? Unfortunately not; the score is an internal value that you can do various calculations with, but you'll need to add a graphical score object to display it. To do this we need to set the current score value into the score counter.

So, let's do the actions for Event Line 12.

- Event Line 12: Action: Brick | Destroy.

- Event Line 12: Action: Player 1 | Score | Add to score | 25 | OK.

- Event Line 12: Action: Sound | Samples | Play Sample | From a file | Bounce lo | Open.

- Event Line 12: Action: Score | Set Counter | Player 1 | Current value of score | OK.

Setting the current internal score to the counter requires you to get the value from another object. Once you do the action "Set Counter" on the score object, a dialog box will appear; in many cases you can type a value in the box above, but in this case you want to retrieve the current system score, so you right-click on the player 1 object and select "Current value of score," as shown in Figure 12.22. This will then place the text score ("Player 1") into the expression evaluator; clicking on OK stores this to the action.

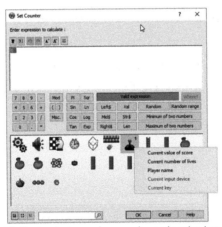

FIGURE 12.22 Getting the internal score value and setting it to the counter.

Now, for the actions for Event Line 14, which follow a similar pattern, we'll add 10 to the score, we won't be destroying the bricks, but we'll change the direction so that next time it's hit it will be destroyed. We'll bounce the ball, play a sample, and then set the current score to the counter object.

- Event Line 14: Action: Player 1 | Score | Add to score | 10 | OK.

- Event Line 14: Action: Brick | Direction | Select direction | 24 | OK.

- Event Line 14: Action: Ball | Movement | Bounce.

- Event Line 14: Action: Sound | Samples | Play Sample | From a file | Bounce hi | Open.

- Event Line 14: Action: Score | Set Counter | Player 1 | Current value of score | OK.

If you run the game now, you'll be able to destroy all of the normal bricks and add to your score. Next, we'll handle the destruction of the special bricks. You can see the code for the brick events in Figure 12.23.

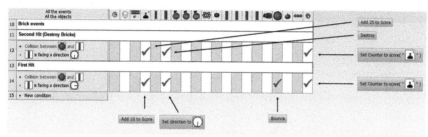

FIGURE 12.23 Code for handling ball collisions with the bricks.

Destruction of Special Bricks

The special bricks will only need to be hit once with the ball; once they are, they are destroyed and will launch a special power-up object toward the player.

For this section of code, we'll need one comment line to tell us what the code does and four separate events, one for each collision between the ball and the four special bricks.

- Event Line 15: Insert | A comment: "Special Brick Events" | OK.

- Event Line 16: Condition: Ball | Collisions | Another object | Brick_ Large.

- Event Line 17: Condition: Ball | Collisions | Another object | Brick_ Sticky.

- Event Line 18: Condition: Ball | Collisions | Another object | Brick_ Shoot.

- Event Line 19: Condition: Ball | Collisions | Another object | Brick_ Double.

The actions for Event Lines 16–19 are mostly the same, except for checking collisions with each special brick type. Let's first look at what we will be doing for each event.

- Creating one of the four special objects and placing it at the center of the appropriate brick (the one that has been collided with).

- Starting the movement of the special object.

- Destroying the brick.

- Playing a sample Bounce hi.

So, let's get on with doing the actions for Event Line 16, before we quickly do the rest. Event Line 16 is testing for a collision between the ball and the Brick_Large special brick, from which we need to create a Formula_Large object to move toward the player.

When you create the following action, you will see a number of dialog boxes as shown in Figures 12.24 and 12.25.

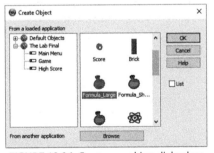

FIGURE 12.24 Create new object dialog box.

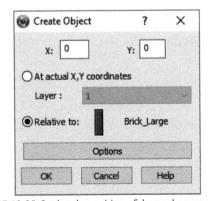

FIGURE 12.25 Setting the position of the newly created object.

- Event Line 16: Action: Create new objects | Create object: Formula_ Large | OK | Relative to | Brick_Large | OK | OK.

Event Line 16 is probably the most complicated action of all the events 16 to 19. When you place an object in the game, it can be set to appear automatically, and it can also be set to not even be loaded and loaded later (which can save memory if you have lots of objects to be loaded at the start of a frame). In this example, we have a number of objects off-screen for which we've decided to set the "Moving at start" property to off, which means that they won't move unless we tell them to. Any new objects created from these 4 special objects will also inherit this property. So, when we create a copy of one of these objects, we'll need to tell it to move. It already has a bouncing ball movement applied, which is set to move to the right only once its movement is set to on.

When we create the Formula_Large object, we set its position relative to the Brick_Large object (as we want it to appear from where the brick was destroyed). In this case we have it relative to the object at 0,0 of the center point of the object. In your games you can offset the position to that of another object, so if you wanted you could add or subtract to the X value to move it to the left or right or add or subtract from the Y value to move it up or down from the object.

 The 0,0 position on an object is defined by its hot spot. All of the bricks have their 0,0 position on the object set to the center.

Now that we have added the first action to Event Line 16, let's now add the rest.

- Event Line 16: Action: Formula_Large | Movement | Start.
- Event Line 16: Action: Brick_Large | Destroy.
- Event Line 16: Action: Sound | Samples | Play Sample | Bounce hi | OK.

For the other three events we will just need to create the relevant special power-up object, destroy the relevant special brick, and play the same sound effect.

For the Sticky power-up:

- Event Line 17: Action: Create new objects: Create object | Formula_ Sticky | OK | Relative to | Brick_Sticky | OK | OK.

- Event Line 17: Action: Formula_Sticky | Movement | Start.

- Event Line 17: Action: Brick_Sticky | Destroy.

- Event Line 17: Action: Sound | Samples | Play Sample | Bounce hi | OK.

For the Shoot power-up:

- Event Line 18: Action: Create new objects | Create object | Formula_ Shoot | OK | Relative to | Brick_Shoot | OK | OK.

- Event Line 18: Action: Formula_Shoot | Movement | Start.

- Event Line 18: Action: Brick_Shoot: Destroy.

- Event Line 18: Action: Sound: Samples | Play Sample | Bounce hi | OK.

For the Double power-up:

- Event Line 19: Action: Create new objects | Create object | Double_Ball | OK | Relative to | Brick_Double | OK | OK.

- Event Line 19: Action: Double_Ball | Movement | Start.

- Event Line 19: Action: Brick_Double | Destroy.

- Event Line 19: Action: Sound | Samples | Play Sample | Bounce hi | OK.

The code for the special brick events can be seen in Figure 12.26.

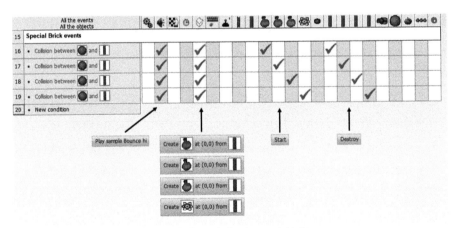

FIGURE 12.26 The code for the special brick events.

Automatically, the bonus items move to the right because they have had their object properties predefined, so when you drop them on the playfield, they have a left-to-right movement ready to be used (which just needed enabling). Chapter 10 has details on how to apply movement to objects.

Destroy Bonus Items If Missed

When you hit a bonus brick and the special item flies out of it, two possible things could happen. You could catch the item with the bat, which means you get a bonus, or you miss the item and it disappears from the play area. We'll start with the code for what happens if you do not catch them; for this case we'll play a sound effect and destroy the relevant power-up object.

- Event Line 20: Insert | A comment | "Destroy collectables if not caught" | OK.

Now we need four events, one for each power-up, where we'll check its position on-screen. As you do the following events, you'll see a dialog box as shown in Figure 12.27. You must select the right-hand box, which is pointing to the right, as this will test the object leaving the frame.

- Event Line 21: Condition: Formula_Large | Position | Test position of "Formula_Large" | → | OK.

- Event Line 22: Condition: Formula_Sticky | Position | Test position of "Formula_Sticky" | → | OK.

- Event Line 23: Condition: Formula_Shoot | Position | Test position of "Formula_Shoot" | → | OK.

- Event Line 24: Condition: Double_Ball | Position | Test position of "Double_Ball" | → | OK.

The actions will be to play a sound effect and destroy the object.

- Event Line 21: Action: Sound: Samples | Play Sample | From a file | Browse| Glass05 | Open.

- Event Line 21: Action: Formula_Large | Destroy.

- Event Line 22: Action: Sound: Samples | Play Sample | Glass05 | OK.

- Event Line 22: Action: Formula_Sticky | Destroy.

- Event Line 23: Action: Sound |Samples | Play Sample | Glass05 | OK.

- Event Line 23: Action: Formula_Shoot | Destroy.

- Event Line 24: Action: Sound | Samples | Play Sample | From a file | Browse | Pop bubble | Open.

- Event Line 24: Action: Double_Ball | Destroy.

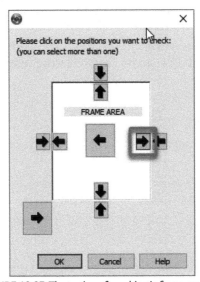

FIGURE 12.27 The testing of an object's frame position.

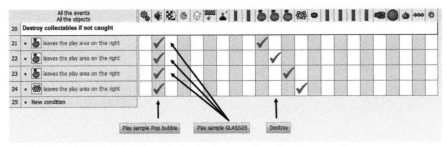

FIGURE 12.28 The code for the destroy collectables if not caught events.

 The Test Position dialog allows you to check where on the play area an object is currently positioned. It is great for quick testing of an object if it has just left the screen, just appeared, is on the outside of the playfield area, or is on the playfield. In the Lab game it is used to see if an object has gone off the playfield, as at this point it is no longer needed in the game.

Run the Game frame and destroy a few bricks and watch the bonus items disappear off the play area. Notice that the number of objects will begin to reduce in the debugger window.

Collecting Bonus Items

When the bat does hit a flying bonus item, we need to activate that power-up, be it a larger bat, the ability to shoot, the ball sticking to the bat, or multiple balls. This section of code handles the collision of the power-up with the bat, and further code will be required to handle sticky and shoot modes.

For this section we will need five comment lines and four events. The four events are simple power-up colliding with bat events. So, let's create all of the events before moving on to each individual event action and finding out how they are different.

- Event Line 25: Insert | A comment: "Collecting" | OK.

- Event Line 26: Insert | A comment: "Large Mode Formula" | OK.

- Event Line 27: Condition: Formula_Large | Collisions | Another Object | Bat | OK.

- Event Line 28: Insert | A comment | "Sticky Mode Formula" | OK.

- Event Line 29: Condition: Formula_Sticky | Collisions | Another Object | Bat | OK.

- Event Line 30: Insert | A comment | "Shoot Mode Formula" | OK.

- Event Line 31: Condition: Formula_Shoot | Collisions | Another Object | Bat | OK.

- Event Line 32: Insert | A comment | "Double Ball Clone" | OK.

- Event Line 33: Condition: Double_Ball | Collisions | Another Object | Bat | OK.

Let's look at the different actions we have in play for the Formula_Large collision, as many of the actions are appropriate for the others.

- Destroy the power-up object.

- Play a sample sound.

- Change the bat's animation to large.

- Stop the animation (there is no animation, but stopping it when not in use is a good way to prevent issues).

- Set the flags 0, 1, and 2 to on or off.

- Make the Gun object invisible.

If you recall, we have flags for each state, so when the bat collides with a power-up, we will reset the flag; this prevents the game getting confused if you have a few power-ups hitting the bat one after another. This is the same reason we are setting the Gun object invisible on the last action, because if you have a gun power-up, you don't want it to still be appearing if you get the Sticky powerup (or any other power-ups, for that matter). It's important to reset flags and values as and when needed; if you don't you may find strange things happening in your game, whereby the game does something totally unexpected.

Most of the other events contain similar bits of code, except for the Shoot and Ball power-ups. The shoot power-up enables the gun and sets a value to 15 (this is the number of bullets), while the double ball event has to create a new ball, set its initial direction, and start the new ball's movement.

Now that you have an idea of the actions involved, let's go ahead and create them all.

- Event Line 27: Action: Formula_Large | Destroy.

- Event Line 27: Action: Sound: Samples | Play Sample | Pop bubble | OK.

- Event Line 27: Action: Bat | Animation | Change | Animation sequence | Large | OK.

- Event Line 27: Action: Bat | Animation | Stop.

- Event Line 27: Action: Bat | Flags | Set off | Flag 0 | OK.

- Event Line 27: Action: Bat | Flags | Set off | Flag 1 | OK.

- Event Line 27: Action: Bat | Flags | Set on | Flag 2 | OK.

- Event Line 27: Action: Gun | Visibility | Make Object invisible.

- Event Line 29: Action: Formula_Sticky | Destroy.

- Event Line 29: Action: Sound: Samples | Play Sample | Pop bubble | Open.

- Event Line 29: Action: Bat | Animation | Change | Animation sequence | Stopped | OK.

- Event Line 29: Action: Bat | Animation | Start.

- Event Line 29: Action: Bat | Flags | Set on | Flag 0 | OK.

- Event Line 29: Action: Bat | Flags | Set off | Flag 1 | OK.

- Event Line 29: Action: Bat | Flags | Set off | Flag 2 | OK.

- Event Line 29: Action: Gun | Visibility | Make Object invisible.

- Event Line 31: Action: Formula_Shoot | Destroy.

- Event Line 31: Action: Sound | Samples | Play Sample | Pop bubble | OK.

- Event Line 31: Action: Bat | Animation | Change | Animation sequence | Stopped | OK.

- Event Line 31: Action: Bat | Flags | Set off: Flag 0 | OK.

- Event Line 31: Action: Bat | Flags | Set on: Flag 1 | OK.

- Event Line 31: Action: Bat | Flags | Set off: Flag 2 | OK.

- Event Line 31: Action: Gun | Position | Select position | Relative to | Bat | OK.

- Event Line 31: Action: Gun | Alterable values | Set | Alterable Value A | 15 | OK.

- Event Line 31: Action: Gun: Visibility | Make Object reappear.

- Event Line 33: Action: Double_Ball | Destroy.

- Event Line 33: Action: Sound | Samples | Play Sample | Pop bubble | OK.

- Event Line 33: Action: Create new objects | Create object | Ball | OK | 382, 228 | OK.

- Event Line 33: Action: Ball | Direction | Select direction | 13, 14, 18, 19 | OK.

- Event Line 33: Action: Ball | Movement | Start.

- Event Line 33: Action: Gun | Visibility | Make Object invisible.

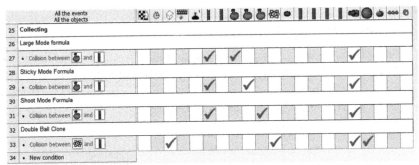

	All the events All the objects																					
25	Collecting																					
26	Large Mode formula																					
27	• Collision between ⬤ and ▐					✓	✓							✓							
28	Sticky Mode Formula																					
29	• Collision between ⬤ and ▐					✓		✓						✓							
30	Shoot Mode Formula																					
31	• Collision between ⬤ and ▐					✓		✓						✓							
32	Double Ball Clone																					
33	• Collision between 🎱 and ▐		✓				✓							✓	✓						
34	• New condition																					

FIGURE 12.29 The events for collecting the power-ups.

As the actions in this section are numerous, we have only provided you with a shot of the events, conditions, and action checkmarks in Figure 12.29. If you need to compare, we recommend that you consult the final example file in the source folder.

Ball Leaves Play Area

The game is now starting to come together nicely, but when the ball leaves the screen, nothing else happens and the game cannot continue. As you can imagine, it is very important to put the ball back on the screen so the play can continue; a knock-on effect is that the player also needs to lose a life as a negative consequence of allowing the ball to get past the bat. Two different events need to be programmed into the game: first, if there is only one ball on the play area and it leaves the screen, a life is lost. Second, if there are two balls on-screen because a bonus modifier is in effect, a life isn't lost, but we'll need to destroy the second ball and play a sound effect.

- Event Line 34: Insert | A comment | "Ball Leaves Play Area" | OK.

- Event Line 35: Insert | A comment | "If Player loses ball and only has one = lose life" | OK.

- Event Line 36: Condition: Ball | Position | Test position of Ball | → | OK.

- Event Line 36: Condition: Ball | Pick or count | Compare to the number of Ball objects | Equal 1 | OK.

- Event Line 37: Insert | A comment | "If Player loses ball and has double ball = destroy the extra ball" | OK.

- Event Line 38: Condition: Ball | Position | Test position of Ball | → | OK.

- Event Line 38: Condition: Ball | Pick or count | Compare to the number of Ball objects | Equal 2 | OK.

When doing a pick- or count-type condition, you will see the Expression Evaluator; at the top are the common arithmetic comparison methods such as equal, lower, greater, and so on, and these will be used with a number in the text edit box to do the comparison. Once the ball leaves the screen, we can then decide what actions to take.

For the actions, on Event Line 36 we need to destroy the ball, as even though it's off-screen, it still exists (for a while), subtract a life, play a sound effect, reset all our flags, create a new ball so that the game can be restarted, reset the animation on the bat just in case it was set to large, and make the Gun object invisible.

- Event Line 36: Action: Ball | Destroy.

- Event Line 36: Action: Player 1 | Number of lives | Subtract from Number of lives | 1 | OK.

- Event Line 36: Action: Sound | Samples | Play Sample: From a file | Browse | Slide down | Open.

- Event Line 36: Action: Bat | Flags | Set off | Flag 0 | OK.

- Event Line 36: Action: Bat | Flags | Set off | Flag 1 | OK.

- Event Line 36: Action: Bat | Flags | Set off | Flag 2 | OK.

- Event Line 36: Action: Create new objects | Create object | Ball | OK | 1722, 539 | OK.

- Event Line 36: Action: Bat | Animation | Change | Animation sequence: Stopped.

- Event Line 36: Action: Bat | Animation | Start.

- Event Line 36: Action: Gun | Visibility | Make Object invisible.

For the actions, on Event Line 38, as the extra ball doesn't require much gameplay, we just need to destroy the ball and play a sound effect.

- Event Line 38: Action: Ball | Destroy.

- Event Line 38: Action: Sound | Samples | Play Sample | From a file | Browse | Slide down | Open.

If you play the game now, you'll be able to destroy the bricks, there will be some issues with the shoot and sticky mode (as we haven't finished programming that yet), but when the ball goes out of play, it should play a sound and remove a life.

You can see the events in Figure 12.30 for handling the ball leaving the play area; if you need more information on the actions, load up the completed example file in the \Full_Source folder.

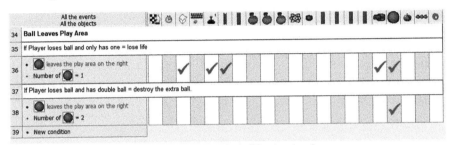

FIGURE 12.30 The events for ball leaving the play area.

Player Dies

One area of functionality of the game that currently isn't working is that when the ball has gotten past the bat and the lives are down to zero, the game continues. This is obviously wrong, as we want the game to end once the player runs out of lives. This part of the code is very quick to do, and the outcome is that once all lives are gone, the game goes to Frame 3 so the player can enter a high score (if appropriate).

- Event Line 39: Insert | A comment | "Player dies" | OK.

- Event Line 40: Condition: Player 1 | When number of lives reaches 0.

- Event Line 40: Action: Storyboard controls: Jump to frame | Frame 3 – High Score | OK.

If you were to play the game now and let the ball go off-screen three times, each time the lives counter would subtract a life and then you'd be taken to the High Scores frame.

All Bricks Destroyed

What do we want to happen in the game when all the bricks have been destroyed? In this game, once they have been removed from the play area, the game will restart the frame—not particularly elegant, but it just means you can try again and test the level. If you were making a larger game, you might have multiple levels with different types of bricks, and you would probably want to store the score once all bricks have been destroyed into a variable and then add it to the new score (as resetting the frame will restart the scoring). As we are keeping this game simple, we will just reset the frame (but if you feel up to it after you've completed making the game, improve it as you see fit).

- Event Line 41: Insert | A comment | "All bricks destroyed" | OK.

- Event Line 42: Condition: Brick | Pick or count | Have all Brick been destroyed.

- Event Line 42: Condition: Brick_Shoot | Pick or count | Have all Brick_ Shoot been destroyed.

- Event Line 42: Condition: Brick_Sticky | Pick or count | Have all Brick_ Sticky been destroyed.

- Event Line 42: Condition: Brick_Large | Pick or count | Have all Brick_ Large been destroyed.

- Event Line 42: Condition: Brick_Double | Pick or count | Have all Brick_Large been destroyed.

- Event Line 40: Action: Storyboard controls | Restart the current frame.

Bullet Events

Now we need to destroy the bricks when they are hit with a bullet. We still cannot fire a bullet, but we can still code this in advance of that working. It's pretty simple code; when the bullet collides with a brick, we'll destroy the brick and bullet.

- Event Line 43: Insert | A comment | "Bullet events" | OK.

- Event Line 44: Condition: Bullet | Collisions | Another object | Brick | OK.

- Event Line 44: Action: Brick | Destroy.

- Event Line 44: Action: Bullet | Destroy.

Now let's do the code for a collision between the bullet and the special bricks and when the bullet collides with the background (as we want to destroy the object rather than let it go off-screen into the distance).

- Event Line 45: Insert | A comment | "Collision with special bricks" | OK.

- Event Line 46: Condition: Bullet | Collisions | Another object | Brick_ Large.

- Event Line 47: Condition: Bullet | Collisions | Another object | Brick_Sticky.

- Event Line 48: Condition: Bullet | Collisions | Another object | Brick_Shoot.

- Event Line 49: Condition: Bullet | Collisions | Another object | Brick_Double.

- Event Line 50: Condition: Bullet | Collisions | Backdrop.

- Event Line 46: Action: Bullet | Destroy.

- Event Line 46: Action: Brick_Large | Destroy.

- Event Line 47: Action: Bullet | Destroy.

- Event Line 47: Action: Brick_Sticky | Destroy.

- Event Line 48: Action: Bullet | Destroy.

- Event Line 47: Action: Brick_Shoot | Destroy.

- Event Line 49: Action: Bullet | Destroy.

- Event Line 49: Action: Brick_Double | Destroy.

- Event Line 50: Action: Bullet | Destroy.

You can see the Player dies, All bricks destroyed, and Bullet events in Figure 12.31.

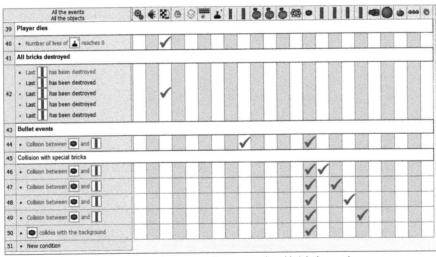

FIGURE 12.31 Various events for game end and brick destruction (order depends on object order placement).

Sticky and Shoot Mode

If you play the game, you may notice that two things are not currently functioning, and in fact are the only two things left to do on the Game frame. We need to introduce the bonus functionality of shooting bullets from the bat (as well as having the gun attach to the brick) and finally for the ball to stick to the bat as it moves and be launched by using the space bar.

For this we are going to place the code into groups; this just keeps the code nice and tidy, even though both groups will be enabled at all times. One word of warning when it comes to groups is that collapsing them changes the subsequent line numbers and expanding them increases the line numbers. When we talk about doing something on event line X, this is taking into consideration that the group is expanded. Please bear this in mind, as this would make some issues in coding these games if you applied them to the wrong event line.

- Event Line 51: Insert | A comment | "Group events for special conditions" | OK.

- Event Line 52: Insert | A group of events | "Mode Shoot" | OK.

- Event Line 53: Insert | A comment | "Shoot Mode events" | OK.

So, we are ready to do the events for shooting (and a few more comment lines), but before we do, we'll just go through what we need to code so you have an idea of why you are coding the various events.

- Set the bat's shoot mode flag to on, and we will set the Y position of the gun to the position of the bat.

- Test for a player pressing the space bar if the gun is visible, if the alterable value of A is greater than 0 (the number of bullets), and the bat flag is on, allowing us to shoot. Set the bullet direction and launch it. Remove 1 from alterable value A (meaning we have 1 less bullet).

- If alterable value A is 0, this means we have 0 bullets left, so remove the gun.

Let's get the rest of the events set up before we do the actions.

- Event Line 54: Condition: Bat | Alterable values | Flags | Is flag on? | Flag 1 | OK.

- Event Line 55: Insert | A comment | "Actually shooting" | OK.

- Event Line 56: Condition: The mouse pointer and keyboard |The Keyboard | Upon pressing a key | Space bar.

- Event Line 56: Condition: Gun | Visibility | Is Gun visible.

- Event Line 56: Condition: Gun | Alterable values | Compare to one of the alterable values | Alterable Value A | Greater | 0.

- Event Line 56: Condition: Bat | Alterable values | Flags | Is flag on? | Flag 1.

- Event Line 57: Insert | A comment | "Ending Shoot mode if you run out of bullets" | OK.

- Event Line 58: Condition: Gun | Alterable values | Compare to one of the alterable values | Alterable Value A | Equal | 0 | OK.

We'll now enter the actions for each of those events.

- Event Line 54: Action: Gun: Position | Set Y Coordinate | Bat | Position | Y Coordinate | OK.

- Event Line 56: Action: Bat: Launch an Object | Bullet | OK | Speed 60 | Launch in selected directions| 16 | OK | OK.

- Event Line 56: Action: Gun | Alterable values | Subtract from | Alterable Value A | 1 | OK.

- Event Line 56: Action: Sound | Samples | Play Sample | From a file | Browse | Pop 2 | Open.

- Event Line 58: Action: Bat | Animation | Change | Animation Sequence | Stopped.

- Event Line 58: Action: Gun | Visibility | Make object invisible.

- Event Line 58: Action: Bat | Flags | Set off | Flag 1.

You have now completed all of the code to handle the shooting, so if you run the game and collect the shoot power-up, you will be able to shoot 15 bullets.

Finally, we need to create a group that will contain the events for handling the sticky bat, which at the moment will not work.

We will have an event that will check for a collision between the ball and the bat and that the sticky flag is on. If this event is true, it will change the position of the ball to the center of the bat at the X position. The final event will check if the sticky flag is on and the ball movement is stopped (meaning that it's currently stuck to the bat); if so, we'll change the Y position, so as the bat is moved up or down, the ball will follow.

- Event Line 60: Insert | A group of events | "Mode Sticky" | OK.

- Event Line 61: Insert | A comment | "Sticky mode is on" | OK.

- Event Line 62: Condition: Ball | Collisions | Another object | Bat.

- Event Line 62: Condition: Bat | Alterable values: Flags | Is a flag on? | Flag 0 | OK.

- Event Line 63: Condition: Bat | Alterable values: Flags | Is a flag on? | Flag 0 | OK.

- Event Line 63: Condition: Ball | Movement | Is Ball stopped.

Now let's get on with the actions, which are mostly aimed at handling the ball.

- Event Line 62: Action: Sound | Samples | Play Sample | Bounce lo | OK.

- Event Line 62: Action: Ball | Position | Set X Coordinate |Bat | Position | X Coordinate: -45 | OK.

- Event Line 62: Action: Ball | Direction | Select direction | 16 | OK.

- Event Line 62: Action: Ball | Movement | Stop.

- Event Line 63: Action: Ball | Position | Set Y Coordinate | Bat: Position | Y Coordinate | OK.

After completing the last action on Event Line 63, run the game and see how it plays. It's not bad for your first game, and on the whole should play okay. There are some improvements that you could consider making; perhaps after you have learned a bit more of Fusion, you can go back to the game and make some changes. You can see the last set of events that we have created in Figure 12.32.

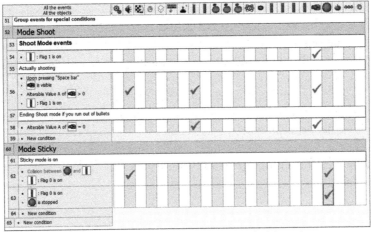

FIGURE 12.32 Various events for shoot and sticky code.

Programming the High Score

There is only one bit of programming that we have to do for the High Scores frame, and that is to go back to the main menu when the player presses the space bar.

Make sure you are on the right frame by double-clicking on the word "High Score" in the Workspace toolbar. The Hi-Score frame will then appear. Click on the Event Editor button on the toolbar to bring up the list of events that are currently programmed into the frame (currently none).

- Event Line 1: Condition: The mouse pointer and keyboard | The keyboard | Upon pressing a key | Space bar.

- Event Line 1: Action: Storyboard controls | Jump to Frame: Frame 1 – Main Menu | OK.

Congratulations, you have completed your first full game in Fusion and, as you can see, with very little coding.

Bat and Ball Retro

The Bat-and-Ball game has been around for over 45+ years and was one of the first to be released. It was slightly different then and consisted of two bats (one for each player) and a ball. It was more like a game of tennis, where the player had to send the ball back and would lose a point if he or she missed it. As computers became more advanced and had more memory available, the traditional idea of bat and ball arrived on the scene. This consisted of one bat and a number of bricks to be destroyed. There have been many variations on this theme, from the bat being at the bottom of the screen and the bricks being above it, swapping left and right, and even 3D versions. There are many games to choose from that you could make with regard to retro-based games. Some of the most popular bat-and-ball games were converted to the home computer format after appearing on arcade machines. An example of one game that took the leap from arcade to home computer is Arkanoid. If you do a search for this on the Internet, you will find a lot of information on how it was designed and what extra options you can build into your bat-and-ball games.

Summary

In this chapter, we went through the process of creating our first in-depth game, and although there was a lot of code, hopefully it wasn't too difficult to understand. The important thing to remember when making games is that you can take what you have learned and apply it to other games you are making. Making games is a learning experience, and the more things you try, the better, so your next game will be much more interesting. Always try to keep copies of any old games you've made so you can go back and look at the code, as you may find that you have useful information in sections of code in them that you can swap over to the latest game you are working on. As you make more games, you will get very much quicker at it and will need less instruction on how to put the events together. This game introduced the concepts of movement, destroying objects, alterable values, flags, and animation. In the next few chapters, we look at the exciting concepts involved in side-scrolling shoot-'em-ups.

CHAPTER 13

SCROLLING GAME CONCEPTS

In This Chapter

- Scrolling Techniques

Before we begin our second game, "Amazing Fighter Pilot," we will look at scrolling. Scrolling the screen is a common technique used to create platform or side-scrolling shoot-'em-up games (not exclusively, but these are two areas that it is commonly used for), and it may be something you will use in your future games. In this chapter, we introduce you to two different scrolling techniques: the standard scrolling you can implement within Fusion, and "fake" scrolling, whereby the illusion of scrolling is created to make the player believe the plane is moving along the scenery.

Scrolling Techniques

For the game "Amazing Fighter Pilot" in Chapter 14, "Creating a Side-Scrolling Shoot-'Em-Up Game," we use the "fake" scrolling technique. This type of scrolling works well for "Amazing Fighter Pilot" but is not necessarily the main type of scrolling you will come across when making your own games. You might consider using the scrolling used in "Amazing Fighter Pilot" in other scrolling shoot-'em-ups that move from left to right or right to left, but you couldn't use it in games that scroll in multiple directions following the main character.

Standard Scrolling

This is the typical type of scrolling found in games made with Fusion whereby the player can move in multiple directions and the screen follows. Although we used the "fake" scrolling for the plane game in the next chapter, we could have used standard scrolling for it. The way scrolling works is that you have a window size, which is the size of the window the users can see on their computer monitor. An example of this would be 1920 x 1080, but within Fusion, you can also create a frame size which is bigger than the viewable screen area, which will be the scroll area. Once this is done, a bit of coding is required to ensure the player is always at the center of the screen and that the frame scrolls in the direction of the player's movement. In the following example, we are going to make a simple scrolling game using a racing car.

To follow the next example, you will need to load a starting file. This file loads a basic 1920 x 1080 screen with a yellow racing car on the frame, which has racing car movement already applied to it. If you run it, you will be able to drive the racing car around the screen, but it will move out of view when it reaches the edge of the window. The file, called "Racing car," can be found in the companion files folder \Scrolling.

When you launch the application, you may have to double-click on the application bar to maximize it (depending on your monitor setup); you can set it to automatically do this in the application properties.

Setting up the Screen

First, we need to load the basic file and then configure the Frame window to be bigger than the Application window. This then allows us to program in the scrolling aspect, which will move around this unseen area. After completing this task, run the file. Notice that the program will not react any differently, as we're simply preparing the area for it to be able to scroll.

1. Start Fusion, and then click on the File | Open option from the menu. When the Open dialog box appears, browse the location of the downloaded files for the book and locate the file "racing car" in the Scrolling folder. Select this file, and then click on OK to open the file.

2. Double-click on the text "Frame 1" in the Workspace toolbar to open the Frame Editor. You will now see a screen with a yellow racing car placed on the frame.

3. In the Properties toolbar, you will now see the frame settings, which will already be on the Settings tab. This will be set to "1920 x 1080," which is the size of the visible frame. Under this you can see Virtual Width and Virtual Height. These allow you to increase the size of the area that you can scroll to outside the application viewable area. Type 3840 in the virtual width box and 2160 in the virtual height boxes. This will now increase the size of the virtual frame to 3840 x 2160, while keeping the Application window size to 1920 × 1080.

 The size that you have set is currently double the application size, but you could, for example, set only the width or the height value if you want to scroll only in one direction.

Now that the screen has been configured to have a scroll area larger than the frame size, it's time for us to create the scrolling events.

Programming the Scrolling

The last bit of work required to implement the scrolling on the screen is to tell the frame to follow the yellow race car. We will create an event that will always run and update the player's position to be the center of the screen.

Click on the Event Editor button on the button toolbar.

You will now be in the Event Editor, where there are currently no events; there will be one line that says, "New Condition."

- Event Line 1: Condition: Special | Always.

- Event Line 1: Action: Storyboard Controls | Scrollings | Center Window position in Frame.

A "Center window position…" dialog box appears, and this allows you to position items either at an actual coordinate or relative to another object's position. In this case we want the window's position to be relative to the car.

- Click on the "Relative to" radio button.

- A "Choose an object" dialog box appears; click on the yellow car object called "Top_Four" and then click on the OK button.

The "Center window position in…" dialog box will reappear, and 0,0 should already be in the X and Y coordinate boxes (if not, ensure that these are set to 0,0). This tells Fusion how far away from the object the position should be; 0,0 is the object-assigned center point. Click on the OK button to save the information to the action.

■ Event Line 2: Condition: Object Top_Four: Position | "Test Position of 'Top_Four'".

A "Test position of…" dialog box will appear; click on the four pointing out arrows, then click on the OK button.

■ Event Line 2: Action: Object Top_Four | Movement | Stop.

This will stop the movement if it reaches the edge of the virtual width or height of the application.

As you can see there isn't much work required to get a basic scrolling example working; add a few graphics and within a very short period of time you have your very own scrolling game.

When scrolling on an area with no background graphics, it can feel like the car object is getting stuck in the screen. This isn't the case; all that is happening is that the car is in the center of the application window and the background (which you cannot see as it's just white) is moving but gives the impression that it's stuck. To see scrolling work better, drop a few active objects around the application, both within the frame and off the frame, and you can see the car and background is moving.

A version of the scrolling example (including additional graphics) can be found with the companion files; it is located in the "\ Scrolling" folder and is called "Stnd Scrolling 1."

Fake Scrolling

There are a number of ways to implement some of the features of Fusion, and scrolling is no different. The solution just discussed is the standard way to implement scrolling within your games. However, if you want to have the same background repeated multiple times, thereby allowing your level to take some time to finish, this type of scrolling is a very memory efficient and easy way to do so (because you do not need to create a very large frame size to accommodate the scrolling area, you use less memory). With standard scrolling the window area moves with the Player object around the frame, and the Background objects are statically placed around the play area. With fake scrolling, the frame does not move; the player object only moves in the window area, and the background moves from right to left to simulate a scrolling screen. The two examples of the scrolling mentioned in this book are shown in Figures 13.1 and 13.2.

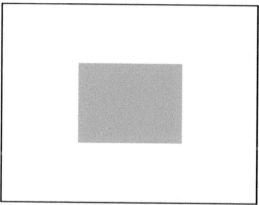

FIGURE 13.1 Standard scrolling where the window moves around the frame area.

FIGURE 13.2 Fake scrolling example, where the background moves and the window is static.

Fake scrolling works by having a number of large graphic tiles that have movement applied to each, so when the game starts, they move in a right-to-left direction. When they get to a specific point on the screen (the end of their movement), they then have to be commanded to return to their starting point. Using four tiles in "Amazing Fighter Pilot" in the next chapter, we are able to generate an endless scrolling effect in which the game is controlled by the destruction of planes (controlled by the programmer) and not the size of the game area.

In the Fighter Pilot game, we will use bouncing ball movement to move the objects from right to left and then reposition them once they have reached a certain location on their X axis. You can also use the Path Movement to do the same task, whereby you draw where you wish the objects to move to before using the reposition and loop options to start it all again.

When applying path movement to the object using the New Line tool, you can work out the distance using the coordinates at the bottom right of the Fusion application window.

Two examples can be found in the companion content showing how fake scrolling works using path movement. These files can be found in the "\Scrolling" folder, and the filenames are called "Fake" and "Fake_2."

The "Fake" and "Fake_2" files show you an example of using the path movement.; notice that "Fake_2" has been color coded to show you how the scrolling works. When a tile is sent back to its original starting point, it overlaps another sea tile; as they are all the same graphically, the end user does not notice this overlapping effect. The fourth tile is always placed on top and isn't affected by the overlapping. Though this solution is okay, it isn't the best method if you want to have tiles that are different. In the next chapter we will be using a repositioning of tiles, taking the further left tile and placing it to the furthest right, creating a loop. The only requirement for that is that the edges of the tiles should match, but you can have different backgrounds, meaning you can be a bit more creative in your floor tiles.

Summary

In this chapter, we examined two different scrolling techniques, and in the next chapter, you will be using one of them for our second game, "Amazing Fighter Pilot." The great thing about the second game is that it is based on a number of retro game styles from the 1980s, and using this fake scrolling technique can be applied to other retro scrolling games with ease. The next chapter takes our scrolling technique and applies it to a side-scrolling shoot-'em-up game, in which the player has to destroy a number of enemy waves and then defeat the end-of-level big boss.

CHAPTER 14

CREATING A SIDE-SCROLLING SHOOT-'EM-UP GAME

In This Chapter

- About Amazing Fighter Pilot
- Fighter Pilot – Initial Setup
- Fighter Pilot – Main Menu
- Fighter Pilot – The Game Screen
- Fighter Pilot – Hi-Score
- Fighter Pilot Programming

You've created your first game, "The Lab," which you hopefully found exciting and a good exercise to learn about the power of Fusion. In this chapter, we move to the next stage of game creation and create a side-scrolling shoot-'em-up game called "Amazing Fighter Pilot" (also known as "Fighter Pilot" for ease of writing). Some of the concepts are the same, which should make your game development a little faster.

About Amazing Fighter Pilot

"Amazing Fighter Pilot" is an exciting side-scrolling shoot-'em-up with left-to-right scrolling, enemy airplanes, and a big enemy boss as the end-of-level enemy that the player will need to defeat. Details of these types of games

can be found in Chapter 1, "Video Games." The story of "Fighter Pilot" is
as follows:

It is 1944, and you have been given an important mission to deliver
a set of top-secret plans to your HQ. Unfortunately, you have to fly
through a number of enemy zones before you can deliver the plane's
cargo.

The second game takes a form similar to the first game, and has been separated into three easy-to-distinguish frames:

The Main Frame: From this screen, we will launch the title frame
(called main menu in most games) of our game, "*Amazing Fighter Pilot.*"

The Game Frame: This is where the player begins to play the game.
"Fighter Pilot" introduces you to a number of new game-making techniques, including fake scrolling, multiple enemy waves, and health.

The Hi-Score Frame: When the players run out of lives, the custom-
ary Hi-Score Frame will appear, where the players score will automatically be entered.

All of the game's graphics and objects have been premade and placed in a
library file to speed up the creation of the game, and to allow you to start
programming rather than drawing images.

We now need to describe the game in more detail so you understand what
is going to happen in each stage.

1. At the start of the game, the main menu screen appears; this displays the
"Fighter Pilot" background image. You will use the mouse to move up
and down a propeller image to select the relevant menu option. On left-
clicking the mouse button, you will then be taken to the relevant screens.
You have three options: New Game, Hi-Score, and Quit. Clicking on
New Game will take you to the game screen.

2. The player's airplane will appear, and pressing the Shift key will fire the
plane's main weapon. There is also a bomb weapon that is limited to
three shots and activated using the Ctrl key. The background will scroll
from right to left, and then return to its original position to begin scrolling again. Waves of enemies will appear over time, which the player will
need to destroy or try to avoid. After a number of waves, an enemy boss
plane will appear. The player's plane has a health bar that is depleted

every time a plane or enemy bullet hits it. When the health reaches zero, the player will lose a life. Once the player has defeated the end-of-level boss, the game will end.

The end-of-level enemy is a big airplane that takes a number of hits to destroy. You might be wondering why it's called an "end-of-level boss." In many old retro games, at the end of each level the player would have to defeat a bigger and more powerful baddie, the end-of-level boss. In fact, many games today still have the concept of an area, end-of-level, or end-of-game boss.

3. Once the player has defeated the end-of-level boss or has lost all their lives, they will be sent to the final frame, which is the Hi-Score frame. If the player's score is higher than the scores already on the scoreboard, they will be asked to enter a name. From here, the player will also be able to go back to the start of the game.

Before you begin to make the game, check out the final game in the companion files. The executable is located in the \Game_2 folder and is called "Pilot.exe."

Please be aware that some anti-virus products can give false positives with Fusion creations. A false positive is when the product states a file has a virus when it doesn't. This is normally only an issue when generating an executable file (a file that you would distribute to other people). In such cases, sending the file to the anti-virus company to set to OK in their products is required.

Graphics Library – Fighter Pilot

To access the ready-made graphics for "Fighter Pilot," download the companion files for this book by writing to the publisher at *info@merclearning.com.*

The Library files for the Fighter Pilot game can be found in the folder \Game2\Lib.

Remember to ensure that you can see the Library Toolbar panel in Fusion. If you don't see it, click on the text menu option "View | Toolbars | Library Toolbar." Then click on the pin icon to keep it on-screen (and prevent it from disappearing as a tab at the bottom of the Fusion application).

1. Right-click on the left-hand pane of the Library toolbar to reveal a pop-up menu.

2. Click on the New option. A dialog box will appear, allowing you to browse your computer for the companion files you've downloaded for this book.

3. Next, locate the folder \Game_2\Lib. Then, click on the OK button, enter a library name, "Fighter Pilot," and then press Enter.

4. You are now ready to drill down into the library and drag any files onto the play area.

Fighter Pilot – Initial Setup

As we did with the first game, we need to set up the frames you will be working with in this game development: one for the Main Menu, one for the Game, and one for the Hi-Score table.

If you want to skip setting up the game, you can load the " FighterPilot_Ready" file (contained in the Game_2 folder), which contains all of the graphics, text, and objects in place, ready for you to start coding. You can skip directly to the section Fighter Pilot – Programming.

Creating the Frames

First, you need to create the three frames that will be used in "Fighter Pilot."

1. Start Fusion, and then click on the File | New option in the menu. This will create the initial game program and its first frame.

2. Highlight the text "Application 1," which is the top item in the Workspace toolbar. Right-click on it and select New Frame from the pop-up menu. This will create a second frame called "Frame 2"; type in Frame 2's real name, "Game." Press Enter to accept the new frame name.

3. Insert another frame and rename it "Hi-Score."

4. Now, rename Frame 1 (either left-click on it, or right-click on the frame text and select Rename) and call it "Main."

Changing Application Settings

You now need to make some application settings as you did in the first game so that we can take advantage of a larger resolution than the default settings when you first created the application.

1. Left-click on the text "Application 1" to select it, and then left-click on it again to rename the game. Change the text to "Fighter Pilot."

2. Save the game to a location of your choice (you'll notice that Fusion is advising you to save with the * after the application name).

3. Go into the Application Properties by clicking on the game name "Fighter Pilot" in the Workspace toolbar. Ensure you are on the Settings tab and uncheck Enable debugger keyboard shortcuts and Show Debugger. We don't need these settings for now.

4. Click on the icon that looks like a monitor; this is the Window Properties tab. First, we need to set the size of our game, which in this case is 1080. In the Size option it should say 640 × 480, change this to 1920 × 1080. On pressing enter a pop-up window will appear, asking you to modify the size of the frames (this would be Main, Game, and Hi-Score); we want all screens to be 1080, so click on the Yes button to continue.

5. If using the full version of Fusion, you can also uncheck Heading, Heading when maximized, Menu Bar, and Menu displayed on boot-up.

6. We need to add a global value to store the player's score, so in the application properties window (make sure Fighter Pilot is selected), select values, and then click on the New button next to Global Values. Right-click and select Rename; rename to HighScore.

Your PC monitor and graphics card will need to support 1080p for this game to work. 1080p is considered the base starting resolution for any PC game these days (and is the standard monitor-supported resolution). This means the top left to the top right of your screen is 1920 pixels (this is called the X axis), while the top left to the bottom left is 1080 (the Y axis). Screens can support larger than this, and 2K and 4K are now more common but can downscale to 1080p.

Web games can be smaller than 1080p; it will depend on what you are considering making your games for. 1080p is a common PC resolution; mobile phones, for example, are much more complicated, and many different resolutions are supported.

Fighter Pilot – Main Menu

The "Fighter Pilot" game main menu is different from the menu you created in "The Lab." It is important to remember that within Fusion, there are many ways to complete the same task, which means that you have much more artistic license when creating your games. For the main menu of "Fighter Pilot," we will be using two new ideas: a moving icon when you move the mouse over a menu item; and, rather than having the menu items as buttons, this time they will be graphic icons, so to initiate the move to another frame we will be using zones. This will be discussed in more detail in the "Games Programming" section. For now, let's place all of the game's menu objects on the game screen.

1. Double-click on the frame Main to open the Frame Editor for this screen.

2. Now you need to navigate to the right library folder that contains the items for this frame. Click on the text "Fighter Pilot" in the Library toolbar; this will show the FighterPilot library file on the right of this item. Double-click on FighterPilot text on the right of the Library Toolbar to open the various library levels, and then double-click again on the item Main. You will now see five objects that can be placed onto the play area.

3. Drag the first item, Menu_backdrop, onto the play area. Try to position it exactly on the frame, or right-click on the backdrop graphic and select Align in Frame | Horz Center and Align in Frame | Vert Center from the pop-up menu to position it correctly.

4. Drag the Selector object onto the play area. Click on the object and set its position to 1384, 386.

5. Then drag the three menu text objects and position them—New_Game_String (1448, 354), HighScore_String (1448, 482), and Quit_String (1448, 608).

Fighter Pilot – The Game Screen

The Game screen involves a large number of graphics; although you may think we need lots for the enemy waves, we only need one of each type, as we'll be creating instances of them at runtime. This makes the entire process much simpler, as they are created at runtime rather than dragging many planes onto the play area. You will need to position some of the objects at a specific location, so make sure you confirm the object's location with the Object Properties and the information in this book; misplacing an object could cause strange results.

 Runtime means when the game is running. So, if we say we are creating objects at runtime, this means we are creating objects such as enemy planes while the game is running.

 Instances were discussed in Chapter 6.

The Game screen is always the longest part of any game creation, so if you become tired, make sure you save your work and then take a break.

1. Double-click on the Game frame in the Workspace toolbar to open the Frame Editor with the empty frame ready for our objects.

2. Then in the Library toolbar you will either need to go back up a level (by double-clicking on the folder icon with the up arrow on it), or you will need navigate to the Game Frame library objects folder by clicking on the Fighter Pilot library and then double-clicking on the Game folder (this all depends on if you closed the editor since the last block of work, as the toolbar resets itself). Once you have double-clicked on Game, it will reveal a large selection of objects; these are the items we will be adding to this frame.

3. First, we need to create the background against which the plane will scroll. Drag the Background_1 object on screen and place it at 0,0. Then add Background_2 (1080,0) and Background_3 (2158,0).

 You may be looking at the X positions of the different sea tiles and wondering why the two of them (Background_2 and 3) are not at precise positions, if we are just adding 1080 onto the X coordinate each time. When running the game, after a short while a small gap appeared in the tiles. This was caused by the speed it took to move the tile from the left-hand side of the screen to the right, ready for it to reappear, and so to fix this issue I overlapped each of the tiles by a couple of pixels. It's not ideal sometimes having to fix issues within your games, but it is something that you will need to do from time to time.

4. Next, we need to take the Island_Background_Graphic, which breaks up our water to make scrolling a little more interesting, and place it at 2160,0. On zooming out, your screen should look like Figure 14.1.

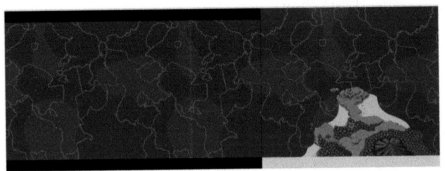

FIGURE 14.1 Background positioned and ready.

5. If you now run the frame, you will notice that nothing happens. Even though each of the objects has a movement type assigned (bouncing ball that is set to move to the left only), we haven't enabled "Moving at Start" by default. This is because we will use events to move them. If you want to learn more about scrolling techniques, see Chapter 13, "Scrolling Game Concepts."

6. Drag Black_Bar onto the frame twice (so that two exist) and place the first at 0,0 and the second at 0,1080. The first of these at the top of the screen will provide a bar for our text and game scoring icons to appear, while the bottom one will prevent our player aircraft from leaving the screen.

7. Let's now place any other items that need to be positioned on the play-field first. We will start with the game information that appears on the top black_bar.

Using events we can prevent the player aircraft from leaving the play area, but an issue arose where the aircraft was still leaving at the bottom. To prevent that we are using the second black bar, which we can then code to stop the movement of the player's aircraft. It is quite possible this is something we have missed or a bug within Fusion, but the key thing to take from this is that if one way doesn't seem to work for you, there are other methods available to you.

Drag, drop, and place the following objects into their positions:

- Life_String (8, 0)
- Health_String (216, 0)
- Bombs_String (568, 0)
- Score_String (795, 0)
- Lives (9, 36)
- Heart_Icon (232, 52)
- Health_Bar (260, 39)
- Counter_bombs (610, 70)
- Bomb_Graphic (641, 52)
- Score (895, 70)

You can see the user information bar as shown in Figure 14.2, which provides the player with all of the required information they need to understand how they are doing in the game. It is important to provide such information so that the player can make a judgment on how to approach a wave or level as well as know how well they are doing.

FIGURE 14.2 The User Information bar.

Let's now drag the game elements onto the screen, such as the character being controlled by the player and the enemy aircraft.

- Flyboy (181, 596)
- Big_Boss (-170, 9)
- Red_Plane (-98, 395)
- Blue_Plane (-98, 517)
- Green_Plane (-98, 642)

If an object is placed either on a minus X or minus Y coordinate, it means that it is most likely off-screen; in the case of the enemy plane objects this is true. We only need these objects when we create them, and then we place them on the right-hand side of the screen at runtime. It doesn't really matter where you place these objects on the left-hand side, as long as they are off-screen. This isn't true of the player's character, as this needs to be on the frame ready for the player to move it around the screen. If you wanted to, you could have the player's character off-screen and at the start of the frame position it precisely where required. This might be something you want to do if you have multiple start points and want to decide where to place the object based on how a player has done in a previous level, for example.

Next, we need to place all of the Bullet objects we intend to use in our game, but these, just like the enemy aircraft, need to be out of sight of the game player (out of frame/out of the playfield). Place the following objects at the specified locations:

- Bomb (-74, 219)
- Bullet (-74, 252)
- Enemy_Shot (-74, 287)

You have now completed the placement of all of the game's objects. Your frame should look like the example in Figure 14.3.

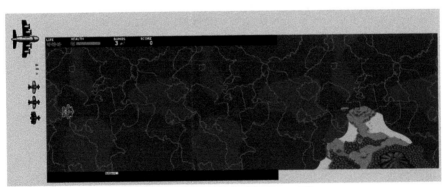

FIGURE 14.3 Current look of the Frame Editor.

Fighter Pilot – Hi-Score

For the Hi-Score screen, we will have a simple screen with a background image and a high score table that will automatically place the score into the table. There are a number of ways to display a score with the HighScore object; for example, you could have a pop-up box appear and display an entry box where the player will enter their name to go on the score table. Though that method is fine, in most cases you would probably want to do it via your own coded events rather than use the inbuilt pop-up box, as it's a little out of date.

1. Double-click on the Hi-Score frame in the Workspace toolbar to open the Frame Editor.

2. Navigate to the Hi-Score folder in the Library Toolbar to reveal three objects; these are the items we will be adding onto this frame.

Drag the following objects and place them in their X and Y positions on the frame:

- Backdrop (0, 0)

- Hi-Score (1298, 272)

- Spacebar_String (4, 1014)

That's it for placing objects on-screen. Now it's time to begin coding the events, conditions, and actions to bring the game to life.

Fighter Pilot – Programming

We will have a selection of colored enemy aircraft appear in waves. Once all three waves of red, green, and blue planes have been defeated (or flown past the player), the end-of-level boss will appear. If you are able to defeat the big boss, the game will end, and you will be taken to the Hi-Score frame; if you are defeated, you are also taken to the end frame. The game is slightly more complicated from a coding perspective than the first, but it is broken into various stages so you can see how the game progresses.

Programming the Main Menu

As previously mentioned, the second game's main menu is more animated than the one in "The Lab." Hopefully, this will show you that you can do many different things to represent your menus and make them interesting to the player. If you run Pilot.exe on the Main Menu frame, you will notice that there is a simple animation of a rotor blade, which will move up or down depending on the location of the mouse with regard to the menu items. Then, when the user clicks on one of three areas, he or she will be taken either to the game or the Hi-Score, or the program will quit. For the first part, you will need to get the Graphic icon moving when the mouse rolls over an item. When creating a movement based on the mouse position, it is a good idea to place the object approximately where you want it to get a general X, Y coordinate (write it down), and then you can tell Fusion to place an object in the exact position.

 At the bottom right of the Fusion application is an X, Y mouse coordinate that updates every time you move your mouse to a new location. This is also very useful for getting a general idea of where a specific location is with regard to its coordinates.

Ensure you are currently viewing the Main Menu frame by double-clicking on the text "Main Menu" on the Workspace toolbar. Then, click on the Event Editor button to go to a blank coding page.

We'll start by creating a comment line (by right-clicking on the event line number) and then create some conditions to check for the position of the mouse cursor on-screen.

- Event Line 1: Insert | A comment | "Create Moving Cursor" | OK.

- Event Line 2: Condition: The Mouse Pointer and Keyboard | The Mouse | Check for Mouse Pointer in Zone | Horizontal 1432 to 1801 | Vertical 330 to 440 | OK.

You will need to click on the OK button to save the information to the event. This will create a box around the New Game text on the frame. Now let's do the next two events for the other two menu options.

- Event Line 3: Condition: The Mouse Pointer and Keyboard | The Mouse | Check for Mouse Pointer in Zone | Horizontal 1429 to 1798 | Vertical 464 to 574.

- Event Line 4: Condition: The Mouse Pointer and Keyboard | The Mouse | Check for Mouse Pointer in Zone | Horizontal 1432 to 1801 | Vertical 584 to 694.

The values stored within the zones are the X and Y coordinates of each of the corners of the box. For example, for line 2 the horizontal line starts from 1432 and finishes at the 1801 pixel location.

You will now have three events with a single condition in each. When the mouse pointer goes within that area of the screen, the condition will be true. Now you will need to create an action, the moving of the graphic rotor blade to a set position to the left of the text. As we are happy with the X position of the selector icon, we only need to change the Y position (up and down) for each of the three events (one for each menu text option).

We will be placing the actions for these conditions on the right-hand side under the Selector object (as the position impacts this object).

- Event Line 2: Action: Selector | Position | Set Y Coordinate | 386 | OK.

- Event Line 3: Action: Selector | Position | Set Y Coordinate | 511 | OK.

- Event Line 3: Action: Selector | Position | Set Y Coordinate | 636 | OK.

If you run the frame now, move your mouse cursor over the text menu options and you'll see the Selector object moving up and down. You can get a bit more creative if you want and change the color of the text or perform other effects. For this example we are keeping it simple, but by all means add your own effects if you feel comfortable with the process.

The next stage of the Main Menu is to get the user to click on one of the three items and then take the user to the relevant screen. We will create a new comment line to separate our code and then create three events that check for mouse point within a zone and then do a relevant action such as go to Frame 2, 3, etc.

- Event Line 5: Insert | A comment | "On Click of Mouse" | OK.

- Event Line 6: Condition: The mouse pointer and keyboard | The Mouse | User clicks within a zone | Left button | Single Click | OK.

This will now create a box where you can drag the edges of the box or type in the values. The box needs to be around the first menu text of "New Game."

- Horizontal: 1430 to 1776

- Vertical 343 to 426

We now need to follow the same process for the other two menu options; you can drag and drop the condition to the next New condition line and double-click to edit it or do it manually. For sake of clarity, we'll do the configuration manually.

- Event Line 7: Condition: The mouse pointer and keyboard | The Mouse | User clicks within a zone | Left button | Single Click | OK.

- Horizontal: 1430 to 1776

- Vertical 470 to 553

- Event Line 8: Condition: The mouse pointer and keyboard | The Mouse | User clicks within a zone | Left button | Single Click | OK.

- Horizontal: 1430 to 1776

- Vertical 596 to 679

We now want to create the actions for these three new events, which will move the player to the appropriate frame associated with the text menu. The first two options are moving to a particular frame, while the third event is to quit the game.

- Event Line 6: Action: Storyboard Controls | Jump to Frame: Frame 2 – Game | OK.

- Event Line 7: Action: Storyboard Controls | Jump to Frame: Frame 3 – Hi-Score | OK.

- Event Line 8: Action: Storyboard Controls | End the Application.

An example of what the events and conditions should look like is shown in Figure 14.4. You have now completed the programming for the Main Menu. You can test it to see if it works correctly, although you won't be able to move back from the other two frames, as this hasn't been programmed in yet.

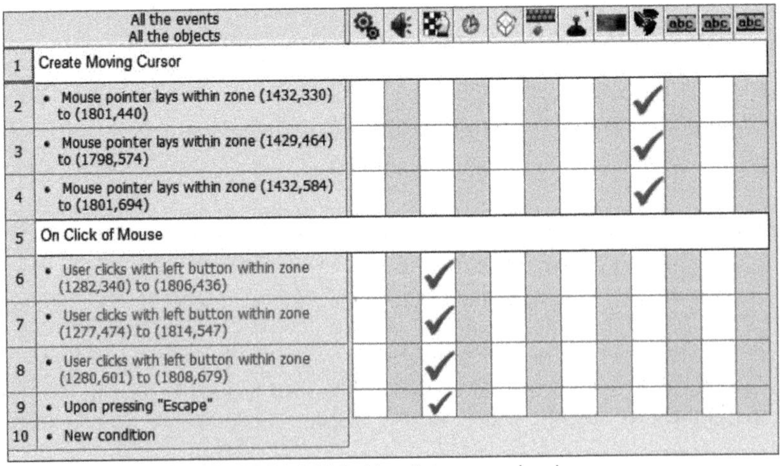

FIGURE 14.4 Main Menu's events and actions.

It is very useful to add a "test" event in each frame that activates when pressing a particular key; this will either quit you out of the game or take you back to the main menu. Otherwise, you may find yourself stuck on a screen that you have yet to program or finish programming. Perhaps you want to test the main menu of your game; you don't want to have to quit the application every time you test one of the menu options, so adding a "go back to main menu frame on pressing a key" condition/action would allow you to test each of your menu's options quickly. If you haven't programmed a frame, you can put a simple text string on-screen, telling you what screen it is so that you can identify it when running the game.

Programming the Game

You are now ready to begin creating the game frame, which contains most of the program code. The coding has been placed into sections to make it easier to code, but it is also a good way to learn how to structure your programs. When making games, you do not need to write everything at once and hope it works. You can take one feature at a time, code it, test it, and then move on to the next. If you become stuck, you can always move on to another feature and come back later.

There is an element of iteration in game development; this is the process where you implement a feature and at various stages need to revisit it, as it doesn't work as expected or you have changed other elements and need to improve the code to work with these new features. In the games provided with the book, this process has already been done, but you may want to change things or add new features once you've completed the examples.

The first thing we need to do in our game code is set up the scoring system, whereby we'll set the default player and set the score to 0 (so that every time the player plays the game, we have reset any value that may be stored so that we don't accidently give the player a previous Hi-Score). At the end of the frame the game will test the player and the current score and see if it's high enough to be added to the score table in the Hi-Score frame.

Make sure you are on the Game frame by double-clicking on Game in the Workspace toolbar. Once you have the Game frame open, click on the Event Editor to bring up the empty editor.

- Event Line 1: Condition: Storyboard Controls | Start of Frame.

We'll now create the actions that relate to the player, which are under the player icon (which looks like a joystick). For the Event line 1 text, include the quote marks.

- Event Line 1: Condition: Player 1 | Set player name | "Player 1" | OK.

- Event Line 1: Condition: Player 1 | Score | Set score | 0 | OK.

Most of the rest of our game code will be placed in groups. This allows us to easily manage the code into its relevant topic, but also some groups will only be enabled when they are required to run; this ensures the code is only run when needed.

Scrolling

The first group of code we'll implement is to handle the scrolling background. First, we shall start the tiles moving using a qualifier group, which is a tag that has been added (by me) to all scrolling background objects with which we'll tell an object to start its movement (it will move from right to left). We will then check for the position of the object on-screen and reset it once it has reached -1080 on the X axis. This X coordinate is off-screen to the left and will allow us to nicely move it back to the right-hand side so that it can loop around again.

- Event Line 2: Insert | A group of events | Title = "Scrolling" | Checked = "Active when frame starts" | OK.

- Event Line 3: Condition: Storyboard Controls | Start of Frame.

- Event Line 4: Condition: Background_1 | Position | Compare X position to a value | Lower or Equal | -1080 | OK.

- Event Line 5: Condition: Background_2 | Position | Compare X position to a value | Lower or Equal | -1080 | OK.

- Event Line 6: Condition: Background_3 | Position | Compare X position to a value | Lower or Equal | -1080 | OK.

- Event Line 7: Condition: Island_Background_Graphic | Position | Compare X position to a value | Lower or Equal | -1080 | OK.

 Make sure you type in the coordinate of minus 1080.

One of the actions is a "run once" action that starts the movement for the tiles (it uses the qualifier group "good"—shown as a red apple), and the other action moves any tiles that have moved off the screen to the left (and out of the player's view) back to the right-hand side of the screen (again outside the player's view). It will take the position of the furthest tile on the right and add 1080 to its position so that it doesn't overlap it. That's because each tile is 1080 in width.

- Event Line 3: Action: Group.Good: Movement | Start.

- Event Line 4: Action: Background_1 | Position | Set X Coordinate | Background_3 | Position | X Coordinate …

You should see X("Background_3") in the Expression Evaluator; add + 108, then click OK.

  - X("Background_3") + 1080

- Event Line 5: Action: Background_2 | Position | Set X Coordinate | Background_1 | Position | X Coordinate | +1080.

You should see X("Background_1") in the Expression Evaluator; if so, add + 1080, then click OK.

  - X("Background_1") + 1080

- Event Line 6: Action: Background_3 | Position | Set X Coordinate | Background_2 | Position | X Coordinate | +1080.

You should see X("Background_2") in the Expression Evaluator; add + 1080, click OK.

  - X("Background_2") + 1080

- Event Line 7: Action: Island_Background_Graphic | Position | Set X Coordinate | Background_2 | Position | X Coordinate | +1080.

You should see X("Background_2") in the Expression Evaluator; add + 1080, click OK.

  - X("Background_2") + 1080

If you run the game now, you should be able to select the menu option for "New Game," and then you should be able to move the player's plane using the cursor keys.

The order you add items into your game defines the position on the layer, so if you add things later you may need to change their order. For example, when setting up this example the Island_Background_Graphic was left out, and when adding it later the player's plane would fly under it.

Player Movement Events

For the next group of events we will be coding a selection of player-related movements and animations.

- Setting a default image of the aircraft if not moving (as when you move up, down, etc., it will change its graphic). This gives the aircraft a default position so that it doesn't stay in an up or down animation state.

- Stopping the aircraft from leaving the screen.

- Firing one of the two weapons (using a system that is easily expandable for more bullet types or directions).

Ensure the scrolling group is collapsed before starting on the code in this section.

- Event Line 9: Insert | A group of events | Title = "Events For Player" | Checked = "Active when frame starts" | OK.

- Event Line 10: Insert | A comment: "If Player is not moving, set it to forward direction.".

- Event Line 11: Condition: Flyboy | Direction | Compare direction of "Flyboy".

  - On the directional dialog, select the following numbers (larger boxes) 4, 8, 12, 16, 20, 24, 28 | OK.

The dialog box should look like Figure 14.5.

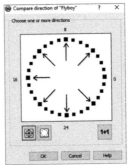

FIGURE 14.5 Direction dialog configuration.

The plane is set to use eight directions in its movements, which is why we want to select the seven directions that are not moving forward.

- Event Line 11: Condition: Flyboy | Movement | Compare Speed of "Flyboy" to a value | Equal | 0 | OK.

 Event line 11 should have two conditions in it.

- Event Line 12: Insert | A comment: "Keep Plane in Area".

- Event Line 13: Condition: Flyboy | Position | Test position of "Flyboy" | Select the top, left, right and bottom arrows that are pointing outward | OK.

As shown in Figure 14.6:

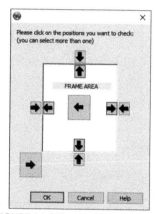

FIGURE 14.6 Test Position dialog box.

- Event Line 14: Condition: Flyboy | Collisions | Backdrop.

- Event Line 15: Condition: Flyboy | Collisions | Another Object| Black_ Bar | OK.

- Event Line 16: Insert | A comment | "Shoot Type" | OK.

- Event Line 17: Condition: Flyboy | Alterable Values | Compare to one of the alterable values | Alterable Value A | Equal | 0 | OK.

- Event Line 17: Condition: The Mouse pointer and keyboard | The Keyboard | Upon pressing a key | SHIFT.

- Event Line 18: Insert | A comment | "Shoot Bombs Mode" | OK.

- Event Line 19: Condition: The Mouse pointer and keyboard | The Keyboard | Upon pressing a key | CONTROL.

- Event Line 19: Condition: Counter_Bombs | Compare the counter to a value | Greater | 0 | OK.

Now that we have created the events for the player, we now need to create the actions, such as stopping movement, shooting a normal bullet, or bomb.

- Event Line 11: Action: Flyboy | Direction | Select Direction | 0 | OK.

- Event Line 13: Action: Flyboy | Movement | Stop.

- Event Line 14: Action: Flyboy | Movement | Stop.

- Event Line 15: Action: Flyboy | Movement | Stop.

- Event Line 15: Action: Flyboy | Direction | Select Direction | 0 | OK.

- Event Line 17: Action: Flyboy | Launch an Object | Bullet | OK | Speed = 100 | Launch in a selected direction = 0 | OK | OK.

- Event Line 19: Action: Flyboy | Launch an Object | Bomb | OK | Speed = 45 | Launch in a selected direction = 0 | OK | OK.

- Event Line 19: Action: Counter_Bombs | Subtract from counter | 1 | OK.

You should now have a set of events as shown in Figure 14.7.

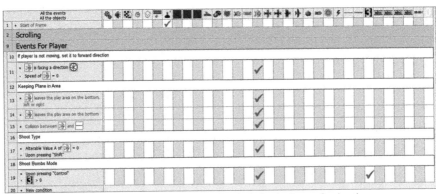

FIGURE 14.7 Event, conditions, and actions for the Events for the player.

You'll notice that in the last action, we fire a bomb and subtract 1 from the counter; this means that next time we try to fire, the game will test to see if the bombs counter is greater than 0, and if so will allow it to fire again.

Remember, for speed of programming you can drag an action down onto another condition line, and then right-click and select Edit to make it specific to that condition.

Bullet Management

If you play the game at this moment, you will be able to fire your weapon. You'll see a bullet that won't hit anything, and it will disappear outside of the frame's visible view. Unless you have specified within the object properties to destroy the object if it's far outside the frame, you will have to do this manually.

The main reason for not having destroy outside of the frame enabled is that you might want a world bigger than the current player's visible view and want that object to continue existing within your game world. This would certainly be true of, say, a scrolling-platform game, where an enemy could move off-screen because the player has moved away from the object. You wouldn't want the object destroyed and have to create it again when the player walks back again; not only is this a massive coding overhead, it's a hassle to keep track of.

The following code is two separate events that check if a qualifier group has left the play area or collided with the background; if so, it will destroy the selected instance. You could have done this with four separate events, but qualifiers are a great way of reducing the complexity of your code and the number of events. A qualifier is one of the things in your programming tool kit that is very useful if you make a game with lots of events, as simplifying code is really important when you try to fix issues or add new features at a later stage, or even go back to making your game after a break, as you'll find it easier to understand.

- Event Line 21: Insert | A group of events | Title = "Bullets" | Checked = "Active when frame starts" | OK.

- Event Line 22: Insert | A Comment: "Bullets leave play area" | OK.

- Event Line 23: Condition: Group.Bullets | Position | Test position of "Group.Bullets" | Click on the four arrows on the edge of the square pointing outward | OK.

- Event Line 24: Condition: Group.Bullets | Collisions | Backdrop.

- Event Line 23: Action | Group.Bullets | Destroy.

- Event Line 24: Action | Group.Bullets | Destroy.

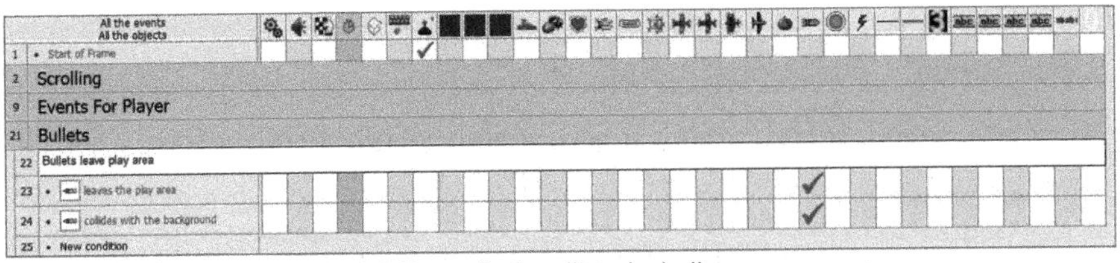

FIGURE 14.8 Events for handling the bullet management.

If you were to run the game with the debugger running (see Chapter 17 for more information), you'd notice that the object count (the number of objects loaded and using memory) is at approximately 17. When firing the bullets before implementing the bullet management code, this number would continue to increase and, at some point, your game would have its performance affected. By adding in the events detailed over the last couple of pages, the number would go up initially as the bullet objects are on-screen, and then decrease as the objects are destroyed. Object management is very important in larger games where memory can be freed up as the player is playing the game.

Creating Plane Waves

The game is starting to work quite well, but the player doesn't have anything to do except fly around and shoot both his weapons. To make it more exciting, we need planes for the player to shoot down. All planes will appear from the right side of the screen and will be in waves. Each wave will be configured to appear in a slightly different way to give the player more of a challenge. The enemy waves are all created in groups, which allows us to enable and disable each group as we want through the code. If you decide to make the game harder, you can create additional waves (groups) or change the order in which each group is run, or enable them at various different times to give the player a more varied challenge. For this section, we have Red, Blue, and Green planes, and the code for each color is defined in its own group. Initially only the Red Planes group will be enabled from the start, and simply using a timer will allow us to enable each group in turn (and disable the previous one).

Before you start, ensure all groups are collapsed.

Let's create the four plane groups (red, blue, green, and the end boss), ensuring only the red planes group is enabled from the beginning.

- Event Line 26: Insert | A group of events | Title = "Red Planes" | Checked = "Active when frame starts" | OK.

- Event Line 28: Insert | A group of events | Title = "Blue Planes" | Unchecked = "Active when frame starts" | OK.

- Event Line 30: Insert | A group of events | Title = "Green Planes" | Unchecked = "Active when frame starts" | OK.

- Event Line 32: Insert | A group of events | Title = "Big Boss" | Unchecked = "Active when frame starts" | OK.

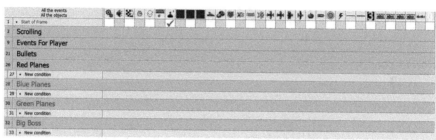

FIGURE 14.9 Plane groups ready to program the code.

Red Plane Code

For the red plane wave, we will be randomly placing planes around the screen, while some of the other waves are placed in set positions. Every 0.75s it will create an enemy plane and set it at a random position off-screen to the right (the planes have movement predefined to the left). We will then check the position of the plane, and if it's off-screen to the left (if it hasn't been destroyed by the player and has left the screen), we will destroy the object. When the timer equals 20, we enable the next wave and disable the red plane group.

Ensure all groups are collapsed except for Red Planes.

- Event Line 27: Condition: the Timer | Every | 0h, 0m, 0s, 1/100 = 75| OK.

- Event Line 28: Condition: Red_Plane | Position | Compare X position to a value | Lower or equal | -200 | OK.

- Event Line 29: Condition: the Timer | Is the timer equal to a certain value | 0h, 0m, seconds = 20, 0 1/100 | OK.

Let's now create the actions.

- Event Line 27: Action: Create new objects | Create Object | Red Plane | 2172 and -82 | OK.

- Event Line 27: Action: Red_Plane | Position | Set Y Coordinate | Random(800) + 180 | OK.

- Event Line 28: Action: Red_Plane | Destroy.

- Event Line 29: Action: Special Conditions | Group of events | Activate | "Blue Planes" | OK.

- Event Line 29: Action: Special Conditions | Group of events | Deactivate | "Red Planes" | OK.

An example of the Activate and Deactivate Group dialog can be seen in Figure 14.10.

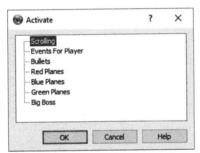

FIGURE 14.10 Activating or deactivating a Group dialog.

If you run the game now, you'll be able to control your plane and fire your weapons, as well as see the red planes appear on the right and move to the left in a random wave. The code for what you have just done is in Figure 14.11.

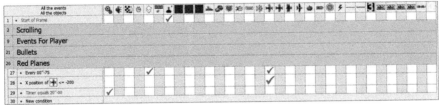

FIGURE 14.11 Red Planes code group.

Blue Plane Code

We now need to create the blue plane wave, and to make the game more interesting, it will need to be different from the first group. Rather than randomly creating planes and making them fly toward the player, we will be creating an entire row. Just like the red planes we will use a timer to generate the waves, though you could use a counter to count how many waves have been generated and then activate the next group. As with everything you do in game dev, it all depends on what you want to achieve and how expandable you want the system to be in the future if you decide you want more waves.

For the blue planes group we want the following code:

- Every six seconds create a row of eight planes at various X/Y positions.

- If a plane is at <= -200 on the X axis, destroy it (as it's off-screen).

- When the timer equals 40 seconds, activate the Green Planes group and deactivate the Blue Planes group.

Ensure all groups are collapsed except for Blue Planes.

- Event Line 32: Condition: the Timer | Every | 0h, 0m, seconds = 6, 0 1/100| OK.

- Event Line 33: Condition: Blue_Plane | Position | Compare X position to a value | Lower or equal | -200 | OK.

- Event Line 34: Condition: the Timer | Is the timer equal to a certain value | 0h, 0m, seconds = 40, 0 1/100 | OK.

Now let's do the actions where you'll be creating eight blue planes, which you can do manually or complete the first and then double-click on the action to take you into the Event List Editor, where you can copy and paste the actions and then just change the data.

- Event Line 32: Action: Create new objects| Create object | Blue_Plane | OK | x = 1995, Y = 170 | OK.

Follow this same process on Event Line 32 for another 7 objects with the following data.

- x = 1995, Y = 287

- x = 1995, Y = 404

- x = 1995, Y = 521

- x = 1995, Y = 638

- x = 1995, Y = 755

- x = 1995, Y = 872

- x = 1995, Y = 989

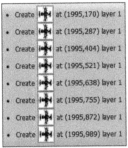

FIGURE 14.12 Creating all the blue planes for the blue wave.

- Event Line 33: Action: Blue_Plane | Destroy.

- Event Line 34: Action: Special Conditions | Group of events | Activate | "Green Planes" | OK.

- Event Line 34: Action: Special Conditions | Group of events | Deactivate | "Blue Planes" | OK.

 A good way to design your waves of enemy planes is to open a blank Fusion game, place them on the screen where you would like them to appear, make a note of the X, Y locations, and then transfer it to your game.

Green Planes

The green plane wave is designed like a V on its side, a common military formation ("<"). The code for this is very similar to the blue planes. The logic is as follows:

- Every 5 seconds launch a new wave.

- Check the position of the aircraft and if they are less than -200 on the X axis (left of the play area), then destroy them.

- Once the timer equals 1 minute, enable the Big Boss group and disable the Green Planes group.

Ensure all groups are closed except for the Green Planes group.

- Event Line 37: Condition: the Timer | Every | 0h, 0m, Seconds = 5, 0 1/100| OK.

- Event Line 38: Condition: Green_Plane | Position | Compare X position to a value | Lower or equal | -200 | OK.

- Event Line 39: Condition: the Timer | Is the timer equal to a certain value | 0h, Minutes = 1, 0s, 0 1/100 | OK.

The actions for these events are pretty much the same as the Blue Planes group, but obviously setting a different position for the aircraft.

- Event Line 37: Action: Create new objects| Create object | Green_Plane | OK | x = 2009, Y = 598 | OK.

Follow this same process on Event Line 37 for another 6 objects with the following data.

- x = 2070, Y = 716

- x = 2130, Y = 831

- x = 2192, Y = 946

- x = 2070, Y = 481

- x = 2130, Y = 364

- x = 2192, Y = 248

Now we'll create the rest of the actions for this group.

- Event Line 38: Action: Green_Plane | Destroy.

- Event Line 39: Action: Special Conditions | Group of events | Activate | "Big Boss" | OK.

- Event Line 39: Action: Special Conditions | Group of events | Deactivate | "Green Planes" | OK.

We have now finished all of the code for the green wave as shown in Figure 14.13.

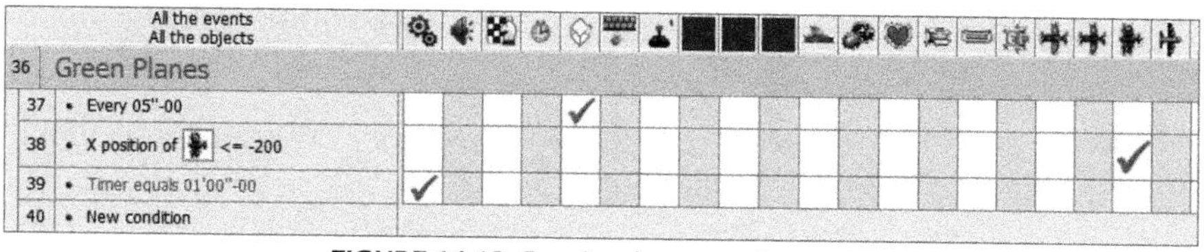

	All the events All the objects																	
36	Green Planes																	
37	• Every 05"-00				✓													
38	• X position of ✈ <= -200															✓		
39	• Timer equals 01'00"-00	✓																
40	• New condition																	

FIGURE 14.13 Creating the green plane wave.

End-of-Level Boss

We now have the enemy plane waves in place, but we still need something to complete the level. We could just finish it there, but it would be much more interesting if we added an end-of-level boss to defeat. If you decided to make a similar game, you could add many levels and a number of different bosses to defeat. Keeping a varied enemy makes for a much more interesting game and allows you to increase the difficulty.

For the big boss section, we need to do the following:

- Create the boss off-screen.

- Check the boss position and move its direction, so that it moves diagonally around the top and bottom of the screen (taking into account that the top of the screen doesn't start from 0 because of the black bar).

- Change direction of the aircraft if it collides with the top black bar.

- Change the direction of the aircraft if it collides with the bottom black bar.

- Check if the health is less than or equal to 0, then destroy the object.

- Check to see if there are 0 planes on screen; if so, jump to Frame 3 (Hi-Score screen).

- We will animate the plane when its health is at 0 and check once it has finished that animation, then destroy it. This is so when the boss plane is at 0 health, we can make it zoom out.

Ensure all groups are collapsed except for the Big Boss group.

- Event Line 42: Condition: Special | Limit Conditions | Run this event once.

- Event Line 43: Condition: Big_Boss | Position | Compare X position to a value | Lower or equal | 1240 | OK.

- Event Line 44: Condition: Big_Boss | Position | Compare X position to a value | Greater or equal | 1540 | OK.

- Event Line 44: Condition: Big_Boss | Direction | Compare direction of "Big_Boss" | 7 | OK.

- Event Line 45: Condition: Big_Boss | Animation | Has animation finished | User Animation | OK.

- Event Line 46: Condition: Big_Boss | Collisions | Another object | Black_Bar | OK.

- Event Line 46: Condition: Big_Boss | Direction | Compare direction of "Big_Boss" | 7 | OK.

- Event Line 47: Condition: Big_Boss | Collisions | Another object | Black_Bar | OK.

- Event Line 47: Condition: Big_Boss | Direction | Compare direction of "Big_Boss" | 25 | OK.

- Event Line 48: Condition: Big_Boss | Alterable Values | Compare to one of the alterable values | Health | Lower or equal | 0 | OK.

- Event Line 49: Condition: Big_Boss | Pick or count | Compare to the number of "Big_Boss" objects | Equal | 0 | OK.

Your events will look like Figure 14.14.

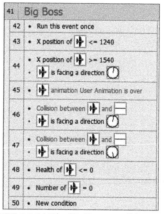

FIGURE 14.14 The Big Boss condition events.

 The animation called "User Animation" on the Big_Boss is two frames that flash the plane, so as it fades out it will flash.

 If you look in the Big_Boss Display properties tab, you'll see the transition has been configured to Fade Out. Fade In and Fade Out in the properties means what to do with the object when it has been created or when it has been destroyed.

The actions for this group of events are as follows:

- Create the Big_Boss aircraft.

- Set direction it should move depending on if it's at the top or bottom of the screen.

- Destruction of the Big_Boss aircraft.

- Jump to the Hi-Score frame when the boss object has been destroyed.

 If an action on an object is the same action needed for another object, you can drag and drop that to another event line to reduce the need to select the object and the pop-up menu options. In a few cases some objects will not accept an action of the same type, but overall most should work.

- Event Line 42: Action: Create new objects | Create object | Big_Boss | OK | X= 2074, Y=552 | OK.

- Event Line 43: Action: Big_Boss | Direction | Select Direction | 7 | OK.

- Event Line 44: Action: Big_Boss | Direction | Select Direction | 23 | OK.

- Event Line 45: Action: Big_Boss | Destroy.

- Event Line 46: Action: Big_Boss | Direction | Select Direction | 23 | OK.

- Event Line 47: Action: Big_Boss | Direction | Select Direction | 7 | OK.

- Event Line 48: Action: Big_Boss | Destroy.

- Event Line 49: Action: Storyboard controls | Jump to frame | Frame 3 – Hi-Score | OK.

You have now finished the code for the final boss. Next, we will be handling the destruction of the enemy planes.

Destruction of Enemy Planes

On playing the game, you can move the plane around, the enemy waves appear, you can fire the weapons, but nothing happens when the bullets hit them. We will need to destroy the enemy planes when they collide with the bullets. We will need to also destroy the bullet, but if it's the bomb, it will continue on its way and destroy any other planes that it collides with. We will also need to add a number of points to the player's score, as it is based on the number of planes destroyed.

In this section of code, some of the events will be using qualifier groups to handle the checking of collision between the bullet and the enemy aircraft. Using qualifier groups reduces complexity and can handle the checking of multiple objects at a time. We mention qualifier groups in Chapter 8 if you need to refresh your memory.

 To check on an object's group status, click on the object in question to reveal its Object Properties, and then click on the Events tab (in the Properties Workspace toolbar) to see if any Qualifiers have been assigned.

First, we will need to create a group (that is initially enabled, as it will be checking for collisions), then we will create the four events that will handle the different bullet collisions between the enemy plane and the Big_Boss (as we want these to be handled differently).

- Event Line 51: Insert | A group of events | Title = "Destroy Enemy Planes" | Checked = "Active when frame starts" | OK.

- Event Line 52: Condition: Group.Bullets | Collisions | Another object | Group.Enemies | OK.

- Event Line 53: Condition: Group.Bullets | Collisions | Another object | Big_Boss | OK.

- Event Line 54: Condition: Bomb | Collisions | Another object | Group.Enemies | OK.

- Event Line 55: Condition: Bomb | Collisions | Another object | Big_Boss | OK.

For the actions we need to do the following:

- Add to score.

- Destroy bullet or bomb.

- Play a sound.

- If enemy plane, destroy it, if Big_Boss, reduce its health.

For the audio actions, we have placed the audio into the Game 2\Audio folder. So, let's create all the audio actions first.

- Event Line 52: Action: Sound | Samples | Play Sample | From a File (Browse button) | Select "Pop.ogg" | Open.

- Event Line 53: Action: Sound | Samples | Play Sample | Pop | OK.

- Event Line 54: Action: Sound | Samples | Play Sample | Pop | OK.

- Event Line 55: Action: Sound | Samples | Play Sample | From a File (Browse button) | Select "Pop bubble.ogg" | Open.

To distinguish between a hit on an enemy plane and the boss plane, we have used different audio noises. It is nice to have these differences within your games, as it makes every type of enemy special.

Now let's add a score for when each bullet collides with an enemy; we'll add an additional value to the player's tracked score, which we can then use to check our HighScore values against.

- Event Line 52: Action: Player 1 | Score | Add to Score | 10 | OK.

- Event Line 53: Action: Player 1 | Score | Add to Score | 20 | OK.

- Event Line 54: Action: Player 1 | Score | Add to Score | 10 | OK.

- Event Line 55: Action: Player 1 | Score | Add to Score | 20 | OK.

 You have three main options when handling score: you can add, which adds to the current score value; you can subtract, which removes a specific number from the current score value; or you can set. Set will overwrite the current stored score value with a new value.

We will now need to destroy any bullets and wave enemies. Both are contained within qualifier groups. We will only destroy the Bomb object when it hits the Big_Boss, as with normal enemies it will destroy the planes and continue on its way. When the Big_Boss gets hit, we will reduce its health (this is so that it can take multiple hits before dying, unlike the normal plane waves that get destroyed in one hit).

- Event Line 52: Action: Group.Bullets | Destroy.

- Event Line 52: Action: Group.Enemies | Destroy.

- Event Line 53: Action: Group.Bullets | Destroy.

- Event Line 54: Action: Group.Enemies | Destroy.

One final bit of code for the Destroy Enemy Planes group is required, and that is to subtract health from the Big_Boss when it is hit.

- Event Line 53: Action: Big_Boss | Alterable values | Subtract from | Health | 5 | OK.

- Event Line 55: Action: Big_Boss | Alterable values | Subtract from | Health | 10 | OK.

You can see an example of all these events in Figure 14.15.

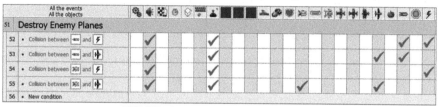

FIGURE 14.15 Destroy Enemy Planes group.

Enemy Fire

Currently the game doesn't give the player much of a challenge; though the player can shoot the enemy, they don't fire back. In this section, we will implement enemy fire. This ensures the player must keep moving or be hit, which in turn makes hitting the enemy planes harder.

For this section we need to do the following:

- Create a group that will contain all of the events.

- Create a timer for each group of waves, which will create the time frame for firing at the player.

- Pick one of the waves to fire at the player, but only if the position of the enemy plane is greater (on the X-coordinate) than the player.

- If the enemy is a normal enemy plane, fire a single bullet in the direction of the player.

- If the enemy is the boss, fire a spread of three bullets in three directions.

 Changing the following code, such as the timer or the X position of the enemy, can create more difficult or easier gameplay. For example, changing the timer to a higher value will mean the enemy fires less often, while reducing the timer will make them fire more often. By changing (or in fact removing) the X position check, you could have the enemy firing even if the player is to the right of them.

For this section, we need to do a number of multi-condition events (more than one condition per event line). So, take care when following the instructions.

Collapse all expanded groups before you start.

- Event Line 57: Insert | A group of events | Title = "Enemy Fire" | Checked = "Active when frame starts" | OK.

- Event Line 58: Condition: the Timer | Every | 1 second | OK.

- Event Line 58: Condition: Red_Plane | Pick or count | Pick "Red_Plane" at random.

- Event Line 58: Condition: Red_Plane | Position | Compare X position to a value | Greater | Flyboy | Position | X Coordinate | OK.

Using Pick or Count, Pick "Object" at random will pick one object at random from that group of objects. So, in the case of the previous code, it will pick one Red_Plane from any that are currently in the game.

For the third condition in Event Line 58, you can either type in the text X ("Flyboy") into the expression evaluator or you can click on the object in the selection of icons and then select "Position | X coordinate." Ensure any previous value in the expression evaluator is removed first.

Let's now do the exact same process for both the blue and green plane waves.

- Event Line 59: Condition: the Timer | Every | 1 second | OK.

- Event Line 59: Condition: Blue_Plane | Pick or count | Pick "Blue_Plane" at random.

- Event Line 59: Condition: Blue_Plane | Position | Compare X position to a value | Greater | Flyboy | Position | X Coordinate | OK.

- Event Line 60: Condition: the Timer | Every | 1 second | OK.

- Event Line 60: Condition: Green_Plane | Pick or count | Pick "Green_Plane" at random.

- Event Line 60: Condition: Green_Plane | Position | Compare X position to a value | Greater | Flyboy | Position | X Coordinate | OK.

We now need to create the conditions for the Big_Boss aircraft, whereby it will fire every 5 seconds and as long as it still has health left.

- Event Line 61: Condition: the Timer | Every | 5 seconds | OK.

- Event Line 61: Condition: Big_Boss | Alterable values | Compare to one of the alterable values | Health | Greater | 0 | OK.

Next, we need to create the actions which are involved in launching the bullets at a particular speed in a selected direction.

- Event Line 58: Action: Red_Plane | Launch an object | Enemy_Shot | OK | Launch in direction of… | Relative to | Flyboy | OK | OK | Speed of object = 60 |OK.

- Event Line 59: Action: Blue_Plane | Launch an object | Enemy_Shot | OK | Launch in direction of… | Relative to | Flyboy | OK | OK | Speed of object = 60 | OK.

- Event Line 60: Action: Green_Plane | Launch an object | Enemy_Shot | OK | Launch in direction of… | Relative to | Flyboy | OK | OK | Speed of object = 60 | OK.

- Event Line 61: Action: Big_Boss | Launch an object | Enemy_Shot | OK | Launch in selected direction | 14 | OK | Speed of object = 100 | OK.

- Event Line 61: Action: Big_Boss | Launch an object | Enemy_Shot | OK | Launch in selected direction | 16 | OK | Speed of object = 100 |OK.

- Event Line 61: Action: Big_Boss | Launch an object | Enemy_Shot | OK | Launch in selected direction | 18 | OK | Speed of object = 100 | OK.

If you play the game, you'll notice that the enemy shoots back, but the bullets will appear on top of the black bar at the top of the screen. This looks untidy and isn't what we want the game to do. The reason for this is that when objects are placed on the play area, that is the order in which they are displayed, but even if you fixed the order when you placed them, any objects that are created via the create objects action will always appear after any objects placed on-screen (because they don't exist until you create them and thus are placed at the very top of the order). To fix this issue, we will change the order of the bullet to be behind the black bar once it has been created.

- Event Line 58: Action: Enemy_Shot | Order | Move behind object | Black_Bar | OK.

- Event Line 59: Action: Enemy_Shot | Order | Move behind object | Black_Bar | OK.

- Event Line 60: Action: Enemy_Shot | Order | Move behind object | Black_Bar | OK.

- Event Line 61: Action: Enemy_Shot | Order | Move behind object | Black_Bar | OK.

We are now done with the enemy fire events, which can be seen in Figure 14.16.

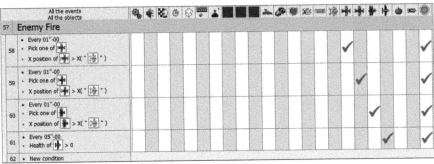

FIGURE 14.16 Enemy fire code.

Player Collisions

The player's plane can currently fly through the enemies' shots and through the planes themselves. We now need to set up a group of events that reduce the player's health if he is hit by an enemy shot or hits another Plane object.

The events for this section of the game are relatively straightforward; the conditions are checking for collisions between different objects such as the player and a bullet, or the player and another plane. The actions relate to the destruction of objects and reducing the player's health and playing a sound effect when this happens.

So, let's start with the group creation and the conditions.

- Event Line 63: Insert | A group of events | Title = "Player Collisions" | Checked = "Active when frame starts" | OK.

- Event Line 64: Condition: Enemy_Shot | Collisions | Another object | Flyboy | OK.

- Event Line 65: Condition: Flyboy | Collisions | Another object | Red_ Plane | OK.

- Event Line 66: Condition: Flyboy | Collisions | Another object | Blue_ Plane | OK.

- Event Line 67: Condition: Flyboy | Collisions | Another object | Green_ Plane | OK.

Let's set up the audio for when an object has had a collision.

 When you have already picked a particular sound file within your game, you will not need to browse for it again; just select it from the list of Samples and click on the OK button.

- Event Line 64: Action: Sound | Samples | Play Sample | Pop bubble | OK.

- Event Line 65: Action: Sound | Samples | Play Sample | Pop | OK.

- Event Line 66: Action: Sound | Samples | Play Sample | Pop | OK.

- Event Line 67: Action: Sound | Samples | Play Sample | Pop | OK.

Now onto the destruction actions for the objects.

- Event Line 64: Action: Enemy_Shot | Destroy.

- Event Line 65: Action: Red_Plane | Destroy.

- Event Line 66: Action: Blue_Plane | Destroy.

- Event Line 67: Action: Green_Plane | Destroy.

Now onto the final section of code for these events, which is to reduce the player's health amount. The code to do something with the current value will be done in the next section, but for now we just want to reduce the health value.

- Event Line 64: Action: Health_Bar | Subtract from counter | 10 | OK.

- Event Line 65: Action: Health_Bar | Subtract from counter | 10 | OK.

- Event Line 66: Action: Health_Bar | Subtract from counter | 10 | OK.

- Event Line 67: Action: Health_Bar | Subtract from counter | 10 | OK.

You should now have a set of events that look similar to Figure 14.17. The Health object is a Counter object with a starting value of 100, so every time the player's plane hits an enemy object, it reduces this counter by 10.

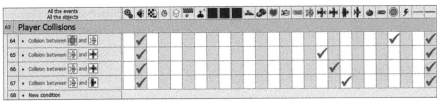

FIGURE 14.17 The Collision events.

Player's Health

Now that we have a set of events that reduce the player's health when his plane is hit by an enemy plane, we now need two conditions for the player's lives. The first condition needs to track the player's health counter, and when it reaches zero, to remove a life and then reset the counter back to full health. The second condition tracks when the player's health has reached zero and there are no more lives left, at which point it tells the game to go to Frame 3, which contains the Hi-Score table.

- Event Line 69: Insert | A group of events | Title = "Player Health" | Checked = "Active when frame starts" | OK.

- Event Line 70: Condition: Health_Bar | Compare the counter to a value | Equal | 0 | OK.

- Event Line 70: Condition: Player 1 | Compare to a player's number of lives | Greater | 0 | OK.

- Event Line 71: Condition: Health_Bar | Compare the counter to a value | Equal | 0 | OK.

- Event Line 71: Condition: Player 1 | Compare to a player's number of lives | Equal | 0 | OK.

Now onto the actions:

- Event Line 70: Action: Player 1 | Number of lives | Subtract from number of lives | 1 | OK.

- Event Line 70: Action: Health_Bar | Set Counter | 100 | OK.

- Event Line 71: Action: Storyboard controls | Jump to frame | Frame 3 – Hi-Score | OK.

- That's it for the Player Health group; the events can be seen in Figure 14.18.

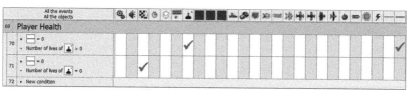

FIGURE 14.18 Player health events.

Final Game Events

We have two additional events that we need to program that are not part of the core groups. The first is a testing (debug) key, whereby we can press the ESC (escape) key and exit the game quickly. If you are running the game a lot, you might get a little bored of having to close the game window using the mouse or other key combinations if you are running in full screen. The second event we need to program is a global value to the player's current highest score at the end of the frame. This is so we can use that data in the Hi-Score table in Frame 3.

- Event Line 73: Condition: the mouse pointer and keyboard | The keyboard | Upon pressing a key | ESC.

- Event Line 74: Condition: Storyboard controls | End of frame.

Let's finish off this frame with the actions; the first is that when pressing ESC, the game will exit, and when the frame ends (which means the frame has completed everything else), it will save the score to a global value which we've already created for you called HighScore.

- Event Line 73: Action: Storyboard controls | End the application.

- Event Line 74: Action: Special conditions | Change a global value | Set | HighScore | Player 1 | Current value of score | OK.

In event line 74, you are getting the current value of the score from the Player 1 object, so you need to right-click on the objects at the bottom of the Expression Evaluator.

Global values are values that are stored at any time when the game is running and can be written to and the data retrieved from on any frame. While most data is only available in the frame in which it is placed, global values are great for storing information that you need access to at any time, such as a score or player stats.

Programming The Hi-Score

We have a small number of events needed to handle the final frame, the Hi-Score frame. This will display the player's score into a high score table, but only if it is one of the top scores.

We need the following:

- At the start of the frame, if the player has a high score, insert it into the table.
- If the player presses the ESC key, quit the game (this is just for our own testing purposes, and you can remove this from the game when required).
- Upon pressing the space bar key, take the game back to the Main frame.

So, let's get on with the final code and finish the game. First make sure you are on the Hi-Score Event Editor. This should currently have no events created.

- Event Line 1: Condition: Hi-Score | Has player a hiscore | Player 1.
- Event Line 2: Condition: the mouse pointer and keyboard | The keyboard | Upon pressing a key | ESC.
- Event Line 3: Condition: the mouse pointer and keyboard | The keyboard | Upon pressing a key | Space bar.

Finally, onto the actions.

- Event Line 1: Action: Hi-Score | Insert a hiscore | Player 1 | Current value of score | OK | "Player 1" | OK.
- Event Line 2: Action: Storyboard controls | End the application.
- Event Line 3: Action: Storyboard controls | Jump to frame | Frame 1 – Main | OK.

An example of the Events can be seen in Figure 14.19.

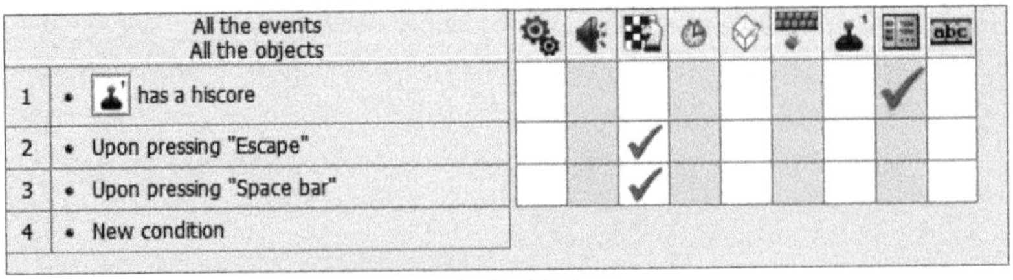

FIGURE 14.19 The Hi-Score events.

Congratulations, you have finished programming the game. Give the game a play and consider how you might improve or change it. There are lots of ways for you to make the game more interesting such as:

- Changing the damage values.

- Adding further waves of enemies.

- Adding further weapon attacks and types.

- Splitting the game into further levels and adding more bosses.

- Adding further sound effects.

- Allowing the player to enter their own name on screen for the Hi-Score table.

Summary

This chapter showed you how to create a side-scrolling shoot-'em-up game. We looked at several concepts, including scrolling, bullets, shooting from another object, and health meters. In the next few chapters, we introduce more concepts and a new game type, the platform game. With this new type of game, we will be looking at platforms, jumping, and ladders, and how to implement them in your games.

CHAPTER 15

CREATING A PLATFORM GAME

In This Chapter

- About Robin Hood
- Robin Hood – Initial Setup
- Robin Hood – Main Menu
- Robin Hood – The Game Screen
- Robin Hood – Hi-Score
- Robin Hood Programming

In this chapter, we will be creating a platform game called "Robin Hood, the Rescue of Lady Marian" (also called "Robin Hood"). It takes a number of the concepts you have already learned and builds on them, but it adds some new techniques such as jumping, ladders, and platforms. Although the game is only a single level, it shows that with some graphics and a small number of events, you can create a very interesting game in no time at all.

About Robin Hood

The game involves the story of Robin Hood, who is controlled by the player. You will need to progress up the ladders and across the platforms, navigating past enemy guards and traversing traps that are lying in wait. The game is completed when Robin reaches the top-left platform where the Sheriff and Marian are waiting for him. The story for Robin Hood goes as follows:

The evil Sheriff of Nottingham has kidnapped the love of your life, Lady Marian, and it's your task to rescue her. Unfortunately, soldiers and traps stand in your way! As you steal from the rich and give to the poor, you must collect as much gold as you can!

This game takes a similar form as the first and second games in that it has been separated into three easy-to-distinguish frames:

The Main Screen: From this screen we will launch the title frame of our game, Robin Hood.

The Game Screen: This is where the player will begin to play the game.

The Hi-Score Screen: Once the player has run out of lives, the Hi-Score frame will appear, allowing the player to enter their score.

All of the game's graphics and objects have been premade and placed into a library file to speed up the creation of the game, and to allow you to start programming rather than needing to draw images.

The game will do the following:

1. At the start of the game the main menu graphic appears, which displays the Robin Hood background image. The user will press the Space bar on the keyboard to begin playing the game.

2. The player (Robin) will appear in a forest; pressing the Shift key will make the character jump, and he can be moved by using the arrow keys. A number of obstacles and enemy soldiers are placed in the play area, and if they touch Robin, he will lose a life.

3. Once the player either has lost all three lives or has reached the platform where Marian and the Sheriff are located, the game will end and take the player to the Hi-Score screen. If the players have a high score, they can enter their name. This is using the inbuilt high-score system; personally, I'm not a fan, as it's not particularly configurable, but to get your game up and running it's nice and quick.

4. The players will be able to exit the Hi-Score screen by pressing the Space bar, which will take them back to the main menu.

Before you begin to make the game, you can check out the final game in the companion files. The executable is located in the \Game_3 folder, and the file to run is called "robinhood.exe."

The graphic library files for "Robin Hood" can be found in the folder \ Game_3\Lib. To connect Fusion to them, use the same approach as we did for the other graphic libraries.

1. Right-click on the left pane of the Library toolbar to reveal a pop-up menu.

2. Click on the New option. A dialog box will appear, allowing you to browse for the library file we need for this game. Browse the list until you see the folder where you placed the companion files.

3. Once you have found your files, find the folder \Game_3\Lib. Then, click on the OK button, enter a library name ("Robin Hood"), and then press Enter.

4. You are now ready to move down into the library and drag any files onto the play area.

Robin Hood – Initial Setup

As with the other games, we need to set up the frames you will be working with throughout this game development: one for the main screen, one for the game, and one for the Hi-Score table.

In this section, we are going to set up the Fusion file with all of the objects set in place. If you feel comfortable with this process and would like to just get programming, you can open the file Robin_Template.mfa in the \Game_3 folder. You can then skip to the Main Menu Programming section to continue with the game.

Creating the frames first, you need to create the three frames that will be used in the game.

1. Start Fusion, and then click on the File | New option in the menu. This will create the initial game program and its first frame.

2. Highlight the text "Application 1," which is the top item in the Workspace toolbar. Right-click on it and select New Frame from the pop-up menu. This will create a second frame called "Frame 2"; type in frame 2's real name, "Game." Press Enter to accept the new frame name.

3. Insert another frame and rename it "Hi-Score."

4. Now, rename frame 1 and call it "Main Menu."

We now need to make some application setting changes as you did in the first two games. We will need to change the default screen resolution, as all Fusion apps by default are set to 640 × 480.

1. Left-click on the text "Application 1," right-click and choose Rename, type in the text "Robin Hood," and then press the Enter key.

2. You will see the Application properties in the Properties window; click on the Window tab, and then change the size from 640 × 480 to 1920 × 1080. On doing so at the application level, you'll be asked to modify the frames that don't match this size. Click on the Yes button to change them.

3. Save your current progress by clicking on the Save button; as this is the first time you have saved this game, you will need to type in a name and a location for the file.

Robin Hood – Main Menu

The first thing you need to complete, as with the other two games, is the main menu, which of course is the first screen the player will see when running the game. The main menu for this game is relatively straightforward, unlike Fighter Pilot, which had a multi-menu selection; this game only requires a single button press to move forward. You will need to make your own decision on how many options in a menu you require, but when you do, always consider how easy it is for the user to navigate and understand what options are available and why they are needed.

1. Double-click on the text "Main Menu" in the Workspace toolbar to bring up the Frame Editor in the right-hand pane.

2. We now need to locate the objects in the Library that we intend to use within our game, so double-click on the text "Robin Hood" in the Library toolbar and then on the text "Robin_Hood_Lib" to bring up the specific levels (Main Menu, Game, and Hi-Score).

We are now ready to begin building our Main Menu, which will consist of two components: the background image and a title image. The title image also contains text that tells the user to press a certain key on the keyboard. We now need to place them on the play area:

3. Double-click on the text Main in the Library toolbar to reveal the four items we need to use in this level.

4. Drag and drop the object Backdrop onto the play area. Center it exactly in the frame by holding down the left mouse button, or by right-clicking on the item and choosing Align in Frame | Horz Center and Align in Frame | Vert Center from the pop-up menu.

5. Drag the Title item from the library and place it on the frame. Right-click on the item and choose Align in Frame | Horz Center and Align in Frame | Vert Center from the pop-up menu.

If you run the frame, your final placements of items on the main menu frame should look like that of Figure 15.1.

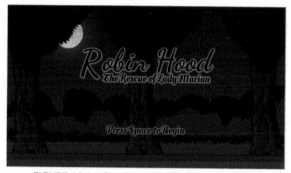

FIGURE 15.1 What the main menu should look like.

For the main menu we have a backdrop and a title text object; as there is no interaction between the two (for example, we do not fade or animate the text), we could create a single image with both assets on. This would save memory and in larger games potentially make the game run faster. Once you have your game up and running, you can consider if there are benefits to merging assets to save memory or improve performance. This is why toward the end of developing a game, performance is greatly improved, as the early stages are generally about getting the game up and running with the core game mechanics.

Robin Hood – The Game Screen

The game screen contains the majority of the objects used within the game and will take the longest to create. To manually place each object:

1. First, we need to locate the correct library objects; currently, we can see the main menu items. In the Library toolbar, click on the upward-pointing arrow to move up a level; the three frames will be listed. Double-click on the Game text to display all the objects.

2. Ensure you are on the Game frame by double left-clicking the Game frame in the Workspace Toolbar to reveal a blank Frame ready for object placement.

3. Drag the Backdrop object onto the frame and position it exactly in the frame by dragging it with the mouse, or by right-clicking on it and selecting Align in Frame|Horz Center and Align in Frame |Vert Center.

When adding objects to your game, you have to consider the order in which you place them; always start from the objects that you expect to be in the background and move forward, and this will ensure you don't need to spend a long time reordering objects later on.

The next thing we need is a lot of platform objects. These are backdrop objects that have been configured in their properties to be platforms. This means later on we can code our character to use them as platforms so that Robin doesn't fall through the game.

 It's relatively easy to create a platform game in Fusion, but the inbuilt features can be a little clunky and not always work as expected. If you want to create a specific platforming effect, you may want to create your own platform code within the Event Editor.

The first core object will be the one called Platform. This is a platform which is used as the main platform, but it doesn't have an edge to it (the left and right platforms connect to it). First, we need to put in 22 of these pieces to cover the whole of the bottom of the frame. This is the main floor of the game that the player will start from and move up the ladders, and so on. You could add these in individually, but a quicker way for placing an object that is in a row or column is to use the duplicate feature. The duplicate feature creates copies of objects, but they are the same instance (so the game sees them as a single object).

So, let's begin by adding the first platform object to the screen:

- Drag the Platform object onto the screen and then place it at 0, 990.

Now we have a single platform at the bottom left of the frame; let's duplicate it.

- Right-click on the single Platform object and select Duplicate. When the Duplicate object box appears, type in 1 for Rows and 22 for columns, then click OK.

You should now have a set of platform objects covering the whole of the bottom frame. Now we need to add all of the other platform elements. Let's start with the Platform object.

- Drag the object Platform once for each location from the library and place it at the following screen positions:

0, 234	90, 234	180, 234	528, 283
618, 283	708, 283	798, 283	888, 283
1183, 142	1271, 142	1359, 142	1651, 210
1740, 210	1830, 210	0, 520	90, 520
180, 520	270, 520	360, 520	450, 520
846, 522	936, 522	1026, 522	1116, 522
1206, 522	1296, 522	1386, 522	1741, 466
1831, 466	150, 749	240, 749	599, 747
689, 747	779, 747	869, 747	1650, 750
1740, 750	1830, 750		

The placement of the platform elements will look like Figure 15.2.

FIGURE 15.2 What the Platform items will look like after they've been placed.

We now need to place the left-hand platforms called Platform_Left.

■ Drag Platform_Left for each of the locations.

62, 749	438, 283	511, 747	758, 522
1093, 142	1565, 210	1657, 466	1566, 750

Now Platform_Right, to complete the placement of the platform tiles.

266, 234	537, 520	325, 749	978, 283
1476, 522	959, 747	1444, 142	

Next, we'll add the characters.

Lady_Marian	88, 165
Sherriff	180, 158
Bad_Guy_1	60, 450
Bad_Guy_2	1029, 214
Player_Robin	162, 915

If you run the game now, you'll notice the player falls through the floor, and the two bad guy guards will move across their platforms and return (then pause for a set amount of time). The player hasn't been coded yet, we'll get to that later, but the two guards have a path movement set to them with a loop and pause at the end.

Let's put the final elements onto the screen.

Painful_Stopper_1	354, 698
Painful_Stopper_2	1222, 476
Collectable_Gold	392, 503
Collectable_Gold	455, 503
Collectable_Gold	518, 503
Collectable_Gold	1242, 124
Collectable_Gold	1305, 124
Collectable_Gold	1368, 124
Collectable_Gold	1345, 505
Collectable_Gold	531, 969
Collectable_Gold	593, 969
Collectable_Gold	655, 969
Collectable_Gold	717, 969
Collectable_jewel	583, 265
Collectable_jewel	1002, 504

Collectable_jewel	569, 731
Collectable_jewel	1624, 194
Trap	634, 680
Trap	1271, 922
Barrel 1	740, -71
Barrel 2	1603, -80
Switch_1	1814, 688
Switch_2	8, 459
Ladder	153, 479
Ladder	929, 720
Ladder	1757, 193
Ladder	1651, 718
Ladder_Top	153, 477
Lives	14, 994
Score	1887, 1068

The placement of all the elements will look like Figure 15.3.

We have one issue that we need to resolve that may be a common issue for you when making your games in a single layer. Since the "Ladder_Top" was added after the Player_Robin character, when he appears at the top of the ladder, the top will appear over him. We added the top of the ladder so that the Bad_Guy_1 would appear behind it.

■ To fix this, right-click on Player_Robin and select Order | To front.

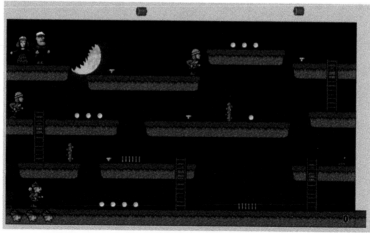

FIGURE 15.3 All of the game elements in place for the Game frame.

Robin Hood – Hi-Score

We now need to place the items for the Hi-Score frame to complete the object placement for all three frames. Once this process has been completed, you will then be able to begin the programming for the game.

1. Double-click on the text "Hi-Score" in the Workspace toolbar to bring up the blank frame.

2. We now need to locate the correct library files for this frame, so double-click on the up-pointing arrow in the Library toolbar to see all the frames, and then double-click on the text "Hi-Score." This is assuming that you haven't closed the application and reopened it since the last bit of work; if you have, you'll need to double-click on the Robin Hood text in the Library Toolbar to get to the frames.

3. Drag the Backdrop object onto the play area and center it in the middle of the frame.

4. Place the Background_Text and center it within the frame.

5. Now place the Score_Border on-screen and center this on-screen.

6. Finally, place the Hi-Score object on-screen and place it within the high score border shaded area, at a location of 646, 440.

Once you have placed the Hi-Score object, you may find it very difficult to move it by clicking on it with a mouse; this is because this type of object is always behind active objects. So, when you click on it and try to move it, you'll probably move the Score_Border object. There are two ways to solve this; you could put the Hi-Score object on a different layer, or you could click on the object in the object list in the left-hand side of the editor or the workspace toolbar and then change its positional properties that way.

You have completed the placement of all the required objects for the Hi-Score frame; when running the frame, it should look like Figure 15.4.

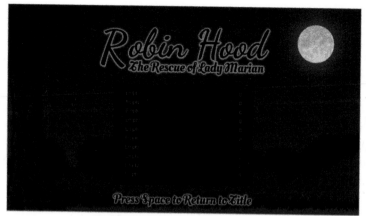

FIGURE 15.4 Layout of the Hi-Score frame.

Robin Hood – Programming

We are now ready to begin programming this game; as with the first two games, the Main Menu and Hi-Score frames are the easiest to program and require very little code. If you have any trouble with the code or don't understand the explanation, you can compare your work with the completed source code version contained in the companion files. The source code for "Robin Hood" can be found in the Game_3 folder under the directory "\ Full_Source."

Programming the Main Menu

The first of the three frames is the Main Menu, and it is the starting point of the game for the player. From this screen, the player can only proceed to play the game or exit it. The Title object placed earlier onto the play area advises the user to press the Space (Space bar) to continue, and this is the only bit of required code for this frame.

1. Double-click on the text "Main Menu" in the Workspace toolbar to take you to the first frame.

2. Click on the Event Editor icon in the toolbar to access the area where you will need to enter your code (currently, there is no code assigned, so you will only have one line, "New Condition").

3. Click on the text "New Condition" to begin entering the required code. When the New Condition dialog box appears, right-click on the The

Mouse pointer and Keyboard object to bring up the pop-up menu. Select The Keyboard and then Upon Pressing a Key, at which point a dialog box will appear asking you to press a key. Press the Space bar to record the condition into the Event Editor, which will now say "Upon Pressing the Space Bar."

With this condition, Fusion will only do something when the condition is true, which is when the user presses the Space bar. Currently, the condition would be true on pressing the key, but as there are no actions, the program would just continue without any reaction. We now need to tell the program to go to Frame 2 when the player presses this key.

4. Move to the right of the condition you just entered, and right-click when you are in the box directly below Storyboard Controls (which looks like a chessboard and a knight). From the pop-up menu, select Jump to Frame, and from the dialog that appears, double-click on Frame 2—Game (or single-click and click on OK).

You can now run the game (Run Application) to see that pressing the Space bar moves the program to the game level.

Programming the Game

Now that the main menu points the player to the game frame, we are ready to begin programming this part of the game. As the code for this section of the game is longer than the Main Menu and Hi-Score, you may want to save your work often so you can come back to it later if you want to take a break. The amount of code required to write for the game is less than you would need to do if you were writing in a traditional programming language. The reason for this is that when using Fusion's built-in engines (e.g., the picture/animation editor, path and player movement), the basic skeleton of the game can be created very quickly without any code.

 Remember, you can consult the final source code in the companion files if you get stuck.

You may have noticed that when you run the game, many items have predefined actions; for example, the bad guys start moving along a path, the coins rotate, and the barrels fall down the screen. The great thing about Fusion is that you can set up objects with particular settings and then use them in various different levels or other games. You may have to modify the settings slightly for each game you make, but on the whole, this allows for fast development time.

- Double-click on the "Game" in the Workspace Toolbar, then click on the Event Editor.

Frame Initialization

At the start of the frame, we need to initialize the player's score and the number of lives we want them to have. In this case, the score will be set to zero and the number of lives to three.

- Event Line 1: Condition: Storyboard Controls | Start of frame.

Now the two actions.

- Event Line 1: Action: Player 1: Score | Set Score | 0 | OK.

- Event Line 1: Action: Player 1: Number of Lives | Set number of lives | 3 | OK.

Basic Player Events

In this section of code, we will be looking at how to handle the basic player events such as:

- Stopping the player falling off the screen.

- Stopping the player moving off the screen to the left or right.

- Collisions with other objects – the collectables.

As usual we'll put the code into a group so that if we want to expand the game at any point, it's easy for us to identify where we can make changes to our code. We'll do all of the conditions and comments for this group before moving onto the actions.

- Event Line 2: Insert | A group of events | "Basic Player Events" | OK.

- Event Line 3: Condition: Player_Robin | Collisions | Backdrop.

- Event Line 4: Condition: Player_Robin | Position | Test position of Player_Robin | ← → (pointing outward left and right)| OK.

- Event Line 5: Insert | A comment | "Activate Lever 1" | OK.

- Event Line 6: Condition: Player_Robin | Collisions | Overlapping another object | Switch_1 | OK.

- Event Line 6: Condition: Switch_ 1 | Direction | Compare direction of "Switch_1" | 16 | OK.

- Event Line 7: Insert | A comment | "Activate Lever 2" | OK.

- Event Line 8: Condition: Player_Robin | Collisions | Overlapping another object | Switch_2 | OK.

- Event Line 8: Switch_2 | Direction | Compare direction of "Switch_2" | 16 | OK.

- Event Line 9: Insert | A comment | "Grabbing Collectables" | OK.

- Event Line 10: Condition: Player_Robin | Collisions | Another object | Collectable_gold | OK.

- Event Line 11: Condition: Player_Robin | Collisions | Another object | Collectable_jewel | OK.

That's if for the Basic Player Event conditions. Your conditions will now look like Figure 15.5.

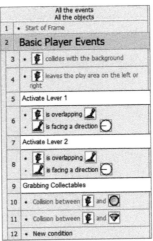

FIGURE 15.5 Current conditions.

So, let's now move onto the actions. The first couple of events only require single actions, and both will be using the Stop movement action on Player_Robin. The first two events will prevent the character falling through the Platform floor as well as leaving the screen to the left or right.

- Event Line 3: Action: Player_Robin | Movement | Stop.

- Event Line 4: Action: Player_Robin | Movement | Stop.

If you run the game now, the game is partially playable. For example, Robin now stays on-screen, you can move him left and right (it's automatically animated) and, using the platform movement that is assigned to Robin, you can jump and climb up ladders.

Next, we will work on what happens when the player collides with the switches (Switch_1 and Switch_2). This will check what direction they are facing (which has been set to left in the object properties) and then play a sound and remove the spinning spikes from the screen, allowing the player to carry on without losing a life. This provides a little bit of a basic puzzle element to the game, which could be expanded significantly.

 Remember that any audio for this game is contained in the specific game folder Game_3\Audio.

- Event Line 6: Action: Sound | Samples | Play Sample | From a file (Browse) | Lever2.wav | Open.

- Event Line 6: Action: Painful stopper 1 | Destroy.

- Event Line 6: Action: Switch_1 | Direction | Select Direction | 0 | OK.

- Event Line 8: Action: Sound | Samples | Play Sample | Lever2 | OK.

- Event Line 8: Action: Painful stopper 2 | Destroy.

- Event Line 8: Action: Switch_2 | Direction | Select Direction | 0 | OK.

For the grabbing of collectables, we need to play a sound effect when the player collides with a collectable, add to the player's score, and then destroy the collided object.

- Event Line 10: Action: Sound | Samples | Play Sample | From a file (Browse) | Blip.wav | Open.

- Event Line 10: Action: Player 1 | Score | Add to Score | 10 | OK.

- Event Line 10: Action: Collectable_gold | Destroy.

- Event Line 11: Action: Sound | Samples | Play Sample | Blip | OK.

- Event Line 11: Action: Player 1 | Score | Add to Score | 30 | OK.

- Event Line 10: Action: Collectable_jewel | Destroy.

You have now completed all of the code for the Basic Player Events section. Play the game and watch your score go up as you collect the gold and jewels and see how you can switch off the spinning spikes using the switches. Your events will now look something like Figure 15.6.

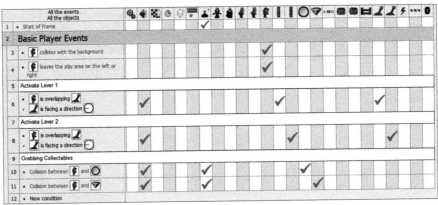

FIGURE 15.6 Current events.

Player Blinking

In the first edition book, we used what would seem to readers as quite a complex system to flash the player character when they hit an object and lost a life. This time we will manage it with five event lines. The first reason for this is that the old method doesn't work that well in a higher resolution; second, as you make more games, you'll learn different and potentially easier ways of achieving the same type of goal. Sometimes just sitting down and thinking about the different ways of completing a task can suddenly reveal a way that's much easier than you had ever considered. In Fighter Pilot, we used a second animation frame to flash the big boss aircraft once it was being destroyed. This is a perfectly reasonable way to achieve a similar effect, but for this game it is important to show you another method that is similar to the original in the first edition book. In this example, we are going to use a simple semi-transparency effect. You may not like the transparency effect; if so, you can always change it to be an animation effect instead.

For this we are going to create two groups; the first contains the check to see if the player has collided with an object that would cause them to lose a life and play a sound effect. We then need to start some data tracking of values so that the player doesn't lose a second life while they are flashing, as this is considered poor design. While the player is flashing, they are safe, and the game allows them to move into a safe area.

For the second set of events, we'll create another group which will contain events; these events can be run based on time, and as such we are going to run two separate events, one to make the player's character semi-transparent and then one setting it back to solid so that we create the flashing effect. Once we have done this 12 times (as that's the number of times we'll change the transparency), we'll disable the group, reset the tracking values, and re-enable the original player flashing group so that the player can be damaged again.

We'll create both groups first:

- Event Line 13: Insert | A group of events | Title = "Player Flashing" | OK.

- Event Line 15: Insert | A group of events | Title = "Flashing Player" | Unchecked = "Active when frame starts" | OK.

 We have created both groups first, as we'll need to create an action in the first group to disable the second group, which obviously couldn't be coded if the group didn't already exist. Additionally, when you add the first event, the event line number for the second group will change.

We have just one event to program; this is to check if the player has collided with any object in the qualifier group "Enemies" (red lightning bolt) and check if Flag 0 of Player_Robin is set to off. We use the flag to keep track of if the player is currently flashing. When the player is flashing, we set Flag 0 to on, which will prevent this running again.

- Event Line 14: Condition: Player_Robin | Collisions | Another Object | Group.Enemies | OK.

- Event Line 14: Condition: Player_Robin | Alterable values | Flags | Is Flag off? | Flag 0 | OK.

We have seven actions to generate for this one event line; we will do the following:

- Activate the group that will handle the flashing.

- Fire two events to start a timer by name.

- Play a sound effect.

- Set the Player_Robin Flag 0 to on (so that this event won't run again until it's reset).

- Set an alterable value to 0; we'll use this to confirm when the flashing has completed.

- Subtract 1 from the player's lives.

Okay, so let's get on with the actions.

- Event Line 14: Action: Special conditions | Group of events | Activate | "Flashing Player" | OK.

- Event Line 14: Action: The Timer | Fire events N times after given delay | 0s | OK | Number of Events = 12 | OK | 0s , 1/100 = 10 | OK | "Flash_1" | OK.

- Event Line 14: Action: The Timer | Fire events N times after given delay | 0s | OK | Number of Events = 12 | OK | 1/100 = 20 | OK | "Flash_2" | OK.

- Event Line 14: Action: Sound | Samples | Play Sample | From a file (Browse) | Ow.wav | Open.

- Event Line 14: Action: Player_Robin | Flags | Set On | Flag 0 | OK.

- Event Line 14: Action: Player_Robin | Alterable Values | Set | Alterable Value A | 0 | OK.

- Event Line 14: Action: Player 1 | Number of lives | Subtract from number of lives | 1 | OK.

Now that we have completed the Player Flashing group, we'll now create the events for the second group to handle the flashing of Player_Robin. For this we will need three events, two for the timers that we generated in Event Line 14. We will also need an event that keeps track of an alterable value (variable) that will increase every time we change the transparency of the player character. Once it gets to 12, we will reset the flashing and disable the group so that we can start the process again.

- Event Line 17: Condition: The timer | On event | "Flash_1" | OK.

- Event Line 18: Condition: The timer | On event | "Flash_2" | OK.

- Event Line 19: Condition: Player_Robin | Alterable values | Compare to one of the alterable values | Alterable Value A | Equal | 12 | OK.

For the actions we need to set the transparency, it runs on a range between 0 and 128. 0 means that it's fully visible, while 128 would be invisible. We will be setting it to 0 and 64. We will also add 1 each time we change it back to fully visible; we know we are running these timers 12 times, so once the alterable value equals 12, then we will reset the flag and disable the Flashing Player group.

- Event Line 17: Action: Player_Robin | Effect | Compatibility| Set semitransparency | 64 | OK.

- Event Line 18: Action: Player_Robin | Effect | Compatibility| Set semitransparency | 0 | OK.

- Event Line 18: Action: Player_Robin | Alterable values | Add to | 1 | OK.

- Event Line 19: Action: Player_Robin | Flags | Set off | Flag 0 | OK.

- Event Line 19: Action: Special conditions | Group of events | Deactivate | "Flashing Player" | OK.

Your events will now look like Figure 15.7.

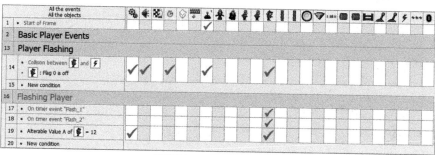

FIGURE 15.7 Current events.

Game Over

If you play the game, you'll lose a life on collision with an enemy object, but when you have run out of lives the game will continue. So, now we need to create a bit of code that checks for when the number of lives equals 0 and moves to the high score frame.

- Event Line 21: Insert | A group of events | Title = "Game Over" | OK.

- Event Line 22: Condition: Player 1 | When number of lives reaches 0.

- Event Line 22: Action: Storyboard controls | Jump to frame | Frame 3 – Hi-Scores | OK.

Rescue Complete

The final code we need for this frame is to allow the player to complete the game when they get to the last platform, which contains the Sheriff and Lady Marian. For this we will be using a simple check to see if the player has entered the area. There are multiple ways of doing this, and it could make it more interactive if you were including more levels by making the Sheriff and Lady Marian leave the screen to the left to show that they have moved to the next stage.

- Event Line 24: Insert | A group of events | Title = "Rescue Complete" | OK.

- Event Line 25: Condition: Player_Robin | Pick or count | Compare to the no of "Player_Robin" objects in a zone | Horizontal = 32 to 343 | Vertical = 50 to 240 | OK | Equal | 1 | OK.

- Event Line 25: Action: Storyboard controls | Jump to frame | Frame 3 – Hi-Scores | OK.

We have now completed all of the code for the Game frame.

Programming the Hi-Score Frame

The final part of the game is to create code to take the players from the Hi-Score frame back to the Main Menu, thus allowing them to play again. This requires only one line of code and is very similar to the code used in the Main Menu to move from Frame 1 to Frame 2.

1. Double-click on the text "Hi-Score" in the Workspace toolbar to take you to the third frame.

2. Click on the Event Editor icon in the toolbar to access the area where you will need to enter your code (currently, there is no code assigned, so you will only have one line, "New Condition").

You are now ready to enter a single event condition and action.

- Event Line 1: Condition: The mouse pointer and keyboard | The keyboard | Upon pressing a key | SPACE (Space bar).

- Event Line 1: Action: Storyboard controls | Jump to frame | Frame 1 – Main Menu | OK.

Congratulations, you have now completed the programming for the game Robin Hood. Play the game all the way through, have fun, but also consider how the game could be made better.

Summary

You have now completed your third style of game, the platform game. This game contains many ideas that you can use in your own programs. Once the player gets used to a level, it won't take him long to get to Lady Marian. Therefore, it is important to make a wide range of levels in your games with varying degrees of difficulty. This can be achieved very easily by changing the movement properties of the enemy guards or the barrels. In this game, we only have two barrels falling at a set speed and in a particular direction; you could in later levels create more barrels or alter the falling speed. Using barrels in games is a good way to make a level harder and have the player concentrate on more than just getting to a certain location. This was achieved very successfully in the game Donkey Kong, in which the player had to get to the top of the screen to rescue a certain character. Donkey Kong would throw barrels at specific times, and the player would need to jump over them to avoid losing a life. As the game proceeded, more barrels would be thrown and at different speeds and directions, thus making each level less predictable and more challenging. Using the same graphics but creating a different path movement or speed (which just involves editing the movement properties), you can change the difficulty of a level without any further programming. This makes Fusion very good for creating levels quickly and easily without needing additional amounts of programming to get it working.

CHAPTER 16

CREATING A MOUSE CLICKER GAME

In This Chapter

- About WhackEm World Tour
- WhackEm – Initial Setup
- WhackEm – Main Menu
- WhackEm – The Game Screen
- WhackEm – Hi-Score
- WhackEm – Programming

In this chapter, we will be creating a game that uses the mouse as its main way of interacting with the gameplay. The common term used is "Mouse Clicker," a game where you are required to press the mouse button quickly and efficiently to score points.

The game is called WhackEm World Tour (shortened to WhackEm) and is based on an arcade machine game/fairground game whereby an animal would pop up from a hole and you'd need to hit it with a bat (or plastic hammer). The concept also reminds me of a game that was played at my school fair in the early 1980s, whereby someone would drop a bean bag down a tube, and you would need to hit it with a stick to win a prize. It's the quick reaction time and the slight jump scare you get from waiting for something to appear that makes the game fun to play.

About WhackEm World Tour

WhackEm World Tour was originally released as an iPhone/iPad game a number of years ago, as it fit perfectly as a game with touch controls. Today it's a Web-based game and perfect for the mouse clicker type game genre. It had a number of different locations that the player would travel to and a number of weird and wonderful creatures that you would hit.

The key to the game is the timing; you wait for the creature to appear before clicking the mouse button on that object to score points. If you time it incorrectly, either too early or when the creature is going back into their hole, you will lose points.

This game takes the same form as the other three games, in that it has been separated into three easy-to-distinguish frames:

> **The Main Screen:** From this screen, we will launch the title frame of our game, WhackEm World Tour.

> **The Game Screen:** This is where the player will begin to play the game.

> **The Hi-Score Screen:** Once the timer has run out (it is set to 60 seconds), the Hi-Score frame will appear, allowing the player to enter their score (assuming it got them on the score board).

All of the game's graphics and objects have been premade and placed into a library file to speed up the creation of the game, and to allow you to start programming rather than needing to draw images.

The game will do the following:

1. At the start of the game the main menu graphics appear; this displays an animated logo, a cloud floating in the background, and a spinning world. The user will need to press the left mouse button to move to the Game screen.

2. A scene with a big lump of cheese set near the Eiffel Tower in Paris, France, will appear. The counter will start counting down and the player will see mouse-like creatures coming up from holes in the cheese. The player's aim will be to hit the mice on the head before they begin to move downward.

3. If the player times it correctly, they will get one sound effect; a graphical dizzy effect will appear over the mouse and their score will increase. If

the player times it incorrectly, then another sound will play, and the player will lose points. The player will not be able to get less than a 0 score.

4. Once the timer is complete, they will go to the Hi-Score screen and enter a high score (if they achieved one).

5. The player will be able to go back to the main menu and start the process again.

Before you begin to make the game, you can check out the final game in the companion files. The executable is located in the \Game_4 folder, and the file to run is called "WhackEm.exe."

The graphic library files for "WhackEm" can be found in the folder \ Game_4\Lib. To connect Fusion to them, use the same approach as we did for the other graphic libraries.

1. Right-click on the left pane of the Library toolbar to reveal a pop-up menu.

2. Click on the New option. A dialog box will appear, allowing you to browse for the library file we need for this game. Browse the list until you see the folder where you placed the companion files.

3. Once you have found your files, find the folder \Game_4\Lib. Then, click on the OK button, enter a library name ("WhackEm"), and then press Enter.

4. You are now ready to move down into the library and drag any files onto the play area.

WhackEm – Initial Setup

As with the other games, we need to set up the frames you will be working with throughout this game: one for the main screen, one for the game, and one for the Hi-Score table.

In this section, we are going to set up the Fusion file with all of the objects set in place. If you feel comfortable with this process and would like to just get programming, you can open the file WhackEm_Template.mfa in the \Game_4 folder. You can then skip to the Programming section to continue with the game.

Creating the Frames first, you need to create the three frames that will be used in the game.

1. Start Fusion, and then click on the File | New option in the menu. This will create the initial game program and its first frame.

2. Highlight the text "Application 1," which is the top item in the Workspace toolbar. Right-click on it and select New Frame from the pop-up menu. This will create a second frame called "Frame 2"; type in Frame 2's real name, "Game." Press Enter to accept the new frame name.

3. Insert another frame and rename it "Hi-Score."

4. Now, rename Frame 1 and call it "Main Menu."

We now need to make some application setting changes, as you did in the first three games. We will rename the default application name, then need to change the default screen resolution, as all Fusion apps by default are set to 640 × 480.

1. Left-click on the text "Application 1," right-click and choose Rename, type in the text "WhackEm," and then press the Enter key.

2. You will see the Application properties in the Properties window; click on the Window tab, and then change the size from 640 x 480 to 1920 x 1080. On doing so you'll be asked to modify the frames that don't match this size. Click on the Yes button to change them.

3. Save your current progress by clicking on the Save button; as this is the first time you have saved this game, you will need to type in a name and a location for the file.

WhackEm – Main Menu

The first thing you need to complete, as with the other three games, is the main menu, which of course is the first screen the player will see when running the game. The main menu for this game is relatively straightforward but has a few elements to place and a little bit of code for the rotation for the world graphic and logo animations.

1. Double-click on the text "Main Menu" in the Workspace toolbar to bring up the Frame Editor in the right-hand pane.

2. We now need to locate the objects in the Library that we intend to use within our game level, so double-click on the text "WhackEm" in the

Library toolbar, and then on the text "WhackEm_Lib" to bring up the specific levels (Main, Game, and Hi-Score).

We are now ready to begin building our Main Menu, which will consist of six items: the background image, an animated logo, a static logo image, a spinning world, a cloud, and some text to advise the player how to continue.

3. Double-click on the text "Main" in the Library toolbar to reveal the six items we need to use in this level.

First let's place a backdrop object, which will be the basis of the game's background.

4. Drag Brp_Background onto the Main Menu Frame and ensure it is positioned at 0,0.

Now let's place all the other items before we discuss what some of them do in more detail.

Act_Planet	993, 1044
Act_Anim_Logo	962, 318
Act_Cloud	-278, 126
Act_Logo	927, -243
Act_Text_Continue	997, 1011

Some things to know about the configuration of some of the objects:

- Act_Planet is a single graphical object that we will rotate manually using the software.

- The Act_Cloud object has a path movement already applied to it that will reset back to the start once it has reached the end of its path (it has loop enabled, also meaning that it will continue to move across the screen).

- Act_Anim_Logo has 14 frames of the logo getting bigger. It will only animate when the object is first created, which in this case is the start of the frame.

Your final placements of items on the main menu frame should look like that of Figure 16.1. If you were to run the game now, the logo would animate and then disappear, and a cloud would move from left to right and loop around once it had gone off-screen.

FIGURE 16.1 What the main menu should look like.

WhackEm – The Game Screen

The game screen contains the majority of the objects used within the game and will take the longest to create. To manually place each object:

1. First, we need to locate the correct library objects; assuming you haven't quit and reloaded since doing the Main Menu, in the Library toolbar, click on the upward-pointing arrow to move up a level; the three frames will be listed. Double-click on the "Game" text to display all the objects. If you don't see the items, you'll have to navigate via the Library "Whack-Em" option and double left-click on Game.

2. We need to change frames; double-click on the text "Game" in the Workspace Toolbar to see a blank frame ready for our objects to be placed.

3. Drag the Bdp_Backdrop object onto the frame and position it exactly in the frame by dragging it with the mouse; its X, Y position should be 0,0, so you can position it exactly or by right-clicking on it and selecting Align in Frame|Horz Center and Align in Frame |Vert Center.

Let's place all the other objects:

Act_Tower	959, 304
Act_Cover	959, 392
Act_Cloud	-184, 74
Str_Time	41, 960
Str_Score	255, 960

Act_Cheese	1137, 812
Ctr_Timer	117, 1057
Ctr_Score	310, 1057
Act_Mouse	786, 649
Act_Mouse	1011, 496
Act_Mouse	1013, 713
Act_Mouse	1258, 649
Act_Mouse	860, 894
Act_Mouse	1178, 887
Act_HoleCovers	1015, 740
Act_Hit_Dizzy	-207, 215

Just like the Main Menu, we have a cloud which has a predetermined path. We have two other objects that have animations: the Act_Hit_Dizzy, which is a bit like those comedy cartoons when a character gets hit and the birds (or in this case stars) appear over the character's head to show they are dizzy; and the Act_Mouse, which is duplicated and appears six times and has a popping up animation, a hit animation, and a shorter down animation.

The placement of the elements will look like Figure 16.2.

FIGURE 16.2 How the Game frame will look after object placement.

If you run the frame, a number of things will happen. The cloud which has already been configured with movement will move across the screen. The mice will all move upward and stay there; the reason is that all of the animations are within the "Stopped" animation set, which means this will play at the start of the frame, because the mice are not moving within the frame. We will sort this issue out within the code, so for the moment we can now move onto setting up the Hi-Score screen.

WhackEm – Hi-Score

We now need to place the items for the Hi-Score frame to complete the object placement for all three frames. Once this process has been completed, you will then be able to begin the programming for the game.

1. Double-click on the text "Hi-Score" in the Workspace toolbar to bring up the blank frame.

2. We now need to locate the correct library files for this frame, so double-click on the up-pointing arrow in the Library toolbar to see all the frames, and then double-click on the text "Hi-Score." This is assuming that you haven't closed the application and reopened since the last bit of work; if you have, you'll need to double-click on the WhackEm text in the Library Toolbar to get to the frames.

3. Drag the Bdp_Backdrop object onto the play area and place it at 0,0 so it covers the whole play area.

4. Drag and Drop the object Act_Logo and place at 981, 268.

5. Drag and Drop the Hi-Score object onto the frame and place at 709, 527.

6. Drag and Drop the Act_Text_Continue object and place at 1005, 1005.

7. Finally, drop the Act_Cloud object onto the frame and place at -130, 138 so that it's just off frame. This cloud is already animated and has a path movement applied.

You have completed the placement of all the required objects for the Hi-Score frame; when running the frame, it should look like Figure 16.3.

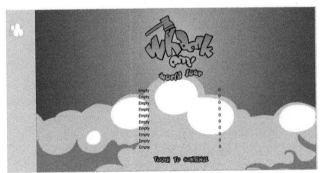

FIGURE 16.3 Layout of the Hi-Score frame.

WhackEm – Programming

We are now ready to begin programming this game; as with the first three games, the Main Menu and Hi-Score frames are the easiest to program and require very little code. If you have any trouble with the code or don't understand the explanation, you can compare your work with the completed source code version contained in the companion files. The source code for "WhackEm" can be found in the Game_4 folder under the directory "\ Full_Source."

Programming the Main Menu

The first of the three frames is the Main Menu, and it is the starting point of the game for the player. From this screen, the player can only proceed to play the game or exit.

We have a few things that we wish to achieve on this screen, as follows:

- Rotate the World.

- When the Act_Anim_Logo animation has completed, place the Act_ Logo at the correct location, which will make it look like a seamless animation.

- When the user clicks on the left mouse button, play a sound and move to the second frame.

So, let's get started with coding WhackEm World Tour.

1. Double-click on the text "Main Menu" in the Workspace toolbar to take you to the first frame.

2. Click on the Event Editor icon in the toolbar to access the area where you will need to enter your code (currently, there is no code assigned, so you will only have one line, "New Condition").

3. Click on the text "New Condition" to begin entering the required code. When the New Condition dialog box appears, click on the Special object and select Always.

   With this condition, Fusion will always run the actions to the right of the condition a number of times per second (if the frame rate were set to 30, it would run this test 30 times a second). We now need to tell the program to rotate the world.

4. Move to the right of the condition you just entered, and right-click when you are in the box directly below Act_Planet. From the pop-up menu, select Scale/Angle | Set Angle. When the Expression Evaluator appears, select Act_Planet from the list of objects, then choose Scale/Angle | Get angle. At the end of the expression, type in -1. If you wanted the object to rotate counterclockwise, you would add to the value; in this case we want to subtract from the angle. Click OK and then type in the value of 1 for maximum quality and then click on OK.

Now we need to check that the Act_Anim_Logo animation has finished playing. In this case we have a set of animations that are assigned to the Appearing animation set; that means when the object is created, it will automatically play this animation set first. Once it's finished playing, we'll need the actions to move the Act_Logo to the correct position and then make it visible (as it's set to invisible in the properties).

5. Click on the New condition text on Event Line 2. Right-click on Act_Anim_Logo and select Animation | Has an animation finished? Select Appearing from the dialog box and click on OK.

6. Now move to the right of Event Line 2 until you are directly under Act_Logo, Choose Position | Set X Coordinate, enter 962, and click OK. Right-click again on the same action box for Act_Logo and select Position | Set Y Coordinate, enter 318, and click on OK. Finally, we need to make the object appear, so again on the same action box, right-click and select Visibility | Make Object Reappear.

Now we need to work on Event Line 3, where when the player presses the left button, we play a sound and then move to the next frame.

7. Click on the New condition text and select the Mouse point and keyboard | The mouse | User clicks. Select the defaults when the dialog box appears and click on OK.

Now let's work on the actions.

8. Move across from line 3 until you are under the Sound option and select Samples | Play Sample. Click on the Browse button next to From a file, browse to the companion files, Game_4 folder, then Audio, then select Pop 2.wav and click on Open.

9. From Event Line 3, move across and then right-click directly under Storyboard controls, then Next Frame.

You can now run the game (Run Application) to see that pressing the mouse moves the program to the game level. But you'll notice that no sound is played; this is because the movement from one frame to the other is so quick the game doesn't have time to play the audio. There are two ways of fixing this; you can add a fade, or you can go into the application properties, select Runtime options, and check Play sounds over frames. In the source code version, we have changed the application properties to play sounds over frames.

Programming the Game

Now that the main menu points the player to the game frame, we are ready to begin programming this part of the game. Make sure you double-click on the "Game" text in the Workspace Toolbar to be on the correct frame, and then click on the Event Editor button to see a blank coding screen, ready to start creating your code.

There are only 11 events needed to make the game part of the game work; this is because we are using quite a few different built-in features such as animation, movement, and scoring to keep track of various items that you only need to partly worry about.

 There aren't a massive number of lines of code to get this game working, but if you need to, you can always consult the final source code to the game.

Frame Initialization

At the start of the frame, we need to set the Act_Mouse animation to stopped. All other starting values such as the timer and score counter are set with defaults within their own objects.

- Event Line 1: Condition: Storyboard Controls | Start of frame.

Now the action.

- Event Line 1: Action: Act_Mouse: Animation | Stop.

Game Events

In this section, we will be looking at all of the code handling player interaction, Mouse animations, and score. We will be doing the following:

Picking a mouse at random every second (as long as it's not animating) and then setting its animations to on.

- If you click on a mouse that is within a set of animation frames that means it's moving upward, you will get a positive sound and the score will be increased.

- If you click on a mouse that is within a set of animation frames meaning that it is moving downward, you will get a negative sound and reduce the score value.

- Reducing the timer every 1 second.

- Resetting the mice when they have gone back down.

- Checking when the timer has reached 0 so you can tell the game to go to the final high score frame.

- Always updating the score that is contained within the counter and updating the player's score global value.

Okay, so let's get the events, conditions, and actions created. First, we'll create a single event that has four conditions in it, in which that every second will pick any currently non-used Act_Mouse object so that it can be activated.

- Event Line 2: Condition: the Timer: Every | 1s | OK.

- Event Line 2: Condition: Act_Mouse: Pick or count | Pick 'Act_Mouse' at random.

- Event Line 2: Condition: Act_Mouse: Animation | Compare current frame of 'Act_Mouse' to a value | Equal 0 | OK.

- Event Line 2: Condition: Ctr_Timer: Compare the counter to a value | Greater than 0 | OK.

For the actions, we will make sure we are on the right animation set and then start the animation. When it comes to animations in Fusion, it is always best to set something to a value even if you think it is already set, as problems may occur (it can be a little flaky).

- Event Line 2: Action: Act_Mouse: Animation | Change | Animation sequence... | Stopped | OK.

- Event Line 2: Action: Act_Mouse: Animation | Start.

In the next event line we are going to check if the player has pressed the left mouse button and whether the current frame is less than frame 13, meaning the Act_Mouse is still moving upward and that the animation is still playing.

- Event Line 3: Condition: The mouse pointer and keyboard: The mouse | User clicks on an object | Left button | Single Click | OK | Act_Mouse | OK.

- Event Line 3: Condition: Act_Mouse: Animation | Compare current frame of 'Act_Mouse' to a value | Greater | 13 | OK.

- Event Line 3: Condition: Act_Mouse: Animation | Which animation of 'Act_Mouse' is playing? | Stopped | OK.

There are a number of actions we want to run on Event Line 3; first, we want to create an object, this being the dizzy animation that will appear over the Act_Mouse head, and then we'll play a sound and add 10 to the counter that keeps track of the score. For the Act_Hit_Dizzy animation, we will offset it by -130 on the Y axis so that it appears around the head of the Act_Mouse object.

- Event Line 3: Action: Create new objects: Create object | Act_Hit_Dizzy | OK | Relative to: | Act_Mouse | OK | X = 0, Y = -130 | OK.

- Event Line 3: Action: Sound: Samples | Play Sample: Pop 2 | OK.

- Event Line 3: Action: Ctr_Score: Add to counter | 10 | OK.

The next event deals with what happens if the player clicks on the Act_Mouse before the mouse has fully reached a particular animation frame. If the player has clicked the Act_Mouse at the wrong time, it will play a sound effect and reduce the player's score by 5.

- Event Line 4: Condition: The mouse pointer and keyboard: The mouse | User clicks on an object | Left button | Single Click | OK | Act_Mouse | OK.

- Event Line 4: Condition: Act_Mouse: Animation | Compare current frame of 'Act_Mouse' to a value | Lower| 13 | OK.

- Event Line 4: Condition: Act_Mouse: Animation | Which animation of 'Act_Mouse' is playing? | Stopped | OK.

The actions for this event line are as follows:

- Event Line 4: Action: Sound: Samples | Play Sample: Browse: From a file | Glass05.wav | Open.

- Event Line 4: Action: Ctr_Score: Subtract from counter | 5 | OK.

Now we need to create a set of conditions which check for when the Act_Mouse object is moving downward. The actions for this will be the same as the previous event; we'll play a sound and subtract 5 from the player's score.

- Event Line 5: Condition: The mouse pointer and keyboard: The mouse | User clicks on an object | Left button | Single Click | OK | Act_Mouse | OK.

- Event Line 5: Condition: Act_Mouse: Animation | Which animation of 'Act_Mouse' is playing? | Down | OK.

The actions:

- Event Line 5: Action: Sound: Samples | Play Sample | Glass05.wav | OK.

- Event Line 5: Action: Ctr_Score: Subtract from counter | 5 | OK.

The next event will just be to run a condition every 1 second. This is so we can count down the timer from 60 seconds down to 0 (to end the level).

- Event Line 6: Condition: the Timer: Every | 1 Second | OK.

It's a simple action, we just subtract 1 each time the event is true (every 1 second).

- Event Line 6: Action: Ctr_Timer: Subtract from Counter | 1 | OK.

We will now have an event that will check to see if the animation of the Act_Mouse has risen; we will do that by checking if the animation has stopped and is greater or equal to a particular frame number (in this case, 25). This event will be used to start the animation to move down.

- Event Line 7: Condition: Act_Mouse: Animation | Has an animation finished? | Stopped | OK.

- Event Line 7: Condition: Act_Mouse: Animation | Compare current frame of 'Act_Mouse' to a value | Greater or Equal | 25 | OK.

For the action, we need to change the animation sequence to down and then start the animation.

- Event Line 7: Action: Act_Mouse: Animation | Change | Animation sequence | Down | OK.

- Event Line 7: Action: Act_Mouse: Animation |Start.

Event Line 8 is all about resetting the Act_Mouse animation once it has gone up and come back down; otherwise, it won't be available for selection again.

- Event Line 8: Condition: Act_Mouse: Animation | Has an animation finished? | Down | OK.

For the actions (which all revolve around Act_Mouse), we need to change the animation sequence, stop it so that we don't have it automatically starting, and restore the animation sequence, which effectively sets it back to frame 0.

- Event Line 8: Action: Act_Mouse: Animation | Change | Animation sequence | Stopped | OK.

- Event Line 8: Action: Act_Mouse: Animation | Stop | OK.

- Event Line 8: Action: Act_Mouse: Animation | Restore | Animation Sequence.

Event Line 9 deals with destroying the Act_Hit_Dizzy animation that appears above the Act_Mouse; we do this by checking if the animation has finished. The animation is short, so we know that it will disappear pretty quickly before the Act_Mouse will go into its down animation.

- Event Line 9: Condition: Act_Hit_Dizzy: Animation| Has an animation finished? |Stopped | OK.

- Event Line 9: Action: Act_Hit_Dizzy: Destroy.

Now we need to check for when the timer has reached 0, as we'd then move to the next frame.

- Event Line 10: Condition: Ctr_Timer: Compare the counter to a value... | Equal | 0 | OK.

- Event Line 10: Action: Storyboard Controls: Next Frame.

Our final condition and action ensure that every second, the score the player gets into the Ctr_Score object is placed into the global player score. For getting the score, we'll need to access the Ctr_Score object in the Expression Evaluator.

- Event Line 10: Condition: Special: Always.

- Event Line 10: Action: Player 1: Score | Set Score | Ctr_Score | Current value | OK.

That's it for the game's code; your conditions and actions will now look like Figure 16.4.

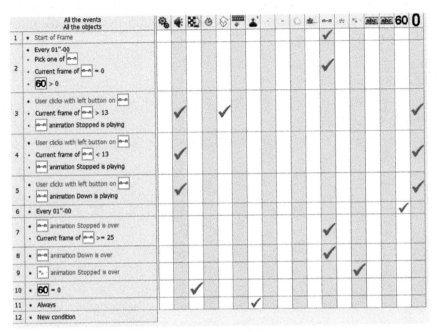

FIGURE 16.4 Game frame's conditions and actions.

Programming the Hi-Score Frame

The final part of the game is to create code to take the player from the Hi-Score frame back to the Main Menu, thus allowing them to play again. This requires only one line of code and is very similar to the code used in the Main Menu to move from Frame 1 to Frame 2.

1. Double-click on the text "Hi-Score" in the Workspace toolbar to take you to the third frame.

2. Click on the Event Editor icon in the toolbar to access the area where you will need to enter your code (currently, there is no code assigned, so you will only have one line, "New Condition").

You are now ready to enter a single event condition and action.

■ Event Line 1: Condition: The mouse pointer and keyboard | The mouse | User Clicks | Left Button | Single click | OK.

- Event Line 1: Action: Storyboard controls | Jump to frame | Frame 1 – Main Menu | OK.

Congratulations, you have now completed the programming for the game WhackEm World Tour. Play the game all the way through, have fun, but also consider how the game could be made better.

Summary

You have now completed your fourth and final style of game, the mouse clicker game. Hopefully all four games will have given you some inspiration and ideas that you can use in your own games. There are many different types of games you can create with Fusion, so you may want to take a little time to think about the type of game you want to make.

CHAPTER 17

Bug Finding And Fixing

In This Chapter

- What Are Bugs?
- Why Find Them?
- Bug Fixing and Product Releases
- The Debugger
- Testing Run-Through

In this chapter, we look at bugs and crashes with your games, how to find them, and how to fix them. No matter how hard you try, bugs will appear in any program you write, but it is very important to ensure that you minimize them before you distribute your game. We will go over the tool Fusion provides to give you the best chance of squashing those nasty bugs—the Debugger.

What Are Bugs?

Computers, and the software used to run them, are made by humans. Unfortunately, no matter how hard we try, we cannot prevent problems with incorrect code or design issues from happening. These issues can cause random crashes and data corruption at any time and can be infuriating for the user. Programmers and hardware designers are human, and thus subject to error, and can unwittingly introduce bugs into programs. This will also be true when you are programming and making games in Fusion. Fusion uses a special programming language, and bugs will be introduced because of assigning incorrect data from one object into another, or just wrong coding in the Event Editor. You, too, will probably introduce bugs into your software; the key is making sure you look for them and try to remove them where possible.

If you were able to reproduce a bug a couple of times, that would be of great concern, as you can be sure that if you multiply that by thousands of users (or for AAA games, in the millions of users), you'll definitely have players seeing the issue consistently.

Why Find Them?

A great game can appear average or poor based on the frequency and location of the bugs in it. If you are not looking to make a game to sell, then it's important to note that the perception from your end users (the players) will be the same; the more frequently the bugs appear, the lower they will rate the software. You may have spent a lot of time developing your game, so you probably want it to be as good as it can be. Although the development of a product can be difficult and complex, the last few months of game development can be the hardest. Your game is nearly complete, and you are excited to try to get it online (or to your friends) as quickly as possible. The problem with this is that you might become less concerned about the product in the last days of development than when you first started out, especially if development has been long and difficult. If you are just releasing games to your friends or online as freeware, you should still try to get rid of any bugs, as the negative feedback from users will probably make the entire project feel like a waste of your time. If you are making a game to sell online, you will definitely need to allow time to remove any bugs you know about.

Bug Fixing And Product Releases

There are a number of areas in which you might consider fixing bugs or need to ensure that all bugs have been removed. This can be broken up into a number of distinguishable phases. Although based on normal product releases, you should still follow this process even if your games are meant for family and friends only.

General Bug Fixing: When you are creating your game, you will also test to see if it works. This is just to confirm that you have completed that section of code and can move on to the next part of the program. You may, at this stage of development, come across a bug that stops this section working significantly enough for you to confirm that the functionality is available by removing the code issue. There may also be issues with the look and feel and just general stability. All of this will be done while you are programming the main part of the game, but you will not be going out of your way to find problems.

Alpha Version: When the product is in a suitable condition and much of the functionality has been implemented, you can then say your product is at version Alpha. This means that it is still unstable, but many of the options work (although not all), and it has the general look and feel of the final product. The product may still have some major bugs and issues, but this is the first version considered suitable enough to show people the work in progress (even if you are a hobbyist creator). The Alpha is used to get feedback on how the product sticks together and if the interface works well. This is the final stage of development before the product will be locked down with regard to features and its look and feel. The main issue with development discussed previously is that you could continue to add new features and never actually release a product. The end of the Alpha stage is an indication that this is the beginning of the final program and its functionality. At the end of the Alpha process, you may have feedback about how the product looks and if the interface works well. After considering all the comments, making final decisions about the interface, and incorporating those changes in the product, you enter the Beta stage.

Beta Version: The Beta stage is where the product is fully locked down with regard to functionality, look, and feel. This stage means that all that needs to be done is to remove any bugs within the program. You can give this version to more testers, who will then try to locate any problems within the game. Beta testers could be a group of friends or anyone who downloads the game from your Website and submits feedback.

Post Release: Once the product has been released, people will be using the game on configurations you may not have expected or ways even the Beta testers didn't consider. There are generally bugs to be fixed once the product is available to a larger amount of people. These types of bugs need to be fixed as quickly as possible, and you will need to upload a patch; you may also have to upload a new version of your game.

 Beta testers are an essential resource for finding bugs within your games. Beta testers will try things that you may not have considered.

The Debugger

One of the key features in Fusion for finding bugs is the Debugger. This functionality allows developers to more easily search out program bugs within their games. The Debugger is very much in line with code-based programming languages and offers many features to make the developer's life much easier. Every program you make contains data information; for example, the current number of lives the player has, the location of the spaceship on the screen, and so forth. All this information is essential if you want to fix issues with your program. The Debugger allows you to access all these details so you can spend more time developing your programs rather than bug finding.

Starting the Debugger

To start the Debugger, you will need to have a program running within Fusion. Once you have opened one of your games, if you run the frame or the entire game, the Debugger will appear in the left side or corner of your screen (depending on how you use it), as shown in Figure 17.1 and Figure 17.2.

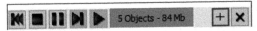

FIGURE 17.1 The Debugger open and ready to use.

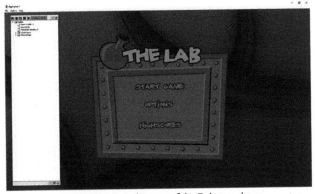

FIGURE 17.2 A close-up of the Debugger bar.

There are a number of buttons and functionality you can access:

The Debugger may start either collapsed or expanded. To change its state between the two, you can click on the "+" or "-" icon on the right-hand side of the Debugger. If you click on the "+" icon on the Debugger bar, it will expand the amount of information available to you. A default set of the program data can be viewed, such as current frame, frame rate, global values, and strings. The expanded Debugger can be seen in Figure 17.3. To collapse it back, you need to click on the "−".

FIGURE 17.3 The Debugger expanded to reveal more information.

- The first button on the Debugger bar—Rewind (the line with the left-pointing arrow)—signifies that the program will start from the beginning of the frame once clicked. This is very useful if you are trying to track a bug and want to watch what is being changed (something we will detail shortly); you can repeat the process until you find the problem.

  There is an example of how the Go to Start of Frame button works in the companion files in a folder called "Debugger." The example is called "debugger1"; open this file in Fusion to see how it works.

- The square icon on the Debugger bar is the Stop button. This stops the frame and program from running and closes the running game and the Debugger.

- The third icon is the Pause button, which will pause your program (i.e., nothing will happen on the game's playfield) until you press Play to start it back up. This will allow you to get to a specific point in the program and then check the result of the current data being stored by Fusion.

- The fourth icon from the left looks like a grayed-out, right-pointing arrow. This is the Next Step button, which allows you to step through your game code one line at a time. To use this function, you will need to pause the program first using the Pause button mentioned previously. This is a very useful option if you want to slowly see what changes are made to your program.

■ The fifth icon is the Play button; once you have paused the program, you would use this to start it back in real time (playing at normal speed). The display in the middle of the Debugger bar shows two bits of useful information: how many objects are being used in the current frame, and the number of bytes for the total memory used by the application.

The default information shown within the expanded Debugger is for the basic application level. What this means is that if you create a blank game with no content, this information is always present. If you add any global values or strings, you will be able to expand the associated folders (if you don't have any, then the folders will not react to your clicking to expand them).

The frame number is the current frame running within the game. Time is the actual time the frame has been running (very important to remember that the time is reset between frames). You also have another expandable folder, which allows you to see all of the global values used within the program. At the bottom of the expanded Debugger are three more buttons that you can use to add and remove additional items. The first icon is to add additional items, the second is to delete any items (if you only have system to begin with, it will delete that group), and the third is an "Edit" button for when you want to edit specific data entries.

Although the time in each frame is reset in the System folder, you can create an object that saves the amount of time the entire application has been running, which you can then add to the Debugger and view it.

Adding Items to the Debugger

You now want to add an item to the Debugger so you can watch it and see what happens to it when your game is running.

Open the game "The Lab" in the companion files. You'll find it in the folder \Debugger, with the filename "debugadd.mfa".

1. Run the game by pressing the Run Application button on the toolbar. This will start the game and open the Debugger. Click on the Start Game button within the game to move to Frame 2.

2. Click on the Add Object to Debugger button, which will open the dialog box. Expand the Counter Objects folder to reveal what objects are contained within. Click on the score line within the Counter objects and then click on OK to add it to the Debugger. An example of this dialog is as shown in Figure 17.4.

3. We also want to watch the number of lives when playing the game. Click on the Add objects icon in the Debugger, then expand the Live objects folder, then select the Lives item and click on OK.

4. Begin to play the game, and notice that the score changes every time you hit a block. The number of live objects will also reduce every time the ball goes out of the play area on the right side of the screen. You can see the extra data as shown in Figure 17.5.

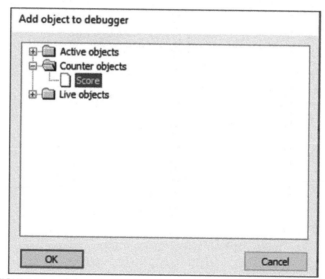

FIGURE 17.4 Click on the "+" signs to see what you can add to the Debugger.

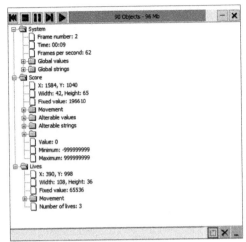

FIGURE 17.5 Once an object is added to the Debugger, more details will be shown.

It is important to note that for each frame, you will need to set up the objects you want to watch. Once you move frames, the Debugger resets the items within its list to just System. This is because each frame will have different objects allocated to it, so it needs to do this to refresh the list.

Testing Run-Through

To ensure that you fully understand the Debugger and the power it has, the following is a short run-through of a program that doesn't have a bug but some configuration that has been incorrectly set. This will allow you to see what a great feature the Debugger is, and how it can fix bugs in your code and code you may have forgotten to implement.

1. Start Fusion.

2. Click on the menu option File and then Open to load a Fusion file into the program.

3. Browse the companion files.

Locate the Debugger folder, locate a file called "debugtest.mfa," and double-click on it so it loads into Fusion.

4. Click Run Application to make Fusion start the game with the Debugger.

5. If the Debugger information is collapsed, click on the "+" sign on the Debugger bar to expand the view. Click on the game's "Start Game" text, which will take us to the second frame, where the game will start.

If you expand the System option within the Debugger, you will see that the game is on Frame 2, the time is incrementing upward, and the frames per second is changing rapidly. This shows that the game is currently running and is awaiting a key press to launch the ball.

6. Click on the Pause button within the Debugger bar to pause the program. This will mean that you cannot make the ball move, as the code has effectively stopped running until you press Play again.

7. Click the Add Object to Debugger button to bring up the dialog box. You will see three items; expand the Counter objects. Once you have done this, highlight the Score object and click OK. Click on the Add button again and do the same for the Live object (expand the Live object, highlight it, and then click on OK).

Notice that the score is at 0, which is expected, as the game hasn't started yet (if there is a score value above 0, then you know it's not being reset correctly). The player hasn't begun to destroy any of the blocks on the playfield and so has no score. You may also notice that the Lives object is currently set to 1. By default, the lives object is set to 3, and it's up to you to change this to a value that you require for your game. In this game the value should be 3. So now you know something is changing this value from the default 3 to 1. As we have started the game and paused it, we can ignore lots of the event code to do with collisions and collectables. If you were to continue playing the game, if you lost one life, the game would be over. The great thing about the Debugger is that we can actually edit the data while the game is paused. This allows us to test the game with different data results without needing to come out, reprogram, and then start the debugging process again.

8. Click on the Number of Lives object in the Debugger dialog box, and you will see that the Edit button is no longer grayed out.

9. Click on the Edit button, which will bring up the Edit dialog box. Type in the number "3," which is the number of lives the player has at game startup.

Immediately, the program is updated with the new results, and the Number of Lives graphic now has three little circles in it (representing each life).

10. If you now press play in the Debugger and play the game and lose a life, the game plays correctly, so close the Debugger and the game and go into the Event Editor. We know that the value is set at the start of the level, so the very first event is "Start of Frame," and you can see under the action that it is setting the lives to 1. So, you can either delete the event (if you are okay with the default value of 3), or you can amend the value to a value that you feel is right for this game by updating the action.

Although this is a very simple example, hopefully it proved how powerful and easy the Debugger is to use. You can now, in one screen, look for a bug, see if you can rectify it, and monitor the results.

Summary

Although bug fixing may be one of the last things you do in the development of your game (and one of the last things on your mind), its importance cannot be overstated. Ensure that you leave enough time between the end phases of your product and its release to get rid of any bugs that might be hiding. You won't be thanked if the program runs smoothly, but you will certainly receive many complaints if there are serious bugs in your game. If you are selling your own games online, a customer who has purchased or tried one game from you that worked badly is unlikely to come back and download another, so quality and minimizing bugs are essential. Additionally, when releasing on different game stores, some have a refund policy based on time. So, if say within two hours a user plays your game and doesn't like what they see within two hours, they can get a refund back. If your game is buggy, it's more likely that you'll see an increase in refunds because of bugs in your game. If you want to make many games and want to increase your user base, it's very important that the user perception of your products remains positive.

CHAPTER 18

ADDITIONAL CONCEPTS

In This Chapter

- Menus
- Web Browser Games
- Icons

In this chapter, we look at additional concepts you might consider for your own games. We'll look at menus, which are standard functionality on games that run within an application window; uploading a game to the Internet so you can create your own online games site; and how to create your own game icons.

 Some of the features mentioned here are not available or will be grayed out in the free version of Fusion 2.5, but they are included for completeness.

Menus

A number of games you can play within an application window contain a standard menu system to allow the player to configure certain aspects of the game, anything from changing keyboard controls to viewing a help file. An example of a menu system can be seen in Figure 18.1, which is the default menu contained in the game "The Lab," provided with this book.

FIGURE 18.1 A menu system in "The Lab."

It is important to state that in many games, designers and programmers implement some of the text menu options we discuss here actually within the game window, rather than in a menu bar; they do this by using a combination of buttons, graphics, and text.

Basic Menu Configuration

When you create a basic game within Fusion, by default there is a menu already preconfigured, without any settings changes. The basic menu system has a number of options predefined, which are separated under three headings: File, Options, and Help. These menu options will work automatically in the games you create, and although they might not be exactly what you want, they are a good starting point.

File

New: Starts the program afresh by reloading the game.

Password: If you have configured a password for a frame, you can enter it here to jump immediately to that frame position. This option will be disabled by default unless you specify a password in the Storyboard Editor.

Pause: Pauses the game in progress.

Players: Configures the default player controls (keyboard and joystick).

Quit: Exits the game.

Options

Play Samples: By default this is enabled, so any samples expected to play within the game will be heard on the speakers; by unchecking this, all samples will be prevented from playing.

Play Music: The same as Play Samples, except it applies to any music that will play within the game.

Hide the Menu: If you don't want to see the menu while playing the game, you can hide it by selecting this option; it can be brought back by pressing the F8 key.

Help

Contents: Disabled by default, this allows you to assign a help file to the menu option or shortcut key (a range of file formats, including hlp, txt, wri, and doc).

About: Selecting this will bring up an information box that details the product name and any copyright message.

Menu Dialog

To change the menu options used within your games, you will need to access the Menu Configuration dialog, which is available via the Application Properties.

1. Start Fusion and click on the option File | New on the menu to create a new game file.

2. Click on "Application 1" in the Workspace toolbar to bring up the Properties sheet. Within the Application Properties sheet, click on the Window tab to bring up options relating to the menu. You should now see a Properties sheet as shown in Figure 18.2.

3. Under the section Menu, you will see two check boxes and an Edit button. If you want to include a menu bar, leave the Menu Bar option selected, and if you would like the menu to appear when the game is started, leave the second option at its default.

4. Click on the Edit button to open the Menu Editor. You will now see a menu dialog as shown in Figure 18.3.

FIGURE 18.2 Application properties sheet.

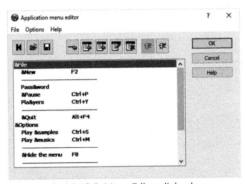

FIGURE 18.3 Menu Editor dialog box.

The top of the dialog box has an example of what your menu will look like when running the game. Below that is a set of buttons that allow you to configure your menu system, and under that are the text commands that make up the actual menu options. The menu buttons consist of:

Reset Menu: This will reset any changes made to the menu back to its original settings.

Load a Menu: Load a menu from a file, allowing you to create an original menu and use it in multiple games without needing to recreate it each time.

Save a Menu: Save a menu so it can be used later in the current or future programs.

Insert a Separator: Creates a line separator between menu options, useful to group similar items together.

Insert an Item: Explanation in sentence case with no end punctuation.

Insert an Item from the Default Menu: If you have created your own menu system but would like to take advantage of some of the default menu options, you can choose which ones to add.

Edit Current Item: Edit the currently selected line item (you will need to left-click on an item that you want to edit before clicking this button).

Delete an Item: Remove an item from the menu.

Push Left: You can create various levels of menus that when selected will bring up another menu to the right of that option. This allows you to move the menu option higher or lower in the menu order.

Push Right: You can move a menu item to the right of its current position using this button.

Editing a Menu

To edit a current menu's options, you can double left-click on the item or single left-click to highlight it and select the Edit Current Item button. After doing so, you will be presented with the Setup Application Menu option, which can be seen in Figure 18.4.

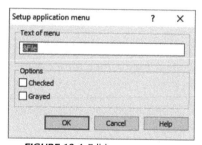

FIGURE 18.4 Editing a menu entry.

Text of Menu: Type in the text you want to appear in the menu system. By using an &, you are telling Fusion that it should underline the next available letter in the menu; in this example, the "N" would be underlined. This is to tell the user that he can access this option using a shortcut key (a key combination configured under the Accelerator section).

Checked: This will place a check next to the word in the menu and is useful for options that can be switched on or off (e.g., in the default menu, the user can turn the music on and off).

Grayed: A check in this box will gray out the option in the menu; when an item is grayed, it is effectively switched off and cannot be selected.

Bitmap: By clicking on the Edit button, you will enter the Picture Editor and be able to create a button for your menu option. This is to allow users to create icon-based menus (first seen in Windows XP), in which many have graphic images next to the menu text.

Accelerator: Allows you to configure shortcut keys to menu options, which are used in many types of games and applications to allow you to quickly access certain options. A default example would be that to quit a Fusion game, you can use the Alt key and F4 keys together to exit the program.

Menu Walkthrough

We are now going to change the default menu—which currently has the three options File, Options, and Help—and add a fourth entry called Book. Under the book item, we will create a number of entries, including one item with an image, a separator line, and two menus on the right of another item. An example of what the menu will look like is shown in Figure 18.5.

1. Start Fusion, and then click on the File | New option from the menu to create a new program file.

2. Double-click on the text "Frame 1" in the Workspace toolbar to open the Frame Editor.

3. Click on "Application 1" in the Workspace toolbar to bring up the Properties sheet. Within the Application Properties sheet, click on the Window tab to bring up options relating to the menu.

4. Under the section Menu, click on the Edit box to begin changing the configuration of the menu.

5. Use the scroll bar to scroll down until you see a blank space below the word "&About." Left double-click on the blank line, or single-click to highlight, and click on Insert an Item.

6. When the dialog box appears, type "&Book" in the Text of Menu edit box, and then click on the OK button. Click on the Push Left button to move the Book item to the left; this will make it into its own menu option rather than an entry under Help.

7. Scroll down again, double-click on the blank line under the &Book entry, type in the word "About," and then click on the OK button. Looking at the menu, you will notice that a new menu option has appeared.

8. Single-click on the blank line. Click on the Insert a Separator option to add a straight line under the About item.

9. Double-click on the blank line under the Separator item. Type in the text "Links" and click on the OK button.

10. Double-click on the blank line under the Links item, type in the text "Book," and then click on the OK button.

11. Double-click on the blank line under Book, type in the text "Publisher," and click on the OK button.

12. We now need to move both the Book and Publisher items to the right of the Links item. Select the Book line (which is just below the Links line) by single-clicking on it. Then, click on the Push Right button. Do the same for the Publisher item.

13. Double-click on the blank line under Publisher, type in the text "Contents," and then click on the Edit button in the Bitmap section. You will now enter the Picture Editor, select the Fill tool, and select a color. Fill the small square image with a single color, and then click on the OK button. Then, click the OK button again to return to the Menu Editor. Ensure Contents is highlighted, and then click on the Push Left button to place it in the correct sequence in the menu system.

14. Your menu is now complete, so click OK to save the menu configuration to Fusion (you will still need to save the game file to ensure all changes are kept).

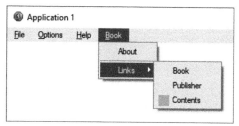

FIGURE 18.5 Reconfigured menu with some new options.

To use the menu you just created, you will need to use the Event Editor to access its options and react to the user selections.

Programming for the Menu

If you want to make changes to the default menu, you will need to create conditions and actions so that when a player selects a specific menu option, the game will react in a certain way. All menu configuration is done via the Event Editor. When adding a condition, from the dialog box you would choose the Special conditions object (the object that looks like two cogs connected to each other), and then from the pop-up menu, you would choose the Application menu to pick relevant conditions for what you want to be tested. In the following walkthrough, we are going to use the menu we just created and create a condition so that when the player selects Book | About, the game will display some text. This is a very simple test but should give you a view into how straightforward it is to add an action to a menu selection.

1. Start Fusion, and then click on the File | Open option from the menu. When the Open dialog box appears, browse to your companion files and locate the file "Menu1," which is stored in the Menus folder. Choose this file, and then click on OK to open the file.

 The file will load into the free version of Fusion but will not work; you need the full version to make changes to the menu system.

2. Double-click on the text "Frame 1" in the Workspace toolbar to open the Frame Editor. Click on the Event Editor button to begin programming the menu system.

3. Click on the "New Condition" text to open the New Condition dialog box. Right-click on the Special conditions object, and from the pop-up menu, select Application Menu | Has an Option Been Selected? You will now see a dialog box as shown in Figure 18.6.

4. Click on the Click Here button to see the already created menu and choose Book | About. You will now see an event that says, "Menu option 'About' selected."

5. Move to the right of the event until you are directly under the String object, right-click, and choose Visibility, Make Object Reappear from the pop-up menu.

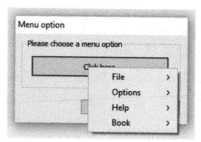

FIGURE 18.6 Menu option selector.

 If you get stuck you can find a completed version of this example, called Menu1_Complete.mfa, in the \Menus folder.

Web Browser Games

Playing games over the Internet is great fun, but it has a number of uses for someone who is making games for fun or as an independent developer.

It's an easy and quick way to add additional content to your site to provide a reason for people to come back.

- You can use it as a marketing tool, to put your message across in a game.

- You can showcase your work.

- You can provide players with a way to see and play a single level of your game without needing to download a demo version of it.

The most popular format for creating Web-based games is HTML5, which is a general standard used across the world. This replaces many other formats that were available that might have required their own plug-in, such as Adobe Flash and Clickteam's Vitalize. It means users don't have to download (or regularly update) a separate installer to run the games, as they will run through the Web browser they are using. Any system that reduces the need for a user to install a plug-in means a greater chance they'll at least take a look at the game. Using a plug-in would mean there were additional hoops for the user to jump through and would mean a loss of some users who might not want to install the latest version or install it at all.

There are a couple of different options to create a game for the Web. If you are using the demo of Fusion, you can create a version of your game using the built-in exporter HTML5; this is the only exporter available to you.

If you are using the full version of Fusion, then you'll need to change the Build Type in the application properties from the default of the Windows EXE application to HTML5.

Before You Create a Game for the Web

With the free version of Fusion, you will be able to create an HTML5 game, but if you are running the full version of Fusion, you will need to install JRE or JDK.

- JRE: Java Runtime Environment.

- JDK: Java Development Kit.

You'll get a message advising you of this fact when you try to build your HTML5 game, as shown in Figure 18.7.

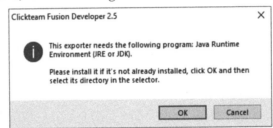

| Clickteam Fusion Developer 2.5 | ✕ |

This exporter needs the following program: Java Runtime Environment (JRE or JDK).

Please install it if it's not already installed, click OK and then select its directory in the selector.

OK   Cancel

FIGURE 18.7 Java installation message dialog for the full version.

Go to a Web browser search engine and type in JDK; you will be looking for a link taking you to the Oracle Website, the site of the owners of Java.

Alternatively, go to:

 https://www.oracle.com/java/technologies/javase-downloads. html

Find the link to the JDK download; download and install as per the instructions. You will need to select the correct version for the operating system that you are using.

Creating a Game for the Web

The first thing you need to do to be able to create a game on the Internet is to save the game in a format that can be uploaded to a Website. This format is called HTML5 and is a file that any Web browser can use. Once you have created a game with HTML5 format, on using the correct settings you will be able to run it via a Web browser.

To be able to test a game that you've converted to HTML5, you will need to either install a local Web server or upload your game to a Website (using any tool that supports FTP/SFTP, depending on your Website provider). If you want to test your game without the need to do this, you can use the standard "Run Application" button.

1. Start Fusion, and then click on the File | Open option from the menu. When the Open dialog box appears, browse to your companion files and locate the file "Web1," which is stored in the \Web folder. Choose this file, and then click OK to open the file.

Web1.mfa provides a copy of the Fighter Pilot game to make into an HTML exported file.

2. Click on the application name, which in this case is application 1. Once you click on this, the Properties toolbar will display the Application settings as shown in Figure 18.8.

3. Depending on the version of the software that you are using (the free or full version), the build type needs to read HTML Application.

4. On Project directory, select the folder where you want the game to be built.

5. Enter the Project name; in this case it's called "Pilot."

6. To build the file, go to the File menu and select File | Build | Application. A pop-up box will appear with the details you've just entered. Click on OK to build or make changes (then click on OK when ready).

Congratulations, you have now created your HTML5 files, which are ready to be played on the Internet.

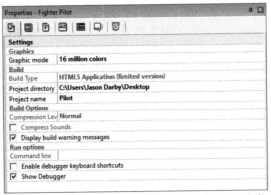

FIGURE 18.8 Application Properties configured for a Web file.

Uploading a Game to Your Website

This section will give some basic information about how to get your game onto the Internet. It won't be able to go into great detail, as it would depend on your own personal setup and configurations, as well as what Web hosting you have available to you. Please consult your own Webhosting site for more information.

We've created our test files, and now we need them on our Website. The first thing you will need is an FTP application, which will allow you to connect to your site and copy files across. FTP stands for File Transfer Protocol and is the standard by which data from a computer can be uploaded. Another type is SFTP (Secure File Transfer Protocol), which some sites may require you to use, which encrypts the data as it's transferred to prevent hackers from reading the information.

In the case of this book, an FTP account had to be created with the Website provider for the Website domain that is being using for this book; it was done via the Web provider's Website tools. The free FTP program called Filezilla (other programs are available) was downloaded and the Fusion files created previously were uploaded.

They were uploaded into a folder on the Website, which then translates to a Web address as follows:

 http://www.jasondarbybooks.com/MakeAmazing/WebExample/ Pilot/

My Web host will automatically run any file called index.html that is contained within the folder. You could also add index/html to that link and it would also run.

When you visit the link provided you will see a landing page, which looks like Figure 18.9; this is the page that you'll see while it is loading your game. Once it has completed loading, it will appear as it does in the Fusion Editor, as shown in Figure 18.10. You will need to click on the page to be able to interact with it.

FIGURE 18.9 The HTML5 loading screen.

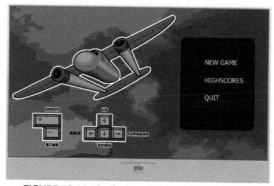

FIGURE 18.10 The final loaded game in the browser.

One of the biggest issues you will have with Fighter Pilot is that it uses the SHIFT key to fire the main weapon. As you can imagine, as this is a shoot-'em-up, the player will be hitting this key quite fast, but in Windows 10 this is a problem, as hitting the SHIFT (or a combination of other keys) quickly will initiate the sticky keys alert box as shown in Figure 18.11. This will pause the game, but once you have clicked on the dialog box and removed the message, this will actually cause the game to play incorrectly. This is a perfect example of why you need to test your game, if possible on different types of machines. The solution to fix this issue is quite simple; either use a different key that isn't a sticky key as the fire button or turn off the sticky key on your machine. The best option is of course to use a non-sticky key, as you cannot be sure that all users will have disabled this option.

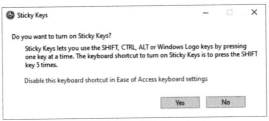

FIGURE 18.11 The sticky keys alert box.

Icons

When you run a game within an application window or look at the executable of any game you've created by browsing the folder in which it is stored, you will see a graphic icon. These icons are created to differentiate the game from others on your machine, as shown in Figure 18.12. There is a default set of icons premade within Fusion that can be changed to better represent your games.

To amend these icons:

1. In the Workspace Properties toolbar, click on the topmost object/text line (the application name) to reveal the Application Properties in the Properties tab.

2. Click on the About tab in the Properties toolbar.

3. Click on the line that represents Icon, and then click on the Edit box that appears.

4. The Picture Editor appears with a selection of icons you can amend. The icons are for different build types and are displayed with their relevant sizes. An example of the icons used in the final version of "The Lab" is shown in Figure 18.13.

**TheLab
Final.exe**

FIGURE 18.12 Desktop icon for game.

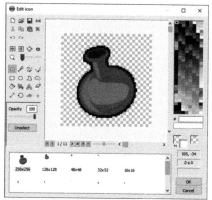

FIGURE 18.13 An example of icons in the Lab being amended.

Summary

This chapter showed you how to add File menus into your programs, how to create an HTML5 game file and what happens when you access it, as well as how to create your own icons for the game. You should now start to feel comfortable in many aspects of the Fusion software and should be able to experiment and try and make changes to the games and examples we have created within this book.

The last few chapters we will be about how to distribute your game, Fusion 2.5+ features, and where to get help.

CHAPTER 19

DISTRIBUTION AND PUBLISHING

In This Chapter

- Distribution Methods
- Publishing
- Marketing
- Taking People's Money
- Copyright Issues

You have finished creating your game, so now what? In this chapter, we look at what to do with your completed project, and what potential issues and pitfalls might be waiting for you as you attempt to get it distributed. Things move at a fast pace in the games industry, and it's possible that some new method of distribution will appear that no one had thought about, so though this chapter details general information, you may need to take into account any industry changes in the meantime that you can take advantage of.

Distribution Methods

In most cases, you will probably be distributing the game yourself. Unless you are one of the few lucky ones to have a publishing agreement whereby someone else handles the heavy lifting of distribution, this section is from the point of view that you are distributing the game yourself. There are a number of options available to you, which will depend on your preference and if you want to (or can) spend money.

DVD Disk

This format is included for completeness but is not recommended as a way of distributing your game. Though buying disks is relatively cheap, it's just not an efficient way to distribute your game these days. Some PC games are still distributed in a professional manner with a disk, but in most cases, they contain a base set of files and a game key (probably for the Steam store). In fact, the disk is generally useless in these releases, as it doesn't generally store the full game. Just like the floppy disk format before it, many computers these days don't even come installed with a DVD drive, and they are an additional extra that you have to purchase. Many software products have already moved over to online-only distribution, to save money but also to reduce piracy.

You can still get a disk professionally created and distribute it, but as fixes and patches are usually generated on a regular basis these days, the disk would quickly be out of date. Of course, you could program an automatic updater into your game to check for the latest patch, but again that's all additional work that many game stores have already built in.

One area which is worth mentioning is the recent trend of people wanting the revival of classic format of a game which has sadly been forgotten or reduced to just a thin plastic box and a serial key. Some companies are now offering classic cardboard big-boxed copies of new games with a full CD containing the game, game manual, and other extras.

Internet

The Internet is the de facto standard for distributing a video game outside of boxed copies, which is usually reserved for games published by professional companies. There are of course multiple options when releasing your game online, and this will be decided by a number of factors:

Cost: How much you want to spend.

Free or Paid: Is your game free, a demo, a test or prototype, or will you be asking money for it?

Visibility: Do you want the whole world to be able to find your game, or are you just wanting to upload it for a select few to play?

With that in mind, here are a number of options:

Itch.io

Itch.io is an extremely popular Website for indie developers who wish to make a name for themselves or to just upload their game for people to play. The site allows anyone with a registered account to upload a game. It also allows games to have a fee or to be given away for free.

Steam

Unlike a number of other game stores where it's still difficult to get your game uploaded, for a minimal fee of approximately $100 you can upload your game to Steam, a massive gaming platform used around the world. Now, wait a second before rushing to upload your game; there are a few caveats. You do have to prepare various items for both marketing and store page visibility before creating a date and releasing your game. Some things you might have to do are as follows (and in many cases, most things Steam expects you to do are extremely useful):

Achievements: Providing a set of achievements that unlock at various stages throughout your game, such as completing a mission, collecting various items, or completing the game.

Store Page: This requires you to upload screenshots and preferably a video of your game in progress; if possible, also a trailer or promotional video.

Release date: Select a specific release date.

Game Specs: What are the expected machine specifications on which your game will run? You should try and at least test this on a low-powered machine and a mid-level machine to gain a good idea of potential minimum and recommended specifications.

Languages: In which languages are you intending to release the game? You may only be releasing in one language. Remember language has to cover both text and audio.

Pricing: Are you intending to release the game for a charge or for free? Any decision here will potentially give you more or less steps to complete before you can release. For example, if you decide to charge for your game, you will need to add regional-based pricing.

If you are looking at making money, then you really need to follow as many of the steps as possible that the Steam store asks you to complete when you are entering your product (it will give you a checklist to complete). You should also consider having at least a minimum of a three months between putting the store page live and releasing the game so you can try and get people to find your page, do marketing, and generally get people to wish list your product. Wish lists are a way of trying to get a number of sales at the launch of your product, and the more it sells on day 1, the more chance you have of appearing in the various lists/charts, and that means more chance of exposure to other users.

If you are selling your game, Steam will take a cut for every game sold; you will also need to register your details with the U.S. tax authorities (relatively straightforward, but another step you need to take). Though Steam takes a cut, the biggest benefit of using them is that they handle all payment transactions; anyone with personal experience of running a Webstore using a card payment provider, this is very much welcome. There are a lot of stolen credit cards used to purchase items around the world, and games software is no different. When selling products via your own Webstore (non-digital products), you might charge the person for postage, you send the item out, and hope they are who they say they are. Sometimes (quite often, unfortunately) a card would have been stolen, and the card issuer will do what is called a chargeback. This is where all of the money is recovered, so you lost both the product and the postage, and in many cases, you might also get charged a fee for this process. With digital games all of the processing and fees are done via Steam; there are no postage fees. If a stolen card is used, of course you lose the sale, but you can cancel the serial key for the game so that it cannot be used, and thereby you haven't lost any money in the process (piracy does exist, but in terms of overall card fraud this is Steam's issue to resolve).

Of course, if you are releasing a game for free, you can still release it on Steam, if you want to have a straightforward platform for people to download your game on. The other benefit of having your game on Steam—rather than, say, for example, your Website—is that people trust downloading a game off Steam more than getting one direct from a Website (people are concerned about viruses).

Web Hosting

You may own your own Web domain where you have your Webpages and store. You can upload your game to your own site, but there are a number of issues relating to this that you may need to consider.

Space: Games can be small, from about 40–100MB to GBs of data. The size of the game on a Website isn't probably too much of a concern unless your game is massive and your hosting Website size isn't. You must also take into account the size of your game and how many downloads you might get (see traffic).

Traffic: You may need to check with your Website provider what limits you have on your account; some have data traffic limitations (the amount of traffic that is allowed to be downloaded from your Website), and others might be unlimited. If you have an unlimited account, you may still have issues if many people download the file at the same time, as this may cause your Website to time out or struggle to handle multiple downloads at the same time.

Virus: As mentioned previously, some people may not want to download your game if you are hosting it yourself, as there is a level of trust required.

Long term: Having a download on a Website is a straightforward process, but the main issue is that search engines and other sites might link to it, and if you change this link, then anyone clicking on these links may find they cannot locate the file anymore. You may stop paying for your Website or move providers and, unless you have backed up your work, you'll lose this data. Not all Web hosting provides backup of data, so if they have a problem, the data can be lost.

Cost: Having a Webhost will normally mean you are paying a monthly fee for those services; if you stop paying, you will lose access to those files and so will your users. If you use a service such as Steam or Itch.io, you will continue to have access to update or change your files. Except for the benefit of having files hosted on your own Website, having someone else handle the data/traffic is certainly a positive.

Publishing

There are two models for publishing: publishing your game yourself via your Website or getting it into stores; or getting someone else to publish the product for you. Publishing yourself means that you would potentially make more money per item sold, but it has more risks and costs associated with it. While getting someone else to publish your product takes away many of the issues concerning printing and packaging (if any), you will be paid less per item sold, but also have the potential for selling more. There are various benefits and pitfalls to both, which we cover here. Things have changed considerably over the years, and while originally publishers would have spent a lot more money on packaging your product and getting it out into the world, in most cases this isn't the case anymore, and it's more about advertising your product (unless you are making an extremely high-quality game).

Self-Publishing

One of your biggest decisions is whether you are going to publish the product yourself, which could cost a substantial amount of money to get it up and running. Some of the things to look at include:

Marketing: You will need to ensure that you try to get your product known; otherwise, you won't get anyone visiting your site or store page and purchasing your game.

Website: A good-looking and professional Website used to be of paramount importance if you were going to convince visitors that they were buying from a proper company, but as most people purchase their games from video game stores these days, a professional-looking Website isn't really that important for actually selling a game. Of course, if you intend to sell via your own Website as well as an online store, then you will need to at least have a Website with some relevant information such as company profile, staff, and games released. If you are not a company in the traditional sense, then at least include some information about the game and how to contact you.

Product Store page: Wherever you decide to sell your game, you will need a detailed product page with screenshots and videos presenting your game in its best light. More details on this can be found in the marketing section of this chapter.

You will need to consider how to take payment options if you want customers to buy direct from you. Many customers are worried about credit card fraud and buying from Websites they haven't purchased from before. You can find out more information from the Taking Peoples Money section of this chapter, but in most cases, it is more cost efficient to use PayPal. Many indies who are selling direct via their own Website are selling Steam keys to their games. This means they can sell a game for more profit this way.

In most cases these days, self-publishing means selling your game on your own Website or being classed as the publisher on game stores such as Steam (you are the publisher); this means being the one who does all the marketing, Webstore data, communication to customers, and so on.

Finding a Publisher

Unless you have a nearly completed game that is of high quality, then it is extremely unlikely that you will find a publisher. Publishers are like any other business—they are looking for a range of highly probable breakeven/successful titles whereby they can make money, and they are not doing this for your benefit (they are a business, so they need to make a profit).

You can contact publishers (there are various Facebook groups and Websites that list indie-based publishers), but in most cases you are probably more likely to get a publisher by showing your work off by doing lots of social media, game dev videos, and showing your game off at shows.

Having said that, here are some things about what publishers might do, or require from you:

Money: A publisher may pay you a royalty advance; this is extra funds to see the game to final completion. These days this is unusual except for a few individuals or games where a publisher can see high income potential. It may be that they've seen your game development videos and users' responses to it and use a royalty advance as a way of getting you to sign on with them. Any royalty advance will be paid back once the game has been released. There have been stories that the % of funds needed to pay back the royalty has meant that some developers get very little or no money in the early stages of a game's release as it's paying back the royalty (as well as paying a % to the publisher).

Contracts: You will have or will need a contract; it's extremely important you read this before signing. Consider things such as %'s and payment schedules, other platforms and publishing rights. For example, what happens if the publisher fails to pay you on time, do the rights to publish revert back, what marketing spending will the company make and how, will they pay for game show stands, and will they provide staff. Do you retain the IP (intellectual property of the game)? It's amazing to think some publishers expect to have your game and own all future versions based on a payment (of course if the payment is significant, you may be happy with this, but be aware of any stipulations and requirements from you as developer in the contract).

Development Schedule: As part of any contract, you may be asked to deliver some items by a specific date to receive further funding or payments. If you don't meet a schedule for a particular build, the contract might be cancelled or you may have a financial punishment. This needs to be very clear, because even in big companies, it has been known that some companies have used development schedules as a way to prevent paying games companies additional funds. If you are going to get a payment for getting to alpha, what does that mean; this should be in the contract and extremely precise.

Ultimately, you will decide what is best for you and your game, so some things that are important to one person may not be important to others, but be aware of any obligations or requirements before you sign on the dotted line.

Over recent years there has been a change in the types of publishers; originally you might get a contract signed based on a basic demo, but nowadays there are many games, and publishers can be pickier in picking the projects they want to support. In many cases they want to see a game near completion before wanting to sign it. Some will pay a royalty advance, many won't; in fact, a new trend from publishers is that they will pay you in marketing spend. In other words, they will provide marketing only for a % of the game's profits. Again, if you accept this type of situation, you should be very clear what is involved in this marketing, as some publishers might do the minimum required just to get you to sign so they can add another game to their portfolio. Also, don't overestimate what marketing may provide you. A number of years ago while involved in getting some advertising space in a magazine; we added a discount code for people to buy the product, but in the end the pickup result (the number of people actually buying the product) was extremely low. You could say that there is an element of product branding and product awareness that increases over time when advertising, but it's not necessarily the golden bullet in terms of making more sales. My advice is not to get too caught up in the moment of "Wow, that sounds awesome"; take a step back and consider how successful it has been for others, consider researching what other games have used the same method, and even ask for supporting data.

Marketing

Your budget will determine what marketing you will be able to do. There are many different options available to you, which can be explored further. Where possible, select a few different ways and then monitor the rate of success. That way, you can continue to do marketing where it works best, which in turn will be more profitable. Of course, if you have a publisher, you may have more options available to you, but always ensure the amount and type of marketing is detailed in your contracts.

One thing to take into account when marketing your game: it should be done over time and should be done at least three months before the game's release. It's not often that games can launch with little or no prior knowledge and be successful; it is possible, but normally it's because the company involved is a large organization that can spend the money or use a major presentation (such as a live online streamed show) to announce the game as "Available now." So, for the rest of us it's about building a brand and getting people to wishlist your game (add your game as wanted by the store platform you are using) so that when you launch, it notifies them.

The key types of marketing (and things that will ultimately help you market your game) include (but are not limited to):

Store Page: The store page is the shop window to your game. Do a bad job here and it doesn't matter what other advertising you do; it will be a wasted opportunity. Make sure you follow any online store requirements for ensuring high-quality screenshots and a set of game videos. You will also need to ensure you describe your game clearly in an opening sentence so that a user has a good idea of what the game is about before they read lots of text. This is similar to an elevator pitch, where you use a short sentence to explain what your game is about.

Videos: You will need gameplay videos for your game's Webstore landing page, but this doesn't mean you cannot upload these videos elsewhere, such as YouTube and Facebook. You will need a game trailer and some gameplay videos; you could even create some developer diary videos detailing the game and its mechanics.

Social Media: Social media is hard work, and it's especially hard to gain any traction, so where possible you should consider starting this early. It's most likely that you may not see traction on your social media until your games is released or starts to get better known through other sources closer to release.

Discord: A common feature these days is to host a chat room where users can come and talk directly to the developers. One of the benefits of being an indie developer is that it is easier to be accessible to users than with a AAA company, which has many restrictions and rules for talking to its users. Though you can use chat systems like Discord to start bringing your users together, it can take time to administer and to keep up with providing new information to users; this could take away from important development time. So, you may need to limit the time on it unless you have a dedicated person looking after it.

Google Adwords: If you want to drive traffic to your Website, you can use Google Adwords. This is a system that, when someone enters a term on the Internet, lists your product or Website on the page. Once users click on the link, Google will then charge you a specific amount. Adwords is a great way to drive traffic to your site for a small cost, and it allows you to enter the total amount you want to spend so you can manage your budget easily.

Facebook Ads: Facebook allows you to create ads that bring in additional people to your Website. You can tailor the ad based on specific criteria such as location and age group.

Viral Marketing: The general opinion on viral marketing is that on the whole it doesn't work, but there have been exceptions. This is where an event or video has gained massive traction; it could be shocking, funny, or different to advertise the game/product. There have been cases of companies getting a negative reception to viral marketing, so tread carefully.

Trade Shows: Trade shows are events where you can go and show off your game to the general public. The games press are also generally at the larger events, and this can provide a good way of getting people to learn more about your product and get some press on gaming Websites (which is extremely difficult to do without a well-known publisher that has contacts). Costs and sizes of trade shows can vary significantly; for indies this can be from a few hundred dollars rising to thousands based on the stand size. Trade shows provide two important elements for an indie developer: first is getting your product and brand better known; and the second is getting people to play your game, seeing how they play it, and getting honest feedback. Just standing back and letting people play your game can provide you with valuable insights that you may not have gotten from other people, and if the event is over two or three days, you can quickly have dozens to hundreds playing your game. You can use this as valuable user testing (though you should have done some before the game was shown in public). Some events allow indie titles to have a limited space free of charge, so it's worth looking out for the possibility of that. Of course, these "free" stands are usually for something a little different, for example one trade show calls these "Left Field," so your game will need to be pretty unique or doing something that other games are not.

The first thing you need to consider is the size of the event. The larger the event, the larger the potential for people to see your game, but actually the reverse is also true, that too many games can mean your game is overlooked. Sometimes a slightly smaller event may provide you with the audience that you need, but you should also expect the cost to be in line with the size of the event.

Always make sure that you have a playable demo available for the event so that people can give your game a try; if you are looking at a busy event, then having a demo that is timed (i.e., will complete within a specific amount of time) is also useful to prevent one person playing on the game for a long time and reducing any lines for other people wanting to play, because the key here is to show how great your game is to as many people as possible.

Taking People's Money

If you are looking at making money from your creations, then in most cases you would be either using a storefront system such as Steam or using a publisher that will handle this work for you. If a publisher is handling purchases (they might also be using payment being taken by a storefront), then you will mostly only be interested in sales, game returns (those people that have gotten a refund), and royalty payment amount. If you are handling the payments yourself as you are self-publishing, then of course you will need to take into account items such as government tax, payments costs, discounts, and sales, as well as other costs for running your business (such as accountancy).

This section is relatively short and is aimed at those that still wish to sell their items independently of a storefront. This is a bigger risk than allowing a storefront to handle the payment, downloads, and returns for your games, and though you can make more money selling software via your own store, the risks and also the amount of work handling this is significantly higher.

The number of options these days for taking money has reduced significantly compared to when the first edition was written, and that's a good thing; though you can still take checks, money orders, and credit cards, in most cases probably the only system that provides an easy way to bring multiple card payments under one system with an easy-to-use interface is PayPal.

PayPal

PayPal is one of the biggest (if not the biggest) payment providers available today. It initially became a very popular payment method due to the auction Website eBay. Users needed a method of paying for items quickly, safely, and easily, and PayPal made this possible. You can purchase many things with PayPal these days, and it's available in multiple countries and currencies. Taking payment is a fairly simple process involving registering for a business account with PayPal at *www.paypal.com*. There is no initial charge for using PayPal, and only a percentage per transaction (which depends on what amount you are charging the customer). The great thing about PayPal is that you can quickly start receiving payments for your games and keep track of who has purchased them. Most companies use PayPal to take payment; as it has become more popular, it has replaced the more awkward banking card payments system, which at times could be extremely costly and require specialized software to get running.

The only downside with selling anything is people asking for their money back, even if they have received the item. The great thing with software and digital software is that in most storefronts you can cancel the serial code for the game so that it no longer works if payment is refused or on a chargeback (where later on the card issuer claims the money back).

 Please consult the PayPal Website for the exact charges.

Copyright Issues

Copyright is an important area to consider for any indie game makers. Are you making a fan game (a game based on a TV show or celebrity) or a remake of a classic title you played some years ago? If you are considering making any game for which someone might retain copyright, you need to take care. Some creators will come on to the game-making forum saying they are going to make a game about a favorite computer character, and then someone else mentions that they could get sued. An argument then erupts between the two parties that they will or won't get into trouble for making it. This is always a difficult discussion to have, as there is no right or wrong answer. If unsure, you shouldn't probably make the game in the first place. There have been a number of "Fan" games made over the years; the larger ones in most cases get shut down by a legal letter from the rights holder, mainly because they have to defend their product's rights by law. This means all the hard work that many fans have put into the game is lost. In a very few examples, making a fan game has led to employment by the company that owned the game's intellectual property.

If you are unsure, then you should always consult a lawyer regarding your rights, but as many fan games are made by fans, they don't really have the funds or the access to lawyers.

The best advice from developers on the forums is to contact the owners of the copyright and see if they mind you making a fan game. In most cases the answer will be no, so it's best to do something else instead. If copyright is a concern, there is no reason why you cannot make a game with a similar concept but with your own graphics, levels, and ideas, as it will be much more worthwhile in the end. Some people consider fan games as missing the point of game creation, and that producing one shows a lack of creativity. The one great thing about trying to replicate a concept from another game is that you are learning gameplay methods that are used in games that are sold to the general public. You will, at the very least, understand how it has been put together, and hopefully come up with something better and more interesting for your own products.

 Always consult a lawyer about copyright law if you are unsure about your rights.

Summary

You will hopefully now have some ideas on how to package, market, and sell your creations. You are not going to compete with the marketing and distribution power of the big AAA games companies. But the positive is that the games market is a diverse and interesting place where the larger companies are not making games that necessarily suit everyone's taste. You can definitely make a success of it.

CHAPTER 20

FUSION 2.5+

In This Chapter

- What Is Fusion 2.5+?
- Key Features

M aking games can be fun, but it can also be difficult, and as you start to learn more, you will want to make bigger and more complex games. In this chapter we will look at Fusion 2.5+, which is extremely helpful if you intend to make a game with lots of events, though it can also be helpful to smaller games if you have an issue with your game but don't know where to start to find the issue. We will look at some of the features available in 2.5+, how to use it, and why you might consider it for your projects.

What Is Fusion 2.5+?

Fusion 2.5+ is an add-on for the standard or development version of Fusion; that means you must have purchased the full product. We have included this paid DLC as a chapter in this book, as it can be extremely helpful when you are developing larger games with many events. Fusion is easy to get started with, but as your games grow the code (Events) can become difficult to read and difficult to troubleshoot.

All games get to a point where the developers need to consider the resources their game is using and optimizing it so that the game can run as well as possible on the lowest specification of machine. This is called "optimizing" and is normally done toward the end of development or where there is a major bottleneck (slowdown or performance issue) when developing the game that causes the testers or developers difficulty in playing a specific part of the game.

Fusion 2.5+ adds some additional features which provide a more professional way of optimizing and bug finding, as well as further improvements to the editor and engine. Consult the documentation for full details of all of the new items within 2.5+, as we'll be only covering the main items.

 If you upgrade to 2.5+, note that you may have issues running any saved file in a non 2.5+ build of Fusion. So, for example, if you have 2.5+ and your friend who is also working on the game doesn't, if you share the game file between you as you develop the game, your friend will not be able to load the game file.

Key Features

In this section, we will go through what is considered the key features of Fusion 2.5+ in terms of making a game; there are many other features which may be important or of interest, so please consult the documentation.

Profiler and Optimizations

One of the biggest criticisms of 2.5 from people making more complex games is the lack of overall performance analytics. A fantastic feature in 2.5+ is the Profiler tool; this allows you to see behind the scenes of your game and see which elements are taking the most time to run. A process that runs slowly can cause your game to function poorly and could mean your game suffers elsewhere. It has already been mentioned that all games go through a process of optimization; sometimes this is due to inefficient programming, new features that you've added that didn't take into account other features, or some item taking more performance than you might have expected. The Profiler will allow you to pinpoint potential problem areas and look to reduce or mitigate them.

1. To start the Profiler you'll need to have the Fusion application loaded, then click on the Application Properties in the Workspace Toolbar, ensuring the Settings tab is selected.

2. Scroll down until you see an option called Profiler. New options include Profiler and Optimizations, as shown in Figure 20.1.

FIGURE 20.1 The new Profiler and Optimizations settings.

 If you enable the Profiler, the inbuilt debugger will not display. So, you may have to run the game with and without the profiler if you want to test different things.

The following settings are available:

Enable profiling: This will enable profiling and its options.

Start profiling at start of frame: Once you enable profiling, this option will be turned on automatically. This will register events and performance from the start of the frame. If you are trying to only see specific events, you can also start it using an event.

Profile top-level conditions only: This will only register the standard events and not provide checks for child conditions.

Record slowest app loops: Loops are a particular issue within Fusion if you want to check performance. For example, when using the Profiler, you'll notice that some code has high timing values (the higher the value, the slower it is performing), but for a loop this is because every time the loop is called, it adds to the timer. This means that the time isn't a true indication of how poor something is performing (you might be calling the loop every so often). By selecting this option, it will only record the slowest time each time the loop is performed, which provides a more accurate reading of how slow your code is. Of course, if you are calling the same loops a lot, this could cause performance issues of its own, so you need to read the performance data with care. Selecting this option will provide you with lots of data for the same events.

Optimize events: This will rearrange events conditions to make them more efficient.

Optimize image size in RAM: This will optimize the images that you use in your game so that it runs faster.

Optimize "Play Sample": In the normal 2.5 build, sound effects would be played immediately when the Play Sample action was called from your game; with this option selected, it will optimize the audio effect (meaning in some cases a small delay) but should mean the game performs better. The delay in playing a sound effect in most cases should not be noticeable.

Build Cache: This will save data related to your game to improve the time that it takes to create a build.

Clear build cache: This allows you to clear the current cache files. Sometimes these files can be out of date or corrupt, so before building the final version of your game you should clear the cache. Doing so will ensure you create a clean build, but this will mean that the final build of your game will take longer.

If you load up a game (or you can create a game file with a single frame) and run it, as long as you have Enable profiling selected (and leave all other options as default), then Fusion will start to collate information about the performance of your game. It will do this over however many frames that you have. As soon as you stop your game, the profiler will populate with information as seen in Figure 20.2. You can expand the groups of information by clicking on the + icon next to each of the Frame names that are contained within your game. You can see an example of the expanded view in Figure 20.3.

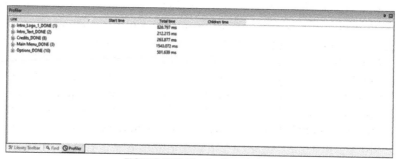

FIGURE 20.2 The Profiler window.

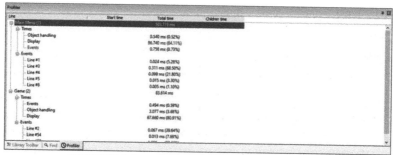

FIGURE 20.3 Expanded information in the Profiler window.

Each frame is separate into Times and Events. The Times section details the amount of total time that each group of items has taken to run within your game; this is split between Events, Object Handling, and Display. The data is presented in ms (milliseconds) and a % for each is also provided.

1000 milliseconds equals 1 second. In Figure 20.3, you'll notice that Display equals 1 second; in this case we know it is because we have a very graphic-heavy animation that is playing, which is a one-off animation and is not a problem in terms of performance, as the game isn't doing anything else at this point (but we could remove some animation frames if we felt it was a performance problem). Remember that not all high values mean you have to try and change the data, but trying to understand the data is extremely important.

The next set of data in the Profiler is the Events, which are separated by the line number that they are run on. You'll notice that in Figure 19.2 there are no lines #1, #2, #3, and so on; this is because in my game these are comment lines and groups, and they are not displayed as they do not contain data that the game will run. Again, just like the data in the Times section, there is a ms and a % value. A high value in line #9 is because the game is running through an ini data file and setting this value into a global value. Loading of data is a high-intensity process, so you should try to move this to a place where it will cause the least problems; you could do this at the start of your game or create a loading screen where you can prevent this from slowing your core gameplay down (you don't want to be reading from data files in the middle of a shoot-out between two characters, for example). If you double-click on the line, it will take you to that line in the Event Editor so you can view the code.

Child Events

If you were creating an event where you then needed to activate other events, you would most likely use Groups. You could also use counters or alterable value checks to activate other events, but this can get quite messy, and overall your code would be difficult to read and very inefficient. Groups were easy to use, but it could get difficult to know what bit of code was activating other groups and follow that process to its natural conclusion.

Child Events are a massive improvement to code readability, as they allow you to run child events only if the parent event is true (and they will continue to run while it is true). This means you can quickly understand what a bit of code is doing and know that, if true, it's running the children, unlike groups which could be being enabled from elsewhere. One downside to child events is that you cannot collapse them, so you should consider ways of keeping them tidy, such as adding comments before and after the code.

To create a child event, you will need to do the following:

1. Open up Fusion.

2. Create a new file.

3. We only need a single frame, so go into the Event Editor from frame 1.

4. Create an event (such as always, start of frame) so that you have a single Event.

5. Right-click on the event line number, and now you will see an additional option of Add a new child event. You can see the pop-up in Figure 20.4.

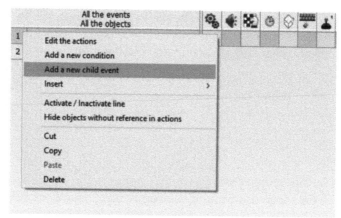

FIGURE 20.4 The add child pop-up.

You can find a simple example of a set of Child Events in the companion files in the Chapter 20 folder and a file called ChildEvents.mfa. This shows a simple example of an object bouncing around the screen, and as it collides with other objects it updates a counter. The counter is updated by Child Events; though not a particularly exciting example, it does show you how you can now use Child Events in your games.

Debugger Output

To use the Debugger ensure that the Profiler option has been disabled. In doing so the standard Debugger window will appear, but some additional items are now available. You can see the standard Debugger on the left and the new Debugger window on the right in Figure 20.5. The changes look subtle but are really useful when making larger games.

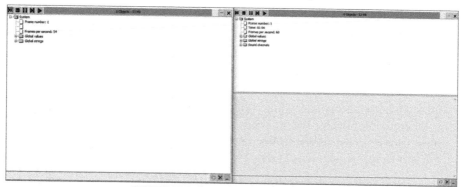

FIGURE 20.5 The updated Debugger window.

There are two new items that appear in the Debugger; the first is that Sound Channels are now listed and can be expanded. This means you can view what audio channel is in use at any point in time.

The second of the two new items is the Debugger Output window. This can be used to print text information to the Debugger Output window at specific times in your game. Previously, you may have put a counter or a piece of text on-screen when something in your game has happened to help track what is happening. For example, you might have placed a counter on-screen which keeps track of a player's level or current button click. These wouldn't be bits of data that you would present to the player in terms of UI, but bits of data that you wanted to keep track of and wanted to see if the data changed at the right time when running your game. For example, we can have a piece of data stored in an ini file that keeps track of if the player has watched the story introduction sequence. If they have, the next time they run the game the introduction sequence will not run. If they haven't watched it before, the value will change once they have so next time it won't play. This data is stored in an ini file and loaded in at the start of the game, and if they watch the introduction sequence, a new value is written to the ini file. To prove this is working we can obviously try and play the game, but it's very useful to show this data on-screen and show it changing in real time, so we load the data into a counter and set it once they've watched the introduction sequence. This provides me with an easy way to prove that it's all working as expected, but the big problem is that it's really inefficient for me to have to add further objects to the screen and then code them in the Event Editor; as the program gets larger, we have to add additional counters or text strings to display this data on-screen. This all becomes very messy, and at a time when you are trying to understand what is going on in your game, you are having to keep track of all these new objects that are not related to your game but are just there for testing purposes.

The Debug Output window allows you to send text or a number (or both) to the debugger at any time. So, you could send the introduction sequence current value at any time. You still need to program an event for it, but it is all contained under the Special Conditions action and is kept to a single object, so it is easy to track. You can see how to access the action for printing text to the output window in Figure 20.6.

On selecting this as an option, you will be presented with a standard Expression Evaluator window, meaning that you can print both text and numbers to the Debug Window (but you must convert any numbers to text for it to work).

You can find a very simple example of the Debug Output window in the companion files contained in the "Debugger" folder. Remember this will only work if you have Fusion 2.5+ installed. At the start of the frame, we clear the output window (you could do this at any point in your game if the window has too much text in it) and it will print a text message of "START OF FRAME," and then after 5s have passed, it will print a combination of text and then the current timer value. It is an extremely simple example, but it shows that you can pretty much do the same things you were doing on the Frame itself.

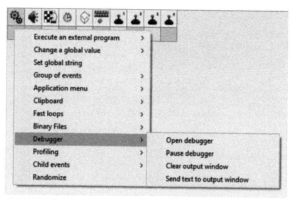

FIGURE 20.6 The action to print to the Debug Output Window.

Find All

Another essential feature that Fusion 2.5+ delivers to anyone serious about making larger and more complex games is the Find All option. Just like a find text option in a text editing program, the Find All option allows Fusion to search through the game for any object, event, value, action, comment, and so on that contains a piece of text.

You can access the Find All dialog box by holding CTRL, SHIFT, and pressing the F key. You can see the pop-up dialog box in Figure 20.7.

Once you have typed in the text that you want to search for, click on the OK button to begin the search. Once you have done this, the Find window will populate with any successful searches, as shown in Figure 20.7. By clicking on each of the items that it has found in the Find window, Fusion will highlight the entry in the Event Editor. If you are currently on the Frame Editor, clicking on a line will still take you to the item.

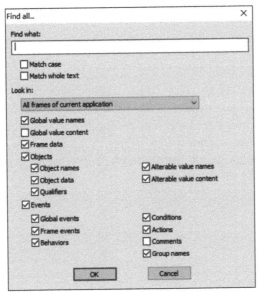

FIGURE 20.7 The Find window.

Summary

In this chapter, we have gone through key features included in Fusion 2.5+. Though this isn't available in the standard version (or indeed the free version), the features were too important to ignore and leave out of the book. The reason for this is that anyone serious about making more complex games will definitely find they will need this functionality. Fusion may be one of the more straightforward game making engines available, but it loses a lot of usability as the game becomes more complex and as more frames, events, conditions, and actions are added. The features in 2.5+ give a much-needed boost to the level of usability back to the developer when it's needed most. As your game gets more complex and more difficult to read, any problems or issues you have with your game will start to be compounded; 2.5+ will save you endless amounts of wasted time and allow you to use that time for making a game, rather than using hours or days trying to find why something doesn't work as you expected.

There are other features available in 2.5+ that you may find of use, so please consult the help documentation for more details.

CHAPTER 21

HELP AND RESOURCES

In This Chapter

- Who Needs Help?
- Fusion Help
- Useful Websites
- Games Research, Game Stores

In this final chapter we will look at how you can further your knowledge of both Fusion and game creation. You should consider this the start of your journey, as with most things, it's a continual learning process and hopefully one that is exciting and rewarding.

Who Needs Help?

To whom can you turn if you are really stuck and don't have a friend who can help with your problem? There are many resources, both within the products covered in this book and on the Internet, that you can use to speed up your development and ensure you don't spend too much time trying to fix a difficult problem.

Fusion Help

There are a number of ways to access help from within the program, and this should be your first choice for getting support. Many problems you will face when you first start using a product can be fixed by using the product's built-in support features, which will be faster than waiting for a response from any online forums.

Landing Page

When you first start Fusion, it will open up the application, ready for you to create your own game, but it will also provide a set of quick links to various tutorials, items on the store, and new creations. You can see an example of the landing page in Figure 21.1.

FIGURE 21.1 Fusion landing page.

Help Files

All products have some form of help file, be it an HTML, Word, PDF document, or Microsoft Help formatted program. The good news is that Fusion comes with an extensive help facility, which also includes the usual title, word, and search functionality of any modern help file. To access the Help system:

1. Start Fusion, and then go to the menu bar at the top of the screen.

2. Select the Help option.

3. Select the Contents option. The Help system will now load.

The great thing about the help system is that you can search for keywords, titles, or previous results. This is very handy when you are looking for something specific. You can see the help files in Figure 21.2.

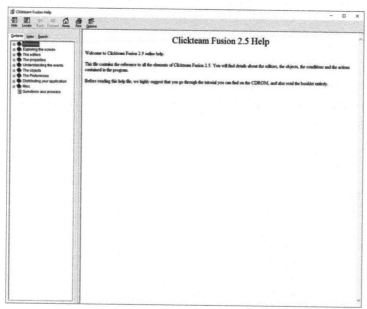

FIGURE 21.2 Fusion's Help File.

Help About

The Help About option is something you will only use when contacting Clickteam's support staff or using their online forums. The Help About option displays information about the current program and the level of patches currently installed. Always mention the product and version number in any correspondence to ensure a faster response to your problem. The Help About option can be accessed from the menu system.

1. Start Fusion, and then go to the menu bar at the top of the screen.

2. Select the Help option.

3. Select the About. The About box will now load.

An example of the About box is shown in Figure 21.3. You will need to make a note of the build number, as this is what you will be asked for on the forums.

FIGURE 21.3 The product's Help About dialog box.

Tutorial

The Tutorial option (which can be accessed from the Menu system, Help | Tutorial) loads a help file that gives you games and examples to follow. If you feel like you need a bit more basic understanding of how to use the product, the tutorials are a great way to improve your skills quickly and easily. It is recommended that you look at how this tutorial is put together from the story and programming point of view. You will learn a lot from looking at other games, as it will help you understand the things that are required to make them interesting.

Examples

Fusion comes with a number of game examples for you to try, which also allow you to explore the code in more detail. You can access this via the menu option Help | Examples (on doing so it will open up the folder where the examples are located).

If you are stuck with a specific concept or game type, look at the examples to see if makes it easier for you to implement in your own game. This is a very good way to find out how a specific game type is made, but if you have problems, copy the code bit by bit into a new game and see what it does.

Clickteam Website

Using the menu option Help | Clickteam Web site will take you to the Web-page of the makers of Fusion. From here you can find out lots of information about the product, including tutorials and links to additional paid (and free) content in the store as well as the user forums, where a simple search can help you find many discussions about topics you may want to implement in your own game.

Clickteam Store

The Clickteam Store is where you can find new objects, example files, and other items that you can use in your own games. You can access this from the Help | Store menu option, or you can also go directly to it from a Web browser.

For example, you may want a fire particle effect, or a laser shot in your game, or you might already have some basic designer art in place but want to replace it with something a little more professional. Most items on the store are at a very reasonable cost or free of charge, so it's always good to take a look if you have an idea you want to implement but maybe don't really know how to do it.

Keyboard Shortcuts

Keyboard shortcuts allow you to use certain key combinations versus finding items within the menu system. Within Fusion is a default set of shortcut commands that you can amend to suit your own requirements. Over time, you may find that you are duplicating certain menu combinations when you are developing your games, so by setting up your own keyboard shortcuts, you will be able to work faster and more efficiently. The other option you have is not to change the defaults but to make a list of all the important key combinations you use for future reference.

To view the default keyboard preferences:

1. Start Fusion, and then go to the menu bar at the top of the screen.

2. Select the Tools option.

3. Select the Keyboard Shortcuts option.

The Keyboard Shortcuts dialog box will then load, as shown in Figure 21.4.

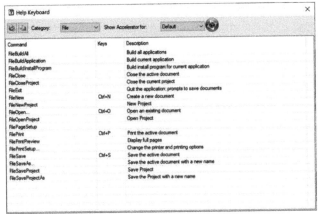

FIGURE 21.4 Keyboard Shortcuts dialog.

If you want to configure the keyboard shortcuts so you can assign your own commands, you will need to access the Customize screen.

To view the default keyboard preferences:

1. Select the View option.

2. Select the Toolbars | Customize option.

A pop-up menu will appear; select Customize to bring up the Customize Configuration dialog box. From here, we can customize the look and feel of Fusion, but we only want to amend the keyboard shortcuts, so click on the Keyboard tab. You should now have a dialog box similar to that in Figure 21.5.

FIGURE 21.5 Customize Keyboard options.

Select the category and command you want to amend, and it will show the current key assigned. You will then need to click on the Remove button to remove this assignment. Press the left mouse key so the cursor is situated in the Press New Shortcut Key, and then press the key combination you want to use. If the key combination you press is already assigned to another command, text will appear below the Press New Shortcut Key box stating the command with which it is associated. Try a different combination. If you still want to assign a combination that is already in use, you will need to change the original to something else before assigning it to the one you want. You also will see a description for every command, which lets you know what each shortcut key does. If you make a mistake or decide that you want to go back to the original settings, click on the Reset All button. Some default key combinations are listed in Table 21.1.

TABLE 21.1 Common Key Combinations

Action	Key Combination	Details
Copy	Ctrl+C	Copy the selection and put it on the Clipboard
Cut	Ctrl+X	Cut the selection and put it on the Clipboard
Delete	Delete	Delete the selected object
Enlarge canvas	Ctrl+W	Enlarge the canvas of the picture
Events editor	Ctrl+E	Open Event Editor window
Events list editor	Ctrl+L	Open Event List window
Find	Ctrl+F	Find the specified Text
Frame editor	Ctrl+M	Open Frame Editor window
Help	Shift+F1	Display help for clicked on buttons, menus, and windows
New	Ctrl+N	Create a new document
Open	Ctrl+O	Open an existing document
Paste	Ctrl+V	Insert Clipboard contents
Play	F5	Play the current frame from the current position
Print	Ctrl+P	Print the active document
Redo	Ctrl+Y	Redo the previously undone action
Run Application	F8	Run the current application
Run Frame	F7	Run the current frame
Save	Ctrl+S	Save the active document

(Contd.)

Action	Key Combination	Details
Select All	Ctrl+A	Select the entire document
Storyboard editor	Ctrl+B	Open storyboard window
Undo	Ctrl+Z	Undo the last action
Zoom in	F2	Zoom the current window inward
Zoom out	F3	Zoom the current window outward
Zoom to fit	F4	Set the zoom factor of the current window to obtain a complete display

Patches & Service Packs

It is always recommended that you install the latest patches if you have been getting problems with creating your game. You will also find that people are more willing to help you with your problem if you have installed the most up-to-date version, as they will ask you to update before offering advice. Patches usually include fixes to bugs, and sometimes new features, so it's to your benefit to keep up to date. Most companies (including Clickteam) issue patch notes which detail the things they have fixed within the patch, so you can consult this before upgrading to see if the issue you are experiencing has been potentially fixed.

If you are in the middle of development of a game, you should consider waiting a few days, weeks, or even months before applying a new patch. Although unlikely, it is possible that this could cause you problems with the program you are already working on and could have catastrophic results. Clickteam's engine is relatively straightforward, so you shouldn't have to stay on an old build for long.

Before applying the patch, make sure you have backed up any programs you're making, so if you need to, you can roll back to a previous release without losing any code.

Useful Websites

If you are looking for product information and support, the Internet will be your best friend. You can find instant results to your problems and be able to locate helpful material and downloads such as tutorials/game examples. The following is a quick roundup of useful sites.

Support & Game Sites

Jason Darby Books
www.jasondarbybooks.com

To accompany this and other books written by the author, a Website has been created (Figure 21.6) to give you the latest information and material.

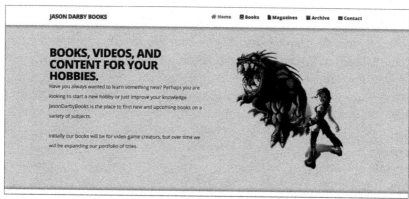

FIGURE 21.6 The author's Website.

Clickteam
www.clickteam.com

This is the home of Fusion and other tools and products for making games as well as DLC for Fusion. From here, you can download demo versions of other products you might need or read articles and information about the products. It is recommended that you register on both the mailing list and the forums. This will mean that you can keep up to date on developments as they happen and have the ability to post questions on any problems you might have during the development process. Users on the forum are generally very efficient and helpful, which usually means you will get a response within twenty-four hours, if not sooner. As with all forums, it is best to read the FAQ before posting, as there are rules to follow to ensure that things go according to plan.

Retro Gamer Magazine
www.retrogamer.net/

Retrogamer has been around for a few years now and has gone from strength to strength. The magazine started with a bi-monthly release, and due to the success of the first issue (which is no longer available in print but available digitally), they changed the issue dates to monthly as well as releasing one-off specials. The magazine has a wide range of articles and details about games from the past, so if you're looking for inspiration or ideas, try to get a copy of this magazine. Although it is a United Kingdom magazine, international delivery is available with additional cost for postage.

Gamasutra

www.gamasutra.com/

Gamasutra is one of the older game news Websites, with jobs, articles, and whitepapers. This site provides more background to the games industry than the standard gaming news sites you probably visit. If you register with the site, you can also post your résumé, look for jobs in the games industry, and find more detailed information about the concepts and technology used in the day-to-day development of games. If you are new to the games industry or just looking for more information, this is a good Website to visit.

Games Research, Games Stores

Many people in the games industry joke that playing games is "research," but it definitely is. The more games you play the more knowledge about different systems you will acquire, sometimes without really knowing about it (where you gain knowledge just from experiencing it).

Play as many games as you possibly can, as this will help you when you are making your own games, or in fact someone else's games. Some games you will play will leave a lasting impression. For many designers these games are usually classic titles and are usually retro based games (games that are 15+ years old). One such game that is still talked about on gaming forums is a game called "Barry McGuigan's Boxing". This was a boxing game based on a popular Irish boxer at the time in what could have been considered the golden age of boxing. It was available on 8bit computers such as the Spectrum 48k, which had limited memory, sound, and color (which at the time people didn't think was a limit at that point in time of technology). For the time, the game was fantastic; you took the role of a boxer just starting out, first taking on the street fighters (they even had appropriate names) while moving through tougher opponents until you took on the number 1 fighter. The aim of the game was to beat the best and become the world champion. Approximately twenty years later, this very mechanic was implemented into a game, Formula 1 for the PS3/Xbox 360 and PC.

The design team had been tasked with creating a standalone game mode that gave the players a challenge different from the standard 19–20 race "Championship" mode, which people had played many times before and weren't necessarily completing (as it was too long). The mode was meant to have more of an arcade feeling with a shorter season (only 10 races) along with shorter race distance. So Season Challenge was created; but though it had more arcade settings, it still needed something more to it. Various game mechanics were added; for example, the player was scored based on the team they drove with (the slower the team, the higher the score modifier), but to make it more interesting, the player had to pick a challenger, and this challenger could only be the driver above or below them in the championship. Picking the driver below them would be easier and picking the driver above them would potentially be harder. If they beat them, they would be offered a drive in their car; this allowed the player to quickly change teams (some players only liked to drive in particular team's cars) but also offered the option of staying in the slower car (for a higher challenge and higher score modifier) and continuing up the championship table. Players could get different scores that would be uploaded to an online leaderboard. Even though it's not exactly the same concept—it's not even the same type of game—the core idea of challenging boxers above and below you and how it would affect your position in the leaderboard became the theme that design went with for this game mode. Even extremely limited games by today's standards can hold the key to useful game concepts and ideas that you can utilize in your own games. Of course, you could say that a players enjoyment of the old game (bias) could have prompted the design concept into any game that was going to be made anyway, but actually the core concept had mostly been designed; it was just lacking the final hook, and knowledge of that game and concept provided the final mechanic that was needed. Could something else have worked? Of course. In the end this was a perfect fit for the mode. Playing games IS definitely research.

Let's take a look at a few online gaming stores where you can view and purchase games (remember, you can also use sites such as YouTube to view game reviews and playthroughs). There are many ways of buying games and many different platforms, but here we are going to be talking about PC games that are available to purchase online. You could have a console or handheld device and learn about games using those systems.

Gog
www.gog.com

Gog is a video games digital store with a difference. It releases games via its own platform called Galaxy, but you can also download games independently of that system and you can download them DRM (Digital Rights Management) free. This means there is no restrictive digital security that has given honest users issues installing games in the past (DRM is used to stop people pirating software).

Gog used to stand for Good Old Games; its primary goal was to release older games that were no longer available, officially with support. These games also included digital "Goodies" such as game manuals, artwork, and music (dependent on the game).

The site is owned by CD Projekt Red, the creators of the Witcher video games series and the recently released (at time of writing) Cyberpunk 2077.

Steam
www.store.steampowered.com

Steam has long been the de facto gaming store for most PC gamers (other providers are slowly trying to increase their userbase). It's been around for many years and has been the main site where indie developers have released their games. In the early days it was very difficult to get indie games released, but then Greenlight came along, which allowed the users to vote for games they wanted to see released (which was open to people finding ways to get the required votes even if the game wasn't very good). In the end, Value (the owners of Steam) found that it was just easier to allow all games to be available on the service as long as users paid the $100 fee per game to upload and as long as they didn't break any legal rules. The upside is that this has stopped vote rigging on Greenlight, and it has allowed many people to release their own games. The downside is that now there is no quality control and many substandard games have appeared (clones and clones of clones). It was never going to be a perfect system, but for a very low outlay you can get your game published on Steam. The other benefit of the platform is that there are many games on the system, so you can view many different games, genres, and levels of quality.

Epic Games Store
www.epicgames.com

Relatively new to the games store market, the Epic Games Store started off as a launcher for their game creation engine called Unreal (which is currently available to download free from within their launcher). The Unreal engine is extremely powerful at making 3D games (but not so great at making 2D games, though). Based on the success of the Unreal engine, Epic then began to sell content via the same launcher, and finally launched their game store. Initially it wasn't viewed in a positive light, due to lack of features and functionality and the always present initial hesitation of wanting to change stores after you've invested in another. Giving away free games, having exclusive content, giving developers more of their share from sales, and being a publisher where they provide finance for companies and a fantastic revenue split after the royalty has been paid have all contributed to an increasingly positive and forward-thinking game store. Most content on the Epic store is curated and, as it's newer than Steam and Gog, they have less available content. For indies this is a great proposition to get in early, but it also means that potentially the range of products (for research) isn't as wide or different compared to the Steam store. I suspect this will change over time, but it's still worth a look to see what's available.

Summary

If you are great at game design but not very artistic, you have a problem if you are the only person involved in your game creation. Over the last few years, a number of Websites have appeared to offer music, graphical, and product help—and Turbo Squid is one of the best. Prices for models, images, and music vary, but there is a large collection, so you should be able to find something you can use.

Congratulations, you have come to the end of the book. Hopefully you've enjoyed it and have perhaps learned something new along the way. Hopefully, this will just be the beginning of your game creation journey and you will spend lots of happy hours thinking, designing, and creating your own games.

INDEX